Panchayati Raj, Participation and Decentralization

Changing Contours of Administration Since Independence
Golden Jubilee Volume Series - 3

Panchayati Raj, Participation and Decentralization

Editors

Ramesh K. Arora
Meenakshi Hooja

Series Editor
Rakesh Hooja

The HCM Rajasthan State Institute of
Public Administration, Jaipur

RAWAT PUBLICATIONS
Jaipur • New Delhi • Bangalore • Guwahati • Kolkata

ISBN 978-81-316-0252-2

Reprinted, 2018

Published by
Prem Rawat for **Rawat Publications**
Satyam Apts, Sector 3, Jawahar Nagar, Jaipur 302 004 (India)
Phone: 0141 265 1748/7006 Fax: 0141 265 1748
E-mail: info@rawatbooks.com
Website: www.rawatbooks.com

New Delhi Office
4858/24, Ansari Road, Daryaganj, New Delhi 110 002
Phone: 011 2326 3290

Also at Bangalore, Guwahati and Kolkata

Typeset by Rawat Computers, Jaipur
Printed at Chaman Enterprises, New Delhi

Contents

Series Editor's Introduction

Rakesh Hooja

It is most likely that all possible types of developmental, governmental, regulatory and administrative initiatives have been tried out in some part or the other of India over the last 60 years since the country gained independence. With governments of different ideological hues having remained in power at different points of time in different states of the Indian Union and at the Centre, and with different ideas about development, governance, planning, state welfarism, market-orientation, administration, nation- building etc. having been fashionable or accepted in different time frames, as well as a willingness to try out and emulate what was being attempted in countries of the West, or of the Soviet bloc, or in other developing areas, all forms of administrative and governmental action and all types of development schemes, as well as types of organizational arrangements, have been tried out somewhere or the other in India and have been commented upon by experts, scholars, researchers, practitioners, journalists and the ordinary laymen. In fact, Public Administration is a well-established discipline in India and has been regularly analyzing changes in the field, as also in administrative thinking and in policy making, over the years. These debates, discussions, descriptions, analyses, comments, opinions, findings and administrative prescriptions have been duly covered in the various articles published in the two journals of the HCM Rajasthan State

Institute of Public Administration (HCM RIPA), which contain useful and valuable reference material.

It is in this context that we have undertaken this project of preparing thematic volumes, which would indicate some of the important changing contours of Indian Administration since independence. We wanted to look at how concepts, approaches, organizational structures, procedures, policies, programmes, projects, working styles, and modes of observation, analysis and evaluation, have all emerged and undergone change over time.

Accordingly, to celebrate 50 years of HCM RIPA, we felt it appropriate to select the best and most appropriate articles from the back issues of the over 34 years that our journal *Prashasnika* is being published, as well as the 11 years that our second journal *Development Policy and Administrative Review* used to be simultaneously printed. Deliberately wanting the articles selected for inclusion in this series to retain the flavour of the period in which they were written and to reflect the thinking and practice of that time, we have chosen not to modify the selected articles, except in some cases to slightly change the titles of the articles. The words, descriptions and analyses are of the authors as they had originally written the pieces. However, the articles selected have their intrinsic value, and by putting them together into separate thematic volumes, we have, hopefully, enabled readers to visualize how certain administrative concepts, or governmental and developmental programmes (or experiments) and policies, have been initially conceptualized and implemented, and have subsequently evolved over time. We have also attempted to provide a judicious blend of the theoretical and the practical in each book as also in the series as a whole.

Having gone through the back issues of *Prashasnika* and of *Development Policy and Administrative Review*, we have selected the following as the themes for each of the separate volumes:

1. Development Administration and Rural Development
2. Training, Civil Services and Personnel Administration
3. Panchayati Raj, Participation and Decentralization
4. Governance and Reforms
5. Welfare and Tribal Development Administration
6. Administration of Public Sector Enterprises and Industrial Development: Changing Trends Since Independence.
7. Administrative Theories: Approaches, Concepts and Thinkers in Public Administration

8. Prashasnik Parivartan or Administrative Change (in Hindi)
9. Plan and Project Formulation and Implementation: Theoretical and Applied Aspects
10. Urban Development and Administration
11. Administration for the Empowerment and Welfare of Women
12. District Level Administration and the Role of the Collector
13. Administration of Desert and Drought-Prone Arid Areas
14. Administration of Water Management and Command Area Development
15. Administration of Health and Education Sectors
16. Managing Change, Organizational Behaviour and Human Resource Development
17. Land Use, Revenue Administration and Land Reforms
18. Criminal Justice and Police Administration
19. Financial Management and Economic Administration in Government

Other titles may be added as we go along.

I have received able support from my colleagues on the Series Editorial Board, namely, Dr. Ramesh K. Arora, Shri S.N. Lathi, Ms. Pankaj Patni and K.K. Parnami, in finalizing the themes for the individual volumes and identifying the possible thematic volume editors. Mr. Parnami got a cumulative index prepared of all matter published in our two journals without which this exercise could not have been started. We are also gratified that the two publishers Mr. Subodh Bhushan Gupta of Aalekh Publishers and Mr. Pranit Rawat of Rawat Publications respectively, agreed to jointly co-publish the books with HCM RIPA at no cost to HCM RIPA, and to distribute them. The editors of each volume also are to be thanked for their efforts at meticulously culling out and selecting the best and most relevant articles for our consideration for inclusion in the respective volumes, and for their writing appropriate volume introductions.

It is hoped that this series of volumes shall prove to be a useful source of reference contributing to better understanding of the themes covered and acting as a stimulus for further reflection to all those interested in Indian administration, and that readers shall enjoy and appreciate reading the books as much as we in the Series Editorial Board, and the volume editors, did while preparing the books for publication.

1 Introduction

Participation for Effectiveness and Effectiveness of Participation

Ramesh K. Arora and Meenakshi Hooja

People's participation is the crux of a democratic system. It lends credence to the legitimacy of a political order; enhances people's involvement in the processes of policy formulation, implementation and evaluation; augments the performance of the governance system; makes the decisional system conducive to the will and the needs of the people; heightens people's competence for participatory governance; and facilitates sustainability and stability of the political system. Participation creates a psychological aura that illuminates a democratic structure.

Little wonder, participation is considered as an imperative of good governance. It is a *compulsive* strategy for enhancing the quality of governance. It is also a *compromising* modality for striking a balance between good politics and good administration and between proliferating inputs and the stipulated outputs. Moreover, participation is a mechanism for creating institutions rooted in a philosophy of *compassion* for the people who form the target groups of development administration. Thus, *compulsiveness, compromise* and *compassion* are the three guiding imperatives of participation.

Participation is facilitated by a democratic legacy in a political order, a political system committed to the flowering of a democratic spirit, an egalitarian social order, an egalitarian cultural ethos, an economic system dedicated to distributive justice and an administrative system believing passionately in the premises of secular-rationalism. Effectiveness and participation are apparently conflicting goals and seemingly opposing strategies of development, but they are not inherently so. Effectiveness is heightened by participation and in turn, participation is facilitated through effective administrative structures. No wonder, both—effectiveness and participation—are integral characteristics of good governance, and of New Public Administration and New Public Management. The challenge before a democratic governance system in a developing nation is to ensure the acceleration of effectiveness and enhancement of participation. Penetration and participation, thus, are complimentary strategies of holistic development.

The rationale of decentralized and participatory governance is to give power to the people so as to create a sense of ownership in them and to ensure their participation in decision-making. Participation of people in decision-making not only helps to resolve local problems more realistically, but also enables better implementation of decisions taken locally and of the government programmes and policies.

Participatory governance acknowledges the existence of a multiplicity of actors and stakeholders who have interest, rights and competencies in public policies and decisions. Much of the success of participatory governance will depend upon the *ability* of the people and their representatives to participate in policy and decisional systems; their *willingness* to be authentic participants; and the *ambience of opportunity* provided to them to network their ambitions and competencies with the goals and energies of the institutions of which they are a part. Much will depend upon the existence of appropriate institutions and in this context, democratic India has chosen Panchayati Raj as its vehicle for participatory and decentralized governance.

Democratic decentralization through Panchayati Raj Institutions (PRIs) has been part of India's development discourse and its debates on participatory governance since Panchayati Raj was introduced in India following the Balwant Rai Committee Report which had recommended that public participation in community works should be organized through statutory representative bodies. These statutory bodies have, following the 73rd Constitutional Amendment, given way to constitutional PRIs. Over the years, much change has occurred in the functions, processes and structures of Panchayati Raj and participatory governance. Various states have evolved their own models of Panchayati Raj.

The present anthology brings before its readers a collection of essays that focus on the dynamics of participation, the dilemmas of decentralization and the potential, changing nature and performance of PRIs. The facets of this analysis are historical, political, economic, socio-cultural and even psychological. Hopefully, the enlightened contribution of the essays contained in this anthology will expand the horizons of our understanding of the comprehensive process of Panchayati Raj and participation-based systemic transformation at grass-roots levels.

Conceptual Dimensions of Participation

Shashi Ranjan Tewari in his essay, "People's Participation: A Theoretical Framework", treats 'participation' as those voluntary activities of the members of a society by which they take part in decision-making involving developmental administration at different levels of government. Thus, people are 'sovereign' in a democratic form of government. The antonym of 'participation' is 'apathy' that refers to people's withdrawal from or their indifference towards associating themselves voluntarily and actively with developmental activities. Several scholars define participation as forms of action by which citizens 'take part' in the governance system. This 'taking part' refers to action at any level from macro to micro and from an advisory role to an intensive involvement in the policy and decision process.

It is paradoxical that most of the literature on participation focuses on developmental administration and refrains from dealing with regulatory administration. Tewari's analysis also refers to three dimensions of development: political, administrative and social. The need therefore is to appreciate the significance of participation as a process even in the areas that are crucial to the existence and stability of a social order. Hence, people's participation in the maintenance of public order and in resource mobilization should be juxtaposed with the participatory process in the developmental realm.

Tewari accords primary importance to political participation in a democratic framework. He has an expanded notion of what is 'political', for he believes that political participation goes beyond participation in the election process and even encompasses an involvement of people in the public policy process. Further, he notes that pluralist and popular democracies supplement a representative democracy. Accordingly, civil servants in a democracy should devise a consultative machinery to explore people's opinions and problems related to government policies and actions and in addition, it is the obligation of the mass media to appraise the people about their own interests and their conjunction with the government's intent and initiatives.

In a similar vein, A.P. Barnabas in his essay "People's Participation in Planning: A Realistic Approach" conceives participation as a means to sensitize people and thus to increase their capacity for receptivity and ability to respond to development programmes as well as encourage local initiative when translated in terms of rural development. Participation implies people's involvement in the decision-making process, implementing programmes and their involvement in the evaluation of programmes.

The common focus of emphasis in the definitions of Tewari and Barnabas is 'initiative'. The spirit of initiative gets strengthened when the policies and plans of the government reflect the needs and demands of the common people and the decentralized organs of governance are accorded adequate powers and discretion to design and redesign programmes in tune with the local needs and environs. Hence, the significance of decentralized planning in fructifying participatory development is immense.

This point is underscored by Y. Sharma in his paper "People's Participation in Development Processes: Experience and Strategy." He observes that rural development through people's participation and initiative should be facilitated by people's representatives as well as by the administrative apparatus, and the local institutions should mobilize resources for effecting rapid socio-economic development at the decentralized level.

Sharma recounts his experience of persuading the people of a backward block in Rajasthan for participating in the development process. The effort, all through, was to awaken and energize the dormant potential of the beneficiaries in the development activities. Ironically, the sincerity of the initiators was not reciprocated adequately by the people themselves, whose skepticism against the new experiment came in the way of genuine participation.

Though Panchayati Raj brought a sea change in the approach to decentralized development, its unintended consequences were too many to be ignored. Paradoxically, the administrative initiative was dwarfed by the power of elected representatives, voluntarism had been replaced by a mercenary approach and planning from above overshadowed the entire development process. No wonder, the whole enterprise of goal-directed change at the local level became 'governmentalized', forcing the relegation of people's initiative to the margin. Soon, as Sharma muses, a capitalistic order supplanted the socialist spirit.

Sharma's reflections indicate how a theory of people's participation gets moderated, twisted and distorted during its implementation in an environment that is bereft of a long tradition of decentralized democracy.

Participation for Rural Development

Satish C. Sharma in his essay "Participative Approach to Rural Development" rightly observes that active participation of citizens is a requisite to successful designing and implementation of rural development programmes, more particularly when such programmes follow an integrated approach. Citizens or client groups have to initiate 'active' intervention through what Milton Esman calls 'induced' development. Here the role of indigenous social institutions and local political institutions for mobilizing public opinion becomes a critical factor in participatory development.

Sharma cautions that bureaucracy is likely to place hurdles in the path of participation, for a participative system will clip the wings of generalist administrators and conversely, the people's dependence on and trust in technocrats are likely to increase. In fact, the age-old tradition of bureaucratic supremacy also prevents the acceptance of leadership of the lay people and their representatives in decision-making in development administration. Bureaucrats also shun situations that would make them 'accountable' for the accomplishment of socio-economic goals of rural development.

Sharma raises a much discussed issue of the competition existing between the representative political institutions and administrators. Moving from the legacy of, what Fred Riggs calls, a 'bureaucratic polity' to a 'party-run polity' is a problematic process, provoking substantial resistance from the bureaucracy itself. While participation strengthens the political system, lack of it promotes bureaucratic power. A competitive relationship between the two systems is natural in any dynamic democracy.

Participation for Watershed Development

The Guidelines for Watershed Development, issued in 2000 and revised in 2001 by the Ministry of Rural Development, had provided for a State Watershed Development Committee and had made Zila

Parishads responsible for implementing the Watershed Development Programme. The chairman of a Zila Parishad was made the head of the District Watershed Development Committee. Moreover, the Panchayati Raj bodies were entrusted with the responsibilities of monitoring and reviewing the implementation of Watershed Development Programme and provide guidelines for improving the relevant administrative arrangements. Various self-help groups (SHGs), user groups, watershed associations (WAs) and watershed committees (WCs) facilitated the participation of the local community in watershed management.

Even before the above system could take deep roots and show its efficacy, the Government of India came out in January 2003 with fresh 'Haryali Guidelines' which did away with WAs and WCs, whereas their functions were transferred to Gram Panchayats. In addition, an intermediate panchayat agency (like Panchayat Samiti) was envisaged as the programme implementation agency for all the projects sanctioned in a block/tehsil/taluka. With the declaration of Haryali Guidelines, District Watershed Committees were dispensed with.

On the issue of modifications in the procedures followed for the decentralized administration of watershed management, Rakesh Hooja and Rakshat Hooja in their essay entitled "Community-Based Organizations and Panchayats as Instruments of Governance in the Sphere of Watershed Development" question the rationality supposedly involved in this wholesale reorganization of watershed development administration. They argue that the scope and nature of administrative organization of Panchayati Raj bodies and watershed user groups are significantly different and reflect their respective unique characteristics. Hence, it is "necessary for panchayat bodies and local user groups to not only co-exist but also to supplement, complement and strengthen each other". Besides, experience proves that Gram Sabhas have not been able to perform their required functions effectively due to their large size, unorganized membership and a high degree of heterogeneity. As for Gram Panchayats, they are only territorial and not ecological units like the watershed areas. Thus, a watershed may cut across boundaries of Gram Panchayats or vice versa. It may be cautioned that the effectiveness of watershed management should not be sacrificed just for the sake of strengthening panchayat bodies as institutions of local governance. Hence, the time-tested programme implementation agencies (PIAs) (NGOs, government organizations/agencies, research institutions, community-based organizations etc.) should not be divested of their role of enhancing the capability of the watershed management system. Thus, the whole policy system, particularly after the enunciation of the Haryali Guidelines, needs to be re-examined and people's participation should be permitted to be institutionalized in more ways than one. No doubt, collaborative co-existence is better than competitive isolation.

Sustainable Agricultural Technology Transfer Through Participation

The Brundtland Commission in their eminent report, *Our Common Future*, had defined sustainable development as "development that meets the needs of the present without compromising the ability of the future generation to meet their own needs". Sujit Kumar Paul, in his essay "Participatory Approach for Sustainable Agricultural Technology Transfer" reminds us that agricultural sustainability and eco-system protection have taken centre stage in international aid and development programmes. Continued mining of soil and overexploitation of water resources is bound to restrict our ability to feed the increasing population and result into adverse environmental consequences that would not be easy to retrieve. Hence, there is a need for ensuring sustainability of the entire farming system so that it provides farmers with economically viable and environmentally sound alternatives in developing their farming system.

Paul presents a case study of the KRIBHCO initiative in a segment of West Bengal that is intended to improve the livelihood of the resource-poor community through participatory approaches employed in order to integrate the entire farming system. The participatory approach adopted in the project involves various stages including the Village Entry, Rapport Building, Participatory Rural Appraisal (PRA), Community Problem Analysis (CPA), Issue Focused Participatory Rural Appraisal (IFPRA) and other aspects of project implementation and monitoring. The findings lead to the conclusion that farmers' education, their participation in different organizations, the environmental problems they encounter, and their thinking about sustainability issue through system approaches are closely interlinked. Thus, a boost to farmers' literacy would augment farmers' knowledge that can be appropriately used for facilitating sustainable agricultural development.

Participatory Irrigation Management

Rakesh Hooja in his essay "Beyond Farmers' Participation in Irrigation: Participatory Irrigation Management Approaches in India" reminds us that farmers' participation in irrigation management is no more considered adequate for improving the performance of irrigation. What needs to be done further is to adopt the approach and technique of Participatory Irrigation Management (PIM) which is an instrument of irrigation reforms and efficient irrigation. PIM is taking over of at least one level of irrigation channels/canals above the outlet, i.e., taking over at least a minor canal by a Water User Association (WUA) that would take over the management of both the operation and the management of a canal. Besides, the WUA and the irrigation agency (mainly governmental) collaborate with each other in a joint partnership at managing the entire irrigation system for equitable, rational, timely and convenient allocation of water and increase in the efficiency of canal management as well as on-field water application.

Hooja explains that farmers' willingness to undertake PIM depends on whether the returns from PIM provide them enough incentives to offset the cost, financial or otherwise, of participating and undertaking managerial and implementational responsibilities. PIM cannot be considered as a panacea for all operational problems faced by the irrigation system. There are issues that warrant only technical solutions, while there are other problems that would warrant an effective government action. It is true however that the technical and the governmental solutions would be inadequate without a sound system of PIM. Hence, Hooja advocates the universalization of PIM throughout all irrigation or water resource projects in India.

Hooja also favours specification of a wider set of functions for WUAs which would encompass the core or compulsory group of tasks (management and maintenance of the irrigation and water distribution system) and the optional agriculture and land-water management related tasks. For performing both the sets of functions adroitly, a rigorous training plan for PIM operations would be required. Ideally, PIM training would be needed for all kinds of stakeholders and functionaries at all levels.

Moreover, Hooja advocates extremely flexible legislation for PIM at the state level. Such laws should be comprehensive, yet should allow various statutory WUAs to follow their own strategies in their own way provided the basic premise of PIM (the taking over of at least a canal minor by the WUA) is met and their implementation ought to be facilitated by interdisciplinary state level groups and supported by advisory and lower bodies.

Community Participation: Lessons from South Africa

John J. Williams in his essay "Governance, Advocacy Planning and Community Participation: A Study of Community Development Workers in South Africa" explores the efficacy of advocacy planning in the context of democratic practice and community participation and offers certain theoretical postulates culled from his research on government in South Africa. Notably, the federal legislation in South Africa enables local governance institutions to be intensely participative in their functioning. Thus, the reigning philosophy in this regard advocates that people should have a say in decisions and actions that affect their lives. Besides, they should receive the information necessary for making participative decisions and obtain the feedback on their execution.

Williams points out that community participation depends, to a great extent, on the nature of organizations and mobilization at grass-roots level as well as on the purpose of such participation. Essentially, it is not so much the presence or absence of community organizations at grass-roots level that determines the nature and impact of community participation on local development programmes, but whether or not development schemes and strategies are taken up by specific local authorities into their Integrated Development Plans (IDPs). Truly, the attitudes of municipal officials and councilors influence both the form and dimensions of participation.

In the above context, Williams offers certain recommendations to foster meaningful dialogues, engagement and empowerment at grass roots level: encourage voluntary participation; ensure that public's contribution will influence planning decisions; encourage equal participation in development programmes; facilitate the involvement of those potentially affected; and communicate to participants how their input affects the decisions. Implementation of these suggestions is most likely to strengthen the overall community participation edifice at the level of local governance. Hopefully, these lessons from South Africa would be relevant to most democracies.

Women's Participation in Local Governance

Pranab Kumar Pandey observes in his essay "Women's Participation in Local Government: The Bangladesh Experience" that in Bangladesh, despite certain facilitating legal provisions, the participation of women in local government has remained minimal. The obstacles in the process of integrating and involving women in local government activities include: traditional dependence of women on men and the former's confinement to the domestic four walls; deprivation of women of land rights, thus rendering them economically powerless; cultural mores that make women subservient to men; the *purdah* system that has adversely affected the status of women; educational backwardness of women; and an absence of a vigorous civil society. In this context, Pandey makes a plea that government policies must address the needs of empowering women in their professional career, political leadership, media relations and resource generation; enhancement of opportunities to women for formal education and training; greater mobilization of women in governance and development at all levels; and heightened awareness of women of their potential role in socio-economic and political transformation. Countries like Bangladesh have a long way to go; the path selected by them seems to be correct though cumbersome.

Early Debate on Panchayati Raj

Mats Kihlberg in his essay published in 1975, "Trends in the Debate on Panchayati Raj", refers to the conflicting views expressed during the Constituent Assembly debates about village democracy. The negative view of the localistic and parochial village socio-political culture, taken by Dr. B.R. Ambedkar, prevented a place of eminence to Panchayati Raj Institutions (PRIs) in the Indian Constitution. Consequently, the Gandhian approach of making villages the centres of local governance could find a place only in the Directive Principles of the Constitution.

Kihlberg refers to a few well-known approaches to Panchayati Raj. J.P. Narayan's emphasis on making Panchayati Raj the basis of 'participating democracy', the community development approaches emphasizing on developing villages with the self-help methods; the bureaucratic view considering Panchayati Raj as a state organization with limited independence; and the local self-government approach with a wider role for PRIs.

Kihlberg favours a broader international comparative approach in examining Panchayati Raj. He argues that the role and status of Panchayati Raj should be examined from the viewpoint of its functions concerning planning, resource mobilization, provision of services and integration of services. The focus of PRI activities should be 'rural welfare' involving health, nutrition, education and other aspects of life like security. This role can be performed effectively only if local leaders in Panchayati Raj act as dynamic agents of change.

Local Governance and Planning

Though planning is a requisite to socio-economic development in transitional societies, its focus only on the macro dimensions may result into a neglect of backward areas and weaker sections, overlooking of the basic needs of people, and an absence of participation in the process of development. These are the views of Abdul Aziz in his essay "Process of Decentralized Governance and Planning", Little wonder, a paradigm shift has taken place in recent years, signifying a move from broad macro planning to specific local area and weaker section-oriented decentralized planning. Such a system of local planning depends for its effectiveness on the efficacy of the local governance system. Aziz outlines certain preconditions for effective local governance. The first condition is the transfer of adequate powers, functions and resources to the decentralized government, thus following the maxim that whatever could be done better at the lower level should be assigned to it and necessary financial resources should be devolved accordingly. Second, decentralized government institutions should enjoy an autonomy of decision-making in respect of planning and administration. Simultaneously, they should be made accountable and thus practice transparency in their functioning. Plans should be formulated on the basis of a rational assessment of people's needs and local resources and thus the various projects designed should be made economically viable. Third, a high degree of coordination in governance and planning at different levels is a requisite for good governance. The District Planning Committees, when activated, can facilitate such a coordination. And finally, people's participation is a requisite for good governance, and for this purpose, the psychological barriers to an active and purposive role of civil society organizations must be overcome sincerely. Hence, Panchayati Raj bodies should awaken themselves to this imperative of effective governance and emerge as result-oriented dynamic institutions.

Strategies for Effective Local Level Planning

K.V. Sundaram in his essay "Local Level Planning for Integrated Rural Development: Case Studies from India and Abroad" deals with experiments of integrated rural development and the role of local level planning undertaken in a block each in Kerala and Tamil Nadu and one block each in Malaysia and Nepal. On the basis of experiences at the cross-state and cross-national levels, he offers certain useful lessons. Sundaram contends that an approach concentrating on a small geographic area seems to be the best way of organizing local level planning for integrated rural development. The plan-frame for area development should be comprehensive and in tune with the available resources and the existing as well as potential administrative capabilities. This would require a synthesis of the target group (like the below poverty line people) and infrastructural development.

Sundaram is of the view that meticulous project planning involving systematic formulation, implementation, monitoring and evaluation make local planning truly effective. Even the selection of projects should be preceded by an evaluation of all the feasible projects and schemes. Only then a multi-sectoral programme can help reduce poverty and enhance productivity. Such programmes also require a high level of coordination among the multiple objectives spanning enhanced production, increased employment and a more equitable distribution of income.

Sundaram cautions that local level planning for integrated rural development can succeed only if it is designed for the people and *with* the people Hence, people's participation in local level planning should also involve reviewing the problems of implementation and sharing of responsibility for the upkeep and maintenance of projects. For this purpose, appropriate training of the local personnel is absolutely desirable. Finally, Sundaram underscores the need to establish viable and effective linkages between the local, regional and sectoral plans and even the national plan. These vertical linkages, complementing the horizontal linkages, can augment the effectiveness of overall socio-economic planning and development of rural areas.

Ramesh C. Shrivastava in his essay "Panchayati Raj and Rural Development in India" remarks that the project and the sectoral approaches have neither triggered an overall development of rural areas nor reduced socio-economic inequality. Hence, efforts should be made to design area-specific programmes and utilize the local endowments for growth, social justice and full employment. Srivastava argues that planning for the integration of various programmes should be undertaken so as to establish appropriate linkages for optimal utilization of local endowment in consistence with the plan objectives, local needs and requirements of environmental balance. It is unfortunate that due to lack of people's participation and of well-organized institutional support, particularly at grass-roots level, rural development programmes could not yield the desired results.

Shrivastava points out that PRIs have not emerged as frontal organizations for undertaking and guiding comprehensive rural development programmes, despite the ambitious 73rd Amendment to the Indian Constitution. Moreover, local planning under the stipulated umbrella of district planning has not taken off. What is worse, there is a persistent ambiguity about the role of PRIs in local level development planning. A greater clarity in this regard is a prerequisite to the devising of a methodical framework for decentralized planning.

Restructuring Development Administration

R.S. Kumat in his article "Panchayati Raj and Poverty Alleviation: Need for New Administrative Structure" observes that despite the 73rd Constitutional Amendment, PRIs were not given the authority and resources to undertake developmental work in their respective territories. This was certainly against the spirit of the Constitution. While the poverty alleviation programmes were run by DRDA, the formal implementing agencies were Panchayat Samitis and panchayats. At the time when Kumat wrote his essay, the district collector was responsible for controlling the officials of Panchayat Samitis and was also coordinating the functions of DRDAs and PRIs. Kumat is critical of these arrangements and therefore his question is: "Why the elected bodies should not have fully independent charge of the development plans and be allowed to take initiatives so that people at large participate in the development process?" Since the time that Kumat wrote his essay, there has been a sea change in the development administrative system at the district and the lower levels. The DRDA has been merged with Zila Parishad and the collector is no more directly and formally responsible for taking initiative and exercising supervision in development administration at the district and sub-district levels. Thus, currently, Kumat's model focusing on the unity of command and direct linkage among elected representatives is in operation. Yet, the recent experience is not entirely satisfactory. Perhaps Kumat's model has eroded the genuine authority of the district collector and this arrangement has dwindled the overall effectiveness of development administration, though state governments still tend to depend upon the coordination and supervision role of the district collectors even for developmental tasks. It is high time that the present arrangements were reviewed and scanned and alternative paradigms designed in consonance with the demands of an effective democracy.

Resources for Panchayati Raj Institutions

A.P. Barnabas in his research article "Finances of Panchayati Raj Institutions: A Study" makes a cross-state analysis of the financial administrative patterns existing in Gujarat, Maharashtra and Rajasthan and examines their variations. He regrets the limited resources available with the PRIs for undertaking development works and offers a few significant suggestions.

Barnabas opines that Zila Parishads should levy taxes or a cess on education, cash crops and income of factories. Besides, the possibility of revenue department collecting taxes on behalf of PRIs should be explored. He also favours the system's reviving of 'untied grants' in order to strengthen the finances of Zila Parishads. Zila Parishad officials and non-officials should also be adequately trained to plan and implement the welfare activities at the district level.

Barnabas cautions that an unduly high percentage of Panchayati Raj resources should not be consumed for meeting establishment expenses, the figure for which currently goes up to 80 per cent of the total outlay. Hence, there should be economy in administrative expenditure and greater rationalization of development investment. Only then PRIs will gain the respect of state governments as their major partners in the process of socio-economic transformation. Barnabas also observes that PRIs, in order to be effective agents of social change, should have before them clear objectives of rural development, enjoy greater delegation of powers in planning and managing the finances, and have an effective administrative set-up to ensure a foolproof control system. These measures can help in restoring the faith of people in decentralized government.

Women and Panchayati Raj

As is well known, the 73rd Constitutional Amendment Act has created an opportunity for a large segment of female population to provide leadership to the institutions of decentralized governance at the village level. Pawan Kumar Banta in his essay "Women in Panchayati Raj Institutions: Beginning of a New Era" outlines the various provisions of the 73rd Constitutional Amendment Act that accord prominence to women's rights and obligations. Banta observes that a mere devolution of powers to women representatives is not enough. In order to enhance their competitive competence, there should be organized continuous training programmes focusing on rural development schemes, management development, gender sensitization, training of trainers and effective administrative skills. Political empowerment must be backed by a high level of administrative competence.

Administrative Adjuncts to Panchayati Raj

D. Ravinder makes an interesting study of the functioning and impact of village secretariat system in Andhra Pradesh. It may be recalled that in January 2002, the Government of Andhra Pradesh in accordance with the requirements of good governance, launched a new system of village secretariat which was headed by the Panchayat Secretary. It was hoped that the *gram sachivalaya* (village secretariat) would change the pace of development in villages and usher in a new work culture for the benefit of rural population. This integrated organizational device replaced the earlier system of executive officers, village development officers and village administrative officers who collectively were undertaking administrative functions pertaining to Panchayati Raj. It was hoped that this new mechanism would result in the reduction of staff and facilitate vertical interaction within the administrative system from village to the state level through an e-governance process. Notably, the revenue and development functions were amalgamated through the newly devised administrative structure. There was an expected uproar over the merger of revenue and developmental functions, more particularly, from the revenue departmental personnel. Resultantly, such a merger was confined to the village level only. Soon, it was realized that Panchayat Secretaries with whom 64 functions of general, administrative, revenue and developmental nature were vested, became a bone of contention and this naturally led to a major conflict between the officials and the non-officials.

It may be pointed out that in the revised dispensation, Sarpanchas enjoy substantial financial powers popularly known as the 'cheque power'. The Panchayat Secretaries were unfavourably disposed towards this expanded power of the Sarpanchas. On the other hand, it was alleged that the Panchayat Secretaries were overruling and ignoring the elected Sarpanchas belonging to lower caste in villages. The community-based organizations (CBOs) also seemed to promote parallel structures of influence and they were managing rural resources independently of PRIs. This led to, in many cases, marginalization of PRIs.

In sum, Ravinder's study highlights the surfeit of contradictions that has emerged as a result of the new administrative innovation at the village level in Andhra Pradesh. It only highlights the competition for influence between the democratic forces claiming legitimate political power and the administrative functionaries who are expected to follow the guidelines of administrative effectiveness. In this context, it needs to be appreciated that the paradigm of good governance advocates a proper synthesis between the power and obligations of political as well as administrative systems and hence envisages collaborative cooperation between the two.

The Cross-State Scenario

There are several essays in the present volume which focus on the Panchayati Raj system and the rural development scenario in different states of India. Although the 73rd Constitutional Amendment envisages a uniformity of three-tier structure of Panchayati Raj in all the states, the divergence and diversities in the actual functioning of PRIs at the state level and below are marked substantially by the socio-political heritage of each state as well as the economic context in which the Panchayati Raj system works.

Sunita Kale provides details of the major programmes being undertaken by panchayats in Goa and of the state control mechanisms over panchayats. She observes that the resolutions of the Gram Sabhas in Goa are generally not honoured by panchayats. Besides, there is a traditional conflict between the Sarpanch and the Village Panchayat Secretary. Moreover, the village level administrators like BDO and Gram Sevak are not adequately motivated. Resultantly, the impact of the 73rd Constitutional Amendment in generating a positive climate for Panchayati Raj in Goa is woefully meagre. Since political awareness among the villagers is low, there is hardly any initiative from the grass roots to introduce effectiveness in the functioning of PR bodies. Kale is hopeful that in due course of time, the constitutionally legitimized democratic decentralized system will transform the politico-administrative ambience at the local level.

C.P. Vithal reflects on the impact of devolution of powers and functions to PRIs in the union territory of Daman. Although legal functions performed by these bodies in Daman and Diu are similar to those found in Goa and other states, Vithal refers mainly to the village panchayat administration organized by the panchayat secretariat performing multifarious functions. Vithal is of the view that panchayat secretariat in Daman and Diu suffers from overburdening of work, stagnation and dual control by officials and the district Parishads.

Further, as against 29 subjects mentioned in the Constitution, only a very few subjects have been transferred to the Panchayati Raj bodies. Besides, they enjoy very little functional powers. All this needs to be rectified. Panchayat should also take the initiative in improving their financial position by undertaking remunerative enterprises like constructing shopping complexes after acquiring vacant land from the government. Besides, economic activities of Panchayati Raj should not be confined to a tourism economy; these should also involve the promotion of irrigation facilities and fisheries.

Rajbir Singh discusses the status of democratic decentralization in Haryana with special reference to the role of Zila Parishad as an apex body. He starts with the premises that after the 73rd amendment, Zila Parishads have become stronger, more autonomous, financially sound and more representative. However, the empirical experience points out that the rotation system of reservation has watered down the political ambition of younger people who can provide continuing leadership at the local level. Besides, the MPs and MLAs, through their participation in the meetings of Zila Parishads, generally try to supplant the initiatives of local leaders. The dominating role of bureaucracy and the lack of regular staff with the elected bodies also come in the way of self-confidence and self-reliance of Zila Parishads.

B.S. Bhargava and Avinash Samal provide a review of Panchayati Raj system in Orissa in a historical context. They discuss the various factors that were responsible for the decline of Panchayati Raj before the 73rd Constitutional Amendment. What is underscored by them is the fact that despite all the ostensible reforms made for the strengthening of the Panchayati Raj bodies, there was an apparent lack of sincerity on the part of the political and administrative leadership in genuinely implementing these reforms. Bhargava and Samal are of the view that the political parties which profess their faith in decentralized democracy should understand that the long-term benefits of an effective Panchayati Raj system are much more than the short-term political gains registered by political parties in their bid to centralize power at the state level.

Almost six years after the 73rd Constitutional Amendment, the state of Rajasthan was also faced with a weak Panchayati Raj structure. G.S. Narwani, in his essay on Rajasthan, notes that PRIs in Rajasthan were short of financial as well as manpower resources. The functions transferred to them under Schedule XI were inadequate and even for the transferred functions, powers necessary to execute them were not devolved. Moreover, the elected representatives, more particularly women chairpersons belonging to SC/ST categories, were not imparted sufficient training in capacity building. Zila Parishads, which until then had not been given control over DRDAs, were essentially weak organizations, and so were the grass roots institutions of Gram Sabhas.

The status of Panchayati Raj during the same phase in Tamil Nadu has been discussed by Santishree D.N.B. Pandit. Pandit explains that Panchayati Raj bodies in Tamil Nadu suffer from unstable and uncertain financial position, low level of service delivery, ad hoc local level planning, subordination of PRI leadership under the state level political leadership, corruption, financial irregularities, casteism and political and official interference. She concludes wryly: "In a state which had a political culture of hero worship, servility to authority and populism, it is very difficult to ensure the realization of decentralization of power."

The essay "People-Centred Governance: The Panchayati Raj Experience in Uttar Pradesh" by S.N. Singh, discusses the status and performance of PRIs in the most populous state of India. Three parameters on the basis of which Singh's analysis of people-centred governance is based are structure, process and behaviour. From a structural perspective, the government of Uttar Pradesh has implemented the essential legal stipulations for women and other sections of society. Looking from the process perspective, elections have been conducted as per law by the State Election Commission. However, from a behavioural perspective, Singh regrets that as yet, the dominance of bureaucracy over the governance system is paramount and the people's representatives, because of their low level of education and awareness, find it hard to assert in dealing with the issues of people's welfare. This vitiates the spirit of people-centred government, for people do not remain at the centre of such a dispensation. Once again, Singh is critical of the DRDAs being kept out of the control of Zila Parishad and of the scarce financial resources with PRIs. Yet, he is hopeful that the grass roots governance will take deeper roots as time lends credence to a democratic order.

It is not surprising that almost all narrations of the Panchayati Raj experiments at the cross-state level reinforce similar concerns. These relate to:

1. Half-hearted decentralization measures, leading to only partial devolution of functions and schemes to Panchayati Raj bodies.

2. Overlapping of authority over the local level developmental system by the endowed state authority and the avowed PRI power.
3. A major chunk of developmental schemes are being kept outside the ambit of PRIs, though lately, with the transfer of DRDAs to Zila Parishads, there has been a tangible corrective action.
4. Shortage of personnel with PRIs.
5. Dominance of bureaucracy over the local governance system.
6. Scarcity of financial resources with PRIs.
7. Lack of integration and coordination between PRIs and the state government structures.
8. Ineffective district and local level planning.
9. Unsatisfactory delivery system.
10. Low level of citizens' involvement in PRI functioning.

Recently, the Government of India has taken the initiative in examining the current status of Panchayati Raj at the cross-state level and has found a glaring gap between the what is professed and what is practised. How these gaps will be bridged will depend not just on the central and the state governments but also on the PRIs which were created with a hope for establishing a truly people's government at grass-roots level.

Vision for Decentralization in Rural Governance

The final contribution in the volume entitled "Decentralization in Rural Governance" by M. Veerappa Moily is based on the slightly edited text of a speech delivered by him at a seminar as Chairman of the Second Administrative Reforms Commission. Moily believes that we must follow a 'middle path' on the basis of recognized principles of subsidiarity while devolving functions to local level PRIs. An exercise in activity mapping can be undertaken that is based on objective criteria such as the economies of scale, capacity available for performing an activity, externalities relating to that activity etc. Following the mapping exercise, appropriate functions should be transferred to the concerned local bodies alongwith the staff and other resources necessary to implement such activities. Further, Moily suggests that the traditional form of government must be associated with self governance and with positive democratic concepts like gender justice and adult franchise. Further, there should be an exclusive functional jurisdiction or an independent sphere of action for each level of panchayats. There could also be common spheres of partnership between the state government and the panchayats or there could be spheres where PRIs would act as agencies for implementing state or central government schemes or programmes.

The whole approach of devolution needs to be built around the twin criteria of speed and simplicity instead of it being a dominantly ideological approach. Moily favours the ensuring of accountability of PRIs, advocates undertaking rigorous annual audits, including social audit and the appointment of a statutory ombudsman. Nevertheless, he cautions that the fiscal autonomy of PRIs ought to be preserved alongwith strengthening their administrative and managerial capabilities. Little wonder, Moily recommends that the grants to PRIs must be untied so that they can decide their own priorities.

Moily is also an advocate of making district panchayat as the seat of district government. He believes that the district tier of local government may represent both rural and urban government and hence there should be a constitutional amendment to facilitate election of a single representative body at the district level. It is indeed a radical suggestion for institutional reconstruction. Likewise, Moily advocates greater accountability and transparency in the functioning of panchayats and enhancing their level of integrity and efficiency. His essay reflects a path-breaking approach to decentralized governance at the rural level and favours the adoption of a genuinely devolutionary approach based on effective multi-level democratic governance. Only time will tell whether it finds favour with the people at the helm.

Panchayati Raj will shortly celebrate its golden jubilee. The question that is uppermost in the minds of all those interested in participatory governance and decentralization is: How truly 'golden' will this jubilee be?

Section I

Participatory Approaches to Development

2 People's Participation

A Theoretical Framework

Shashi Ranjan Tewari

It has to be admitted at the outset that a cross-section of the people do not as yet participate in the functioning of development activities in India. The major fiscal efforts leading to planning and its implementation are undertaken by the government on different levels of its administrative organizations. It has to be admitted here too that the administrators of the government still mostly interpret 'public interest' as end-results of developmental activities on the basis of organic theoretical assumptions which are being challenged today. The redeeming feature, however, of their approach is that they do provide a refined utilitarian theory of policy process which shows that certain 'inputs' of interest into final decisional equations are best provided by them within a framework of general political authority and guidance.[1]

Before an attempt is made to go deeper into the study, it is logical a priori to understand the concept of 'participation' as has been implied in this paper. The word 'participation' refers to those voluntary activities by which the members of a society take part in decision-making in the different processes and aspects of developmental activities at different levels of government. It implies also that the people do so as matter of their role as sovereign in a democratic from of government. The area of their participation involves administrative decisions and their implementations conducive to development.

The word 'apathy' refers to a situation of withdrawal or indifference of the people towards developmental activities opposite to the sense of participation involving wilful association sustained in unity with the objectives of a programme or scheme or a project of development.

There are many types of participation—political participation, administrative participation and social participation. The concept of political participation is crucial since the highest and the broadest fabric of society is the state. It thrives on its political ideals which bear the spirit and the principles of that society based on place, consent of the people and their institutional device of government operative in nature and effective in administration. In a democratic form of government, with a mixed economic structure and a determined hierarchy of values—liberty, equality and progress arranged in priority of first, second and third respectively, the political participation is the most important variable.

The sphere of administrative participation is the exclusive area of civil servants who participate under the conditions of their service, and in contract with the government as individuals. This formal participant must be either a member of the government or must be deemed to be so for a fixed tenure either as an expert consultant or as a political associate legitimately holding his position vested in the structure of the law—the rule of the law manifested by constitution, statutes, rules and regulations of the government.

The area of social participation is the widest in meaning and is entirely dependent on the understanding, identification and sense of social responsibility of the volunteering individual or volunteering group of individuals motivated by the values of social justice and national objectives.

Political Participation

In a simple language, political participation refers to those voluntary activities by which the members of a society take part in the selection of rulers at different levels of the government, directly or indirectly associate themselves in the process of formulating a public policy. Their association in operation is classified as a political process. In other words, the political process involves those activities in various groups as they struggle for and use power to achieve group purposes.

The importance of the above types of participation must be driven home to the administrators because they do not resist the strongest temptation to call a decision jointly taken with the formal political associates as political in nature, inherent in a political process. Such a phenomenon is discernible in a case where an Enquiry Commission tries to locate responsibility.[2] The civil servant is basically concerned with policy-making and its implementation. He needs a view of democratic theory, both as a citizen and as an administrator.

There are at least three reckonable ideas of democracy, which cannot be ignored.[3]

Representative Democracy

It is the fundamental thesis of democracy, which assigns policy-making to the elected representatives of the people. The initial sinew of popular control is provided by periodic elections and the representatives do convey the wishes of the electorate. The dynamics of democratic representation today are indicative of the fact that the policy-making functions are exercised often through political parties than through individual representatives. There is no indication in the democratic theory as to how far elected leaders should be bound, either positively or negatively by the directive of the parties as opposed to the use of their own discretion.

Pluralist Democracy

This view refers to the recognition of the rights of the groups to organize with a view to pressing their interests and viewpoints. In a plural society like India and the USA, such groups are formed at all levels of government. These groups work through the formal channels of representative organizations, vindicating their views for acceptance of the elected members of the legislature and selected members of the executive. According to this theory, political parties may be turned into cross-group representative bodies cutting across party lines but reflecting broader group compromises.

The ambitious part of the theory is that it accepts that parties may be largely turned into coalitions of group interests and that ministers or presidents may function mainly as arbitrators between competing group interests. "Pluralism as a normative theory of democracy can therefore only be plausibly supported as a supplement or correlative to other theories."[4]

Populist Democracy

According to this theory, people should directly participate in the decision-making processes but it should be confined to the concerned public.

There are two types of views about 'populist theory': the first approach (classic populism) seeks to shift key decisions from elected representatives to the general electorate, e.g., through referenda and to restrain the actions of representatives who are supposed to be delegates theoretically through such devices as frequent elections and revocation of political authority; the second viewpoint about populism has some analogy with economic theories of consumers' sovereignty of market system. The political person passes for a 'consumer' of public services and his decisions as such smack the same air of independence in the use of franchise as the consumer exercises in the choice of his spending power motivated by both gain and tastes.

A serious shortcoming of the classical populism is that it calls for vesting excessive authority in the electorate. In the case of the Indian polity, it tends to substitute for the discretion of the representatives with the manipulated local interests with demagogic leadership (e.g., the opinions of the controller of mass media).

This brief review indicates that pluralist and populist theories should still be treated as supplementary to representative theory of participation. Even a casual look at the working of the modern governments shows that the civil servants mostly accept their subordination to the formal political authority only on the basis of electoral procedures. So far as pluralist theories are concerned, even in the most mature countries like Switzerland and the UK, the ideas of pluralist or populist form of participation have lately commended themselves to the thinking of the elected heads of the government to some extent and to a microscopic minority in the legislature.[5]

To recapitulate the statements made earlier, public interest is a complex and elusive notion hardly doing justice with the participative aspect of its connotation. The moot question is what is the relationship between the administrative version of the public interest and the treatment of organized groups who have their own version of public interest on a certain issue, which touches the core of their existence.

The critics of pluralist thesis take it for granted as a universal phenomenon that the interest of a group cannot be justified in tune with the concept of general interest. This notion is again debatable today. A consideration of the interests of farmers producing and supplying food grains to the whole community cannot pass for narrow or sectarian approach because it is concerned with the principle of equity; bow far should special efforts be made to help small farmers having poor soil?

There could be problems of perspective—how far should farmers bow to the call of immediate sacrifices for a better future. Again, there could be a problem of tying them in cooperative associational with other competing as well as supporting organizations, for example, it could be a question to what extent should farmers be solely concerned with their own prosperity or work for an affluent economy which benefits the farmers along with other association.[6]

The next problem crops up regarding how far pluralist thesis tends to cover the 'public interest'. The values and stakes involved in public interest are broader than those which affect farmers' organization referred to above and what is indeed primarily concerned with prices and marketing. It is all the same tenable that the basic problems of defining interest are not so dissimilar. It has to be admitted that the interest of a group or public interest or general interest comprises both distributive and substantive elements.

Peter Self has observed:

> *Public interest* stands for predicated rules or standards of distributive justice and *general interest* for the assumed collective requirements of the whole community.
> This difference of terminology is related to the conflict between utilitarian and organic views of public interest. A narrow pluralist view of public interest confined the notion simply to acceptable rules, but rules imply standards of comparison unless justice is defined purely pragmatically.[7]

The distributive element requires successive balancing and reconciliation of sectional interest—for instance, of wheat producers with livestock keepers, of farmers generally with farm workers, of all agriculturists with consumers and tax-payers and so on. The substantive element requires the determination of an agricultural policy which serves as well the interests of the entire society.[8]

Even in a democratic government, this understanding generally goesabegging since the administrators bank on organic theoretical assumptions. This can be explained thus: a law is made by the legislature, for instance, the U.P. Roadways Act in which it is mentioned that roadways shall be run by the state on all highways which connect district centres and national highways. It is an enabling provision of the act that the supply of the roadways would be adequate in number, accessible to the smallest pocket of income-earner, would keep timings, and run efficiently in public interest. The methods of running them in public interest would be devised by the administrative authorities on the premises of efficiency, economy, and as public utility. The administration is entrusted with the delegated legislative powers to cover these requirements by means of rules and regulations.

The administrator working in the above sphere under delegated legislative generally uses the enabling powers, banking on its own departmental data and procedures, because to him, the legislative support is good enough to fulfil the participative requirements of the policy-development.

The above limitation in restricting the notion of public participation is hardly seen when he assumes some of the onerous tasks of identifying, balancing and aggregating interest. The latter is an exception and if it is in practice, it elevates the civil service above the status of a bureaucratic body. Thus, the theories of populism serve as a necessary corrective to pluralist theories as well in imposing a legitimate claim upon administrative attention.

A realistic attitude about the dynamics of bureaucratic working and the dire need of people's participation induce us to suggest at least three avenues for ascertaining peoples' wishes:

1. the civil servant is fully conscious of his responsibility if there is a formal machinery for direct public consultation or participation in administrative decisions;
2. social surveys for popular needs, opinions and attitudes;
3. cost-benefit analysis oriented in the perspective of clienteles; and
4. educative role of the mass media in appraising the people about their own interest and the related governmental operations.

Notes

1. For the official strategic contribution in the preparation of the "Integrated Area Development and Drought Prone Area Programme" see Ishwar Dayal et al., *Dynamic of Formulating Policy in the Government of India,* New Delhi, IIPA, 1975, p. 31.
2. Note the general tone of the statements made by the officers of the Ministry of Information and Broadcasting facing the Shah Commission in New Delhi between 1 and 3 November, 1977. *The Hindustan Times, The Statesman* and *The Indian Express,* 2 to 5 November 1977.

3. See Robert A. Dahl, *A Preface to Democratic Theory*, Chicago, University of Chicago Press, 1956.
4. Peter Self, *Administrative Theories and Politics*, London, George Allen and Unwin, 1972, p. 285.
5. Herman Finer, *Government of Greater European Powers*, London, Metheun, 1958.
6. Chester L. Bernard, *Functions of the Executive*, Oxford, Oxford University Press, 1968, p. 194. In the perspective of environment, organizations existing in relationship with one another have interdependent interests leading to general interests.
7. See Peter Self, op. cit.
8. Peter Self and H. Storing, *The State and the Farmer*, London, 1962, Chapter 10.

3 People's Participation in Planning

A Realistic Approach

A.P. Barnabas

With the advent of the Panchayati Raj Institutions (PRIs) in the early sixties, it was hoped that there would be enthusiasm among the rural communities to participate in the process of development. However, these hopes were denied. A number of committees were appointed to look at the problems and many recommendations have been made by them. The 73rd Constitution Amendment Act is expected to provide a new lease of life to PRIs. However, observations indicate that while there was positive response initially, there has been much less enthusiasm of late.

It may be averred that people's participation according to the 73rd Amendment Act is effected more through elected representatives at the three levels: Zila Parishads, Panchayat Samitis and Gram Panchayats. Some states have, in their Acts, assigned some functions to be performed by Gram Sabhas. Among them are:

1. to consider/approve development plans,
2. to review the implementation of the development schemes,
3. to identify needs and priorities along with location, and
4. to mobilize people's participation and involvement through contribution in cash and kind and/or voluntary work in the programmes of economic development.

The legislation has a tendency to assign various functions including planning but not much attention is paid to the capacity or the available mechanism to undertake planning and implementation of the concerned units. The Gram Sabha's capacity to plan is extremely limited. It needs to be noted that almost all the studies on the PRIs indicate that the experience with regard to the functioning of Gram Sabha is far from satisfactory.

People's participation is a term that has been used over a long period. The Balwant Rai Mehta Committee's recommendations (1961) came about because of lack of people's participation in community development programmes. The Asoka Mehta Committee (1978) also made reference to the same concept. So also, the Working Group on District Planning (1984). The literature and experience (in India and abroad) on people's participation tends, by and large, to refer to micro-level experiences and usually of programmes initiated by voluntary organizations.

To analyze people's participation, there is need to look at it in terms of: (a) definition, (b) prerequisites (with particular reference to planning), (c) levels for planning, (d) implementation process—manpower requirements, and (e) resources.

Definition

There are many approaches to looking at people's participation. However, two of them relevant to the present discussion are being mentioned:

1. Participation, in its broadest sense, means to sensitize people and thus to increase the capacity for receptivity and ability to respond to development programmes as well as encourage local initiatives.
2. With regard to rural development, participation includes people's involvement in decision-making process, implementing programmes and sharing in the benefits of development programmes, and involvement in efforts to evaluate programmes.

If the first definition is accepted, then the task of evoking people's participation would in a sense gets limited. It would involve building awareness of the people regarding the activities planned for them at different levels and enabling them to participate by responding to the programmes that have been initiated by government or an outside agency. The assumption is that the programmes are, to some extent, at least based on the needs of the people.

The second part of the definition refers to encouraging local initiatives. This would mean that where the programmes do not meet felt needs, people could take initiative to indicate their requirement.

If the felt needs are to be met, then the plans at the state or district level will have to be flexible enough to undertake activities which are in keeping with the needs of people. It would also mean less rigidity in the utilization of funds provided by the state. The other alternative would be to provide for some united funds to Zila Parishad or Panchayat Samiti to enable them to fund programmes suggested by the community.

If the second definition is accepted, there would be many dimensions that need to be considered. It refers to people's involvement in decision-making, as well as evaluation of programmes. The Working Group also defines participation in similar terms. "People's participation to be really meaningful should take place at every stage of planning including preplanning, strategy setting, schemes formulation, monitoring and review and not merely at the time of plan finalization." Undertaking all these would be a very complicated process. To assume that Gram Sabhas or Gram Panchayats can perform all these functions is not realistic.

Prerequisites

Both the Asoka Mehta Committee and the Working Group suggest certain prerequisites for planning to be meaningful:

- Formulation of the major objectives of the plan.
- Resources inventory and data collection (potential for development and constraints).
- Identification of priorities.
- Formulation of programmes/projects for developments.
- Assessment of resources required (manpower and financial).

Apart from all this is the awareness of people of their rights, duties and obligations. There is also a need for empowerment of people to enable them to realize the benefits of development programmes. Civic education would therefore be another prerequisite.

Levels for Planning

It is also suggested that the district would be the more realistic unit for planning. Some states (e.g., Gujarat) provide for more pivotal role to the district while in others (such as, Uttar Pradesh) the block is more operational.

If the prerequisites are to be met, it would seem that the district would be the most suitable unit for planning. The manpower available at the district level has greater capacity to meet the prerequisites and also for implementation.

If this is accepted, then the most important need would be to strengthen the District Planning Committee for Rural Development. The Committee should be under the Zila Parishad and include officials of ICDS, DWCRA, AES etc. (DRDA is now a part of the Zila Parishad). There is need for a total view of the socio-economic needs of the district.

The Asoka Mehta Committee felt that village was too small a unit for planning. Mandal Panchayats were not considered adequate, and hence planning was to be done at the district level.

If the planning is to be done at the district level, it would mean that people's participation would be through elected representatives. According to the Working Group, "participation through representation at the district planning bodies may be the only feasible method of inducting popular participation". The Working Group also suggested that over time, the scope of participation would be enlarged.

The guidelines of the NIRD with regard to administrative powers of Zila Parishad suggest "to prepare district plans taking into account, plans at the Panchayat Samiti and Gram Panchayat levels and conforming to priorities set by the state and national level planning". If the Zila Parishad (as well as the Panchayat Samiti) is to conform to the state and national plans, the scope for planning at the district level *per se* becomes limited. There is need for working out mechanisms so that district plans are considered and incorporated in the state plan.

Mechanisms of Planning

In most states, there is a District Planning Officer, who is not necessarily a part of the Zila Parishad. He is expected to plan for all aspects of the district. Within the Zila Parishad, either the administrative head (or an officer designated) would be in charge of planning. At present, there is no Planning Officer in the Zila Parishad cadre. Some of the states studied felt apprehension about the capacity to undertake planning even at the district level with the existing staffing. This was true of both the officials and non-officials.

As already mentioned, the District Planning Committee for Rural Development needs to be strengthened by streamlining the structure and assigning specific functions. The present DPCs where they exist tend to be sprawling organizations with amorphous functions.

As the set-up of the PRIs is varied in the different states, guidelines from Ministry could indicate the manner of strengthening the District Planning Committee for Rural Development.

Implementation

The functionaries of the PRIs are recruited, appointed and paid by the state. The administrative control of the Zila Parishad *per se* is limited. At the block level, the technical officers are under dual control of the District Technical Officer and the BDO. There is a need to reconsider the manner of strengthening the block level administration. The district officers are also not responsible to the Zila Parishad President. If decentralized planning with popular support is to become functional, then the Zila Parishad officials need to have some control, so that the officers at the district and block levels would be responsible to the Zila Parishad officials for implementing the plans. The mechanism for making the officers responsible to both the state administration and the elected officials need to be worked out. The dual control has to be functional and meaningful.

Resources

The PRIs have hardly any resources of their own. Decentralized planning would be of little value, unless the PRIs have the power to determine the manner of expenditure of the funds provided by the states and the centre. The capacity to raise their own resources is limited as shown by most studies. In the present arrangement of schematic budgets, there is no flexibility available to the PRIs even to change allocation from one sector to another. Therefore, if felt needs are to be met, then there has to be either flexibility in the budget, or united funds provided to the PRIs.

It would seem that there are two possible alternatives to looking at participation:

1. Accept that participation is through sensitizing people to be more receptive and respond to development programmes.
2. (a) Accept the district as the planning unit and the role of elected representatives in the planning process be considered to be people's participation.

(b) Strengthen the mechanisms for planning at the district level having a Planning Committee of Zila Parishad for Rural Development. The committee would take into account the plans of the Panchayat Samitis and Gram Panchayats.

Further, the other development programme officers (ICDS, DWCRA, AES etc.) should be members of the Planning Committee. The committee should be assisted by competent technical personnel in various fields. The possibilities of this are greater at the district level.

Given the prerequisites, staffing pattern and their capacities, the district would be the most functional unit for planning. Even at this level, there has to be a political will for devolution of powers and resources.

In this context, the Working Group's observations may be of relevance:

> For success in a decentralized programme it is not that functions, finances and powers must be decentralized, but also certain attitudinal, behavioural and cultural conditions conducive to decentralization have to be built up. This culture of decentralization has to grow in strength and take deep roots in the country to successfully resist the pressures for centralization and to sustain the march towards the goal. This, of course, is a matter of evolution through time. But action so planned and purposeful action has to proceed much ahead of times.

4 People's Participation in Development Processes

Experience and Strategy

Y. Sharma

Nowhere it is written in our Constitution that people of this country will voluntarily contribute towards their own development works. Mentally, we are a people reading too much in between the lines of the law. Are we law abiding also, is, however, a different matter. The type of government chosen by us is democracy, which signifies a set-up in which the government is meant to provide all the solace to the mankind, broadly speaking. This evidently clarifies that people are meant to sit cross-legged and wait for the goods to be delivered by others.

This is what has been happening. There are reasons for this. We still have a feudalistic approach, mainly because our past had been altogether feudalistic. The Britishers put a stamp on our society, leaving the lasting impression that people were 'most obedient' to administrators. Freedom at midnight hardly meant anything except arousing a spate of emotions and demands galore from all sides. There was complete dearth of vital statistics for formulating a broad based plan on the very basis of the real requirements of the people. The infrastructure of administrative machinery was more of a 'regulatory' character. There was no room for people to participate in decision-making.

Yet, an experiment was made. The type of community development introduced in the country on the eve of the First Five Year Plan aimed at bringing the people forward on a working platform. The effort was to have a joint approach, a type of equity participation between people and the government. This was to be practised at broad levels and preparations were started in the same measure.

According to a document of the Planning Commission, "the aim of achieving rural development through people's participation and initiatives should not only be continued but further strengthened. The link between the administrative apparatus and the elected representatives of the people should be more cordial and of mutual faith, pointing to the common goal of the development of the community. Adequate mobilization of the resources by the local institutions and sufficient channelization for the welfare of the last man in the last row should be attempted.

The visionary, S.K. Dey, popularized the concept, which surprised many among the administrative ranks. The officers were drawn from different princely states to form the officialdom of Rajasthan. Many asked as to how people were to participate when they had nothing to contribute?

Nilokheri was the answer. A small village in Punjab was chosen to train the trainers, I happened to be among those from Rajasthan to undergo training there in 1953. Most of the population of this village had migrated from Pakistan. They were provided substantial assistance from the government. But the people had no job to do. Community services were introduced. The carpenter, blacksmith and weaver, all were given some task to prepare one or the other item. Farmers were taught better ways of farming. A team of extension workers sought their participation and taught them advanced ways of field farming. We worked with them. That was an experiment to let administrators learn how they were meant to seek participation of the people at the field level.

Back in Rajasthan, I found myself landing into one of the most backward pockets. It was a shocking experience to act as Block Development Officer for Kumbhalgarh in 1954, soon after a former posting as City Magistrate (a regulatory job with ample of authority) at a district headquarters. Trekking several miles from the bus terminus, I reached the office of the tehsil, only to experience like Alice in the Wonderland. However, keeping Nilokheri as my Sandhurst for field-craft, which was to be applied in this hinterland of Udaipur district, inhabited mostly by tribals, I settled down.

It was a clean slate for me, as would have been, I am sure, with so many other administrators. The rural folk would not listen to us for lack of credibility. The administrator, to be precise, the 'officer', in their eyes was the exploiter. It was very hard to canvass the thought of development through their own participation. However, with lot of persuasion and personal involvement they came forward.

People of Kelwara village constructed their own road.

A meeting of the Gram Sabha, attended by all the adult male members of the village, complained of lack of road. They agreed to do *shramdan* (self-help) but bluntly expressed lack of finances to contribute. They, however, brought with them whatever small tools they had like pickaxes, shovels, *sabbals, phaoras,* hammers for stone crushing etc. The women hammered stones to make pebbles, while men helped in levelling, after the blasting, mapping and other formalities had been done by the technical and extension staff. Some of the well-off local people came forward to donate in cash. The Gram Sabha negatived their benevolent offer. Instead, they were also requested to contribute manually, to which they had to agree, though with winking eyes.

It was envisaged that each adult would work an hour every morning. The school bell was rung to give a call. And soon they assembled. Technical staff of the BDO assigned them their work. This continued every morning. Within a few days, there were apparent signs of achievements. A small stretch had been levelled up. The very sight of a road, first-ever road in the history of that village, made people cock-a-hoop. They worked with renewed enthusiasm. Believe it, the road, nearly one km long, was completed within fifteen days, while the targeted period was one month.

Not knowing the outcome, I had put all the stakes of my career with that challenge, which I often describe as my first 'experiment with truth' in that truly Gandhian style. More similar tasks were executed. People did come to participate in the work. The effort, all through, was to energize the dormant potential of the beneficiaries in the development activities. It must be confessed that we failed to generate a self-propelled system to involve people in the developmental activities. Scepticism was writ-large and party factionalism gradually emerged as a hurdle to reckon with.

The year 1959 provided a definite ray of hope when the first-ever programme of democratic decentralization was implemented in the country and Rajasthan took the lead. Pick of the lot officers, who had rendered their services under the community development programme, were supposed to man to the new system on the basis of their yeomen services, hard experiences and the lessons learnt. However, administrative change at this crucial juncture gave rise to a new class of administrators, which was posted in different blocks on criteria of party polity, not one's merits of work in a particular area. The system of polls for different posts of elected representatives gave rise to politics of a type in which the administrative machinery could hardly emerge unscathed.

Priorities changed. Allocation of funds for the rural development made the wiser rural-folk awakened. A race for developmental activities started, leaving little room to accommodate all areas in a particular block for want of sufficient funds. The participation waned. This was primarily because the administrator felt dwarfed under the new set-up in which the elected representatives of Panchayati Raj Institutions intended to hold the sway. At the same time, the representatives encouraged funding on development works, often undermining the role of people in rendering voluntary services. Priorities went on changing. The plan, which was perhaps, conceived to be framed from lower levels, continued to be formulated at the top. Downward flow of funds made everyone crave for the same for his areas. A visible craze for government help was on the rise. The public participation almost dwindled. If any one came forward, it was so arranged meticulously that adjustments were manoeuvred within the governmental assistance.

We became more articulate. More slogans were coined to popularize the Panchayati Raj and muster people's participation. Lesser people turned up at works intended with that spirit. The people in rural sector became wiser too. The economic value of labour increased sharply. The worth of time was accounted for in terms of profit. At this stage, excessive participation of elected representatives in 'higher politics' gave birth to a phenomenon, described by sociologists as 'alienation from society'. A spate of queries about programmes from the above and a lot of official procedure kept the administrative staff cut off from the grass roots. People saw more benefit in applying for loans from cooperative societies or making use of the high-yielding variety of seeds. Why should they care to construct a road or dig a well? This society harped on its traditional and inherent attitude like that of capitalism. The socialistic order, so much conceived and attempted by the leaders of the country, appeared crying off. Self-interest superseded the community service. Spirit of selfless contribution for community held evaporated, thinning away in the air. What development work is going on these days? How is it being undertaken, whether in urban clusters or in the countryside? The complete reliance on government funds is being practised. Participation of people is nowhere to be seen. What used to be a joint venture with matching participation of manpower from the society and financial grant from the government is now a talk of yesteryears. There is, however, no cut in the staff of the agencies which had originally been planted to mobilize people to respond to development works.

This continues despite a chronic deficit economic system of the government. Everyone sits idle after his day's business whether in village or in the city. Who should ask whom to clean their street or repair the damaged portion of the embankment of tank? People realize the gap. But no effort is made to fill it.

I feel like putting a question: why should people participate in development works, especially when they get goods delivered at their doors? They seem to have reconciled with the adversities of life. The succour they receive out of whatever measure of welfare is provided by the government is, perhaps, good enough for their sustenance. It is a malaise in our system of the government, which is giving a sharp rise to several economic ills, also creating imbalances. The worse effect of it will be on the attitudes of people.

The disparity has increased. The new rich in the farm sector intend to be alienated from the working lot of labour at fields. Circulation of money has widened and purchasing power has also sharply increased. Why should then people think of voluntary work or participation. Who has time to seek such help?

5 Participative Approach to Rural Development

Satish C. Sharma

It is a fact that for a programme of development administration, particularly rural development, which is cognitively diffuse, to be successful, active participation of the clients is the *sine-quo-non*. The reason being that development administration does not mean simply 'growth' in quantitative terms, but it essentially involves the 'distributional' aspects too along with institutional changes and changes in political system. It is through this process only that 'capabilities' strengthening and 'equality' promotion objectives can be achieved.

In the case of 'rural development' it is all the more true. It is now an accepted fact that rural development simply does not mean 'agricultural development'. It is an all-encompassing term, indicating a well-structured development of rural areas integrating in it all other activities like that of landless labourers, marginal farmers, petty artisans, traditional handicraftsmen, locally 'based' small scale

This note was prepared while I was engaged as a Post-Doctoral Research Associate at the Centre for Applied Development Studies, Texas Tech University (USA). I feel highly obliged to Dr Richard Vengraff, USA ID-Consultant and Professor of Development Administration at the Department of Political Science and Public Administration for providing me guidance in preparing this paper. However, shortcomings, if any, are entirely mine.

industries and allied activities. Besides above-mentioned activities leading to accelerated economic growth, we have also to take into account the cultural, social, anthropological, institutional and political aspects too because induction of technology as a purely 'instrumental means' is not sufficient to achieve the objective of 'integrated' rural development. In short, following Harold Lasswell and Abraham Kaplan's concept, rural development includes both the 'technique' and 'technic' aspects.

Before analyzing the reasons for clients' 'participation', let us historically review, what were the reasons of past failure of efforts made towards agricultural projects launched in rural areas. In 1950s, efforts were initially made in India followed by other sixty nations, to ameliorate the conditions of rural people through the programme of community development. So great was the impact that Moldcroft[1] labelled 1950s as Community Development's Decade of 'Prominence'. However, as concluded by Korten,[2] record of earlier community development and cooperative efforts is largely a history of failure. The basic reason was non-integration of masses with the programme except a handful of rural elites. The lesson should now enable us to conclude reasons for participation of clients: Development administration which encompassed rural development involves 'Active Intervention' through 'Induced Development'.

According to Esman,[3] induced development involves initiative, planning, support (by clients) and actual guidance (by the implementors). This necessarily means that clients should not be 'Passive', which Esman treats to be an out-moded theory.[4] Contrary to it, to enlist their support, they should be actively associated with formulation, implementation and evaluation stages. Their association will efficaciously bring interaction so very necessary for successful implementation and they will be in a position to play tutelary role.

The participation will enable to reduce the 'physical', 'social' and cognitive 'distances' and would eliminate super- imposition of new administrative pattern. Reduction of 'distanccs' is also imperative for fostering innovations, so very necessary for successful administration keeping in view the socio-cultural and socio-political conditions.

Effective participation by clients would lead to knowing their needs, desires, capacities, in the existing socio-cultural 'environment', which will serve as 'key' for successful development administration.

'Institutionalization' of the Programme

The early efforts had failed because little was done to build independent local organizations to solve local problems and make demands on the broader system. Through clients' participation, it would be possible to frame programme out of village experience. Consequently, the development process itself would be viewed as a "learning" experience (to use Landau concept)[5] for all participants. To effectively implement such experiences, clients will feel need for new 'institutions', which are essential for corrective measures, keeping in view the socio-cultural aspects. Ultimately, such 'emerging' programmes will enable to achieve an unusual degree of fit between beneficiary needs, programme outputs and the competence of the assisting organization. Thus, only 'participative' experiences would lead to feel the necessity of new 'institutions' which will enable to successfully implement the programme by utilizing the potential of newly created indigenous social organizations.

Changes in Political System

The other reason for 'participation' by clients is that if 'distribution of justice' and 'distribution of economic power' objectives, so very necessary for rural development, are to be achieved, changes in existing local political system are to be ushered in. The earlier community development effort, as concluded by Kuldeep Mathur,[6] failed to achieve objective because a new class of rural elites emerged which was able to distort and redirect development programme to their own advantage thus insulating the poor from the benefits of development. Contrarily, by adopting the participation approach, it should be possible to break up the existing power structures and usher in a new one, by not placing the resources at the command of few.

Another variant of changes in local political system relates with the effective control of bureaucracy by creating 'interest groups'. To effectively control the bureaucracy, it is essential to usher appropriate political system changes. Further, for strongly established political parties, it would be possible to accelerate the process of 'politicization', which will serve the purpose of primary vehicle or transmission belt. Ultimately, viable political institutions based on changed socio-political situation, will mobilize the public opinion, will be prepared to give voluntary 'support' to the programmes of development administration and will also be able to control burgeoning bureaucracy.

Clients' Participation

To the question "should we have unequivocal participation in all kinds of projects", the answer is "no".

The projects, which are created for solving specific problems of technical nature, clients' participation is not that important, for instance as in creation of multipurpose irrigation dam. The reason being that in such case authorities are created to adhere to their specific objectives. For example, like TVA in the states, Damodar Valley Authority (DVA) was created to construct a multipurpose irrigation dam solely with the purpose of designing dams keeping in view certain ecological conditions. Such projects are highly capital-intensive and involve sophisticated technology. For administering such projects, separate organizations or 'authorities' are instituted with distinctive competence and specified task requirements. These projects, which are technical by nature, do not deal with socio-cultural 'environment' or human resource development aspects. Such grandeur projects are short-lived and are normally dissolved when the specified objective is accomplished.

Contrary to it, all other projects involving 'programme-approach', having impact on 'distributional' aspects or involving 'socio-cultural environment' or 'human resource development' aspects, the clients' participation adds to effective implementation. Besides the reasons mentioned above, the basic philosophy is that non-involvement will create 'cognitive' distances and thus the administrative institutions will not be able to anticipate socio-political pressures in response to 'intervention' and the intention of introducing 'modifications' while implementing to achieve maximum effectiveness will continue to be a wishful thinking.

Constraints in Participation: Bureaucratic Attitudes

The following inherent attitudes in bureaucratic system are identified as constraints in the participation process.

Rigidity to Change

Amongst the important characteristics of bureaucracy may be listed 'rigidity', 'hierarchy' etc. This means that bureaucratic machinery always acts according to fixed principles and levels of graded authority. 'Participation', if it is to be 'effective', will cut at the very root of the system and therefore bureaucrats will never prefer it or like it. Further, participation involves continuous 'in-plant evaluation', i.e., working out remedial procedure to reach the stated goals. Ultimately, it would be possible only by introducing 'innovative' concepts at all levels, and the bureaucrats are alien to such innovative techniques.

Declining Supremacy of Bureaucrats

With development process and techniques getting more complex, the technocrat is drawn into it more deeply, for without the utilization of his specialized knowledge, planning and through it achieving stated goals, become increasing difficult. This means that technocrats, specialists, independent advisors, consultants etc., start getting more importance and recognition rather than generalist bureaucrat. The bureaucracy always wants proliferation and expansion of bureaucratic machinery so that hierarchial command may not vanish. This obviously means that 'conflicting' situation is to emerge with the possibility that bureaucrats might be tossing ground. It wants to maintain its own 'paramount position' and dislikes the emergence of a competing centre of power.

Fragmentation of Bureaucracy Constituted Special Sub-cultural Segment

The bureaucrats feel that they belong to high prestige strata of the society. Psychologically, belonging to higher rung, they would not like to rub shoulders with common masses, who will be the participant clients. Earlier created 'cognitive-distances' would thus vanish, which bureaucrats will never like. Experiences of 'grass roots of democracy', an experiment conducted in the early 60s in India, reveals that highly placed civil servants (of a district), do not even like to attend the meetings which are presided by people-elected representatives, who obviously do not belong to that 'strata' of the society to which bureaucrats belong.

Unpreparedness to Face the Realities of 'Accountability'

Effective participation will ultimately lead to not only breaking the rigidity of administrative structure, but also making bureaucrats 'accountable' to non-accomplishment of goals. In the colonial ruling era, where from the bureaucracy hails in most of the developing countries, bureaucrats are not apt to be 'accountable' nor function in the goal-specified regime. This means that they would resist such 'participation' system which will require drastic changes in their present working conditions.

Emerging New Culture of Politics

In the participative system, supremacy of administration will be replaced largely by the sovereignty of politics. With rapid expansion of bureaucracy, when the political system lags behind, it tends to inhibit the development of effective politics. It becomes imperative to give incentives for changes in political system, a lesson to be learnt from earlier 'experiments'. However, building of viable political institutions, which will meaningfully participate in modern style politics will not be preferred by the bureaucrats, as such institutions will be controlling the burgeoning bureaucracy and will be making efforts towards administrative changes, which the bureaucrats will resist. The emerging ethos will therefore present bureaucracy with a series of problems specially because in the new setting it will not be in a position to maintain its 'image' of power.

Notes

1. David C. Korten, "Community Organisation and Rural Development: A Learning Process Approach", *Public Administration Review,* September-October 1982, pp. 480–95.
2. Ibid., pp. 480–85.
3. Milton Esman, "Administrative Doctrine and Developmental Needs", pp. 11–25.
4. Ibid.
5. Martin Landau, "Development Administration and Decision Theory", pp. 78–81.
6. Kuldeep Mathur, "Administrative Institutions, Political Capacity and India's Strategy for Rural Development" in *ACDA*, pp. 1–62.

6 Community-Based Organizations and Panchayats as Instruments of Governance in the Sphere of Watershed Development

Rakesh Hooja and Rakshat Hooja

The Government of India has long considered watershed development as a catalyst for development activities in rainfed areas. Accordingly, during the last twenty-five years, most programmes of the Ministries of Rural Development, Agriculture and Environment have followed the watershed development approach. During this period, a number of non-governmental organizations (NGOs) and panchayat bodies/ District Rural Development Agencies (DRDAs) as well as State Governments and grass roots researchers gained considerable experience in the implementation of watershed projects. Based on their feedback and the report of the Hanumantha Rao Committee on Drought Prone Areas Programme (DPAP) and Desert Development Programme (DDP), the Government of India had, in 1994, developed 'Guidelines for Implementation of Watershed Programmes'. These guidelines were subsequently (following the publication of 'Common Principles for Watershed Development', prepared jointly by the Rainfed Farming Division of the Ministry of Agriculture and the Ministry of Rural Development in 2000) revised in 2001 by the

Department of Land Resources of the Ministry of Rural Development and circulated as the Guidelines for Watershed Development (Revised 2001) (popularly referred to as Common Guidelines or GWD).

The GWD aimed to bring people to the centre stage and push the administration towards a facilitating and assisting role. The focus was on the enhancement of the viability and quality of rural livelihood support systems as indicated by the objectives of watershed development mentioned in the Common Guidelines, which referred to developing wastelands/degraded lands/drought prone and desert areas on watershed basis; and also called for attention to improving the socio-economic condition of the resource-poor sections inhabiting the programme areas, employment generation, poverty alleviation, community empowerment, as well as encouraging the village community to make use of simple and affordable technological solutions and institutional arrangements.

The Panchayati Raj Institutions (PRIs), which are India's constitutionally recognized local government bodies, had an important role in Watershed Development Programmes (WDPs) as per the Common Guidelines, having the right to monitor and review the implementation of the programmes and provide guidance. At the village level, the Gram Panchayat was to be involved in the implementation of the programme. The Zila Parishad, Panchayat Samiti and the Gram Panchayat could also take on the responsibility of implementing a cluster of watershed projects in the capacity of a Project Implementation Agency (PIA). However, for this, they had to compete with other NGOs, government organizations (GOs), community-based organizations (CBOs) or other support organizations to get selected as a PIA.

The Common Guidelines proposed a user-friendly organizational structure with Watershed Associations (WAs) and elected/nominated Watershed Committees (WCs) undertaking the field/village level implementation of each watershed under the supervision of the PIA (which was to manage 10–12 watersheds), and with technical inputs from experts who comprised the Watershed Development Team.

A District Watershed Committee with multi-source membership helped ensure coordination as well as the selection of PIAs and members of WDTs and in the approval of detailed action plans for watershed projects in the district.

To recapitulate, the main institutional and administrative arrangements as per Common Guidelines of 2001 can be summarized as follows:

1. A State Watershed Development Committee (SWDC) constituted to ensure coordination among various government departments/ institutions and voluntary agencies. This committee was to meet twice a year to monitor, review and evaluate the progress of implementation of WDPs.
2. The WDPs to be implemented through the Zila Parishads/DRDAs.
3. To ensure coordination at the district level, a District Watershed Development Committee (DWDC), headed by the Chairman, Zila Parishad or DRDA, constituted with a multi-source membership of officials and non-officials. The role of DWDC was to advise and assist the Zila Parishad/DRDA on matters regarding selection of PIAs, and of members of WDTs, as well as training, activities of community organization etc. The committee was also to approve the detailed action plan for watershed development projects in the district.
4. The PRIs had the right to monitor and review the implementation of the WDPs and provide guidance for improvements in the administrative arrangements and procedures with a view to ensuring convergence with other programmes of the Ministry of Rural Development. At the village level, the Gram Panchayat was to be involved especially in community organization activities and training. The Zila Parishads, Panchayat Samitis and the Gram Panchayats could also take on the responsibility of implementing a cluster of watershed projects as a PIA however, for this, they had to follow norms prescribed for PIAs under the Common Guidelines, and had to compete with other NGOs, GOs, or CBOs or other support organizations to get selected as a PIA.
5. The projects were implemented at the field level by the WCs under the overall supervision and guidance of PIAs. PIAs to normally be assigned 10–12 watershed projects covering an area ranging between 5,000–6,000 hectares and to be responsible for constituting four-member WDT for planning, implementing and reviewing of watershed programmes through village level organizations, and also maintenance of accounts. The members of PIAs to preferably be selected from amongst PRIs, government departments or a reputed NGO, which had been active in the field of watershed development or similar area of development.
6. The WDT had a minimum of four members, one each from the disciplines of forestry/plant science, animal sciences, civil/ agricultural engineering and social sciences.

7. The Common Guidelines envisaged the following village level institutions to enable the communities to take up participatory watershed management:
   (i) *Self-Help Groups (SHGs):* Constituted in the watershed area with the help of the WDT, these were to be homogenous groups, who were dependent on the watershed but not owning land in the watershed areas, such as agricultural labourers, shepherds etc.
   (ii) *User Groups* (UGs): These groups to consist of persons most likely to derive direct benefits from particular watershed work and holding land within the watershed areas. The UGs were to eventually take over the operation and maintenance of completed community works.
   (iii) *Watershed Associations (WAs):* Members of the community directly or indirectly dependent on a watershed area organized into a *WA,* which should be a registered society as per Registration of Societies Act, 1860. The WA to meet at least twice a year to improve, monitor and review the watershed development plan, nominate members of the Watershed Committee etc. Wherever a watershed was coterminous with a Village Panchayat, the Gram Sabha of the Gram Panchayat concerned could be designated as the WA.
   (iv) *Watershed Committees (WCs):* The WC to consist of members nominated by WA from amongst the UGs, SHGs, Gram Panchayat and a member of the WDT for carrying out the day-to-day activities of the Watershed Development Project. Each WC had a secretary to be a paid on an honorarium basis by the WA.

Just as the initial projects under the Common Guidelines were beginning to bear fruit, with growing awareness about the procedures, schemes, benefits etc., among the beneficiaries and the potential PIAs, as well as CBOs, NGOs, local government staff etc., the government (the Ministry of Rural Development) decided to launch a new 'Haryali' scheme in January 2003 under which it replaced the Common Guidelines with the Haryali Guidelines. The Haryali Guidelines stipulated that CBOs, comprising UGs, SHGs, WCs and even the WAs, as well as NGOs, which have often proved to be efficient PIAs, would cease to have any role in watershed development and that, henceforth, the PRIs (Gram Sabhas, Gram Panchayats, Block

Panchayats/Panchayat Samitis and Zila Parishads) are to manage and implement watershed development activities.

Some changes brought about by the Haryali Guidelines are:

- The Haryali Guidelines have done away with WAs and WCs, their functions being transferred to the Gram Panchayats. The Gram Panchayat is now expected to perform both executive functions (even being responsible for day-to-day activities) as also governance functions. The UGs and SHGs are now to be constituted by the PRIs and the role of the UG has been reduced to mere maintenance of the created assets while its earlier role in planning and executing development works has been ended.
- Under the 2001 Guidelines, a large variety of organizations were allowed to function as PIAs, but preference was given to PRIs, a line department of government, or a reputed NGO/other corporate body, in that order. The Haryali Guidelines, however, indicate that an intermediate panchayat (Block Panchayat/Panchayat Samiti/Mandal Panchayat/ Taluka Panchayat) may be the PIA for all the projects sanctioned in a block/taluka/tehsil. In case the intermediate panchayat is not adequately empowered, then the Zila Parishad either may itself act as PIA or appoint a suitable line department (agriculture, social forestry/soil conservation etc.) or an agency of state government/university/institute as PIA, failing which a reputed NGO with experience of having worked as a PIA could be considered. Thus, eventually, it is only the intermediate panchayat bodies, which so far were not associated with watershed development, who are to be the PIAs.
- The District Watershed Committee has been dispensed with, though one wonders why the Haryali Guidelines have chosen to deprive the Zila Parishad of the advice/guidance of a district level body of social and technical experts and representatives of various stakeholders (GOs, NGOs, CBOs and other support organizations) intimately connected with watershed activities.
- The 2001 Guidelines had provided for a watershed secretary for each watershed to be locally engaged on honorarium basis by the WA to work under the supervision of the chairman of the WC. As per the Haryali Guidelines, the Secretary, Gram Panchayat (a government employee) is to assist the Chairman, Gram Panchayat.

— Haryali has left state governments wondering whether their Watershed Directorates should continue to be attached to the Agriculture Department and to provide technical/ techno-economic inputs, or whether the Watershed Directorates should be transferred to the State Panchayat Department where it would emphasize on participatory and socio-political aspects of watersheds.

— While there is considerable commonality about the objectives of watershed development, the two guidelines differ somewhat wherein the 2001 Guidelines stress developing waste-lands/degraded lands, drought prone and desert areas keeping in view capability of the land and local needs and conditions, while the Haryali Guidelines talk of harnessing every drop of rainwater for irrigation, horticulture, floriculture, pasture development/fisheries etc., to create sustainable sources of income for the village community, and provide drinking water supplies. However, where the two guidelines totally part company is that the Haryali Guidelines talk about ensuring overall development of rural areas though GPs and creating regular sources of income for the panchayats as a major objective. The earlier guidelines were silent regarding any such objective.

Evidently, the purpose behind introducing the Haryali Guidelines was to strengthen the PRIs. There exists a group of activists and scholars who feel that such 'parallel' bodies like WAs should either not be permitted to exist or should function as subordinate entities of the PRIs who they see as the third tier of Indian federalism. They often advocate that to strengthen PRIs, it is necessary to abolish the special watershed-related bodies.

The present authors tend to disagree with the view that it is necessary that only panchayat bodies represent the local community or act on its behalf. Not every member of the Gram Sabha is a user or beneficiary, while in the case of a watershed user group every member is user and beneficiary as well as an implementer-cum-manager. In fact, because of their nature, traditions, functions, size and frequency of meetings etc., Gram Panchayats function in a manner very different from watershed user groups and have different sorts of relationships with their members. The Gram Panchayat leadership may also have a wide band of concerns and interests of which watersheds may form a minuscule or peripheral part, while for the watershed user group the watershed is a major part of their existence, It is thus necessary for panchayat bodies and local user groups to not only co-exist but also to supplement, complement and strengthen each other. Perhaps, a small amount of creative tension between PRIs and user groups, or other CBOs, may even prove to be good for the community and for the watershed development efforts.

It needs to be questioned whether using of Haryali as a tool for empowering PRIs, to the extent of displacing the WCs, WAs, and other user groups and SHGs, is the appropriate or best way to empower PRIs. Without the devolution or decentralization of appropriate powers and authority from the state governments to the various levels of PRIs, as is called for in the 73rd Constitution Amendment Act, it is difficult to expect real empowerment of PRIs. It is such devolution of powers (which has still to be effected properly in most states), rather than trying to take over functions from the primary community-based stakeholder groups (UGs/SHGs), which would really empower panchayat bodies.

It may also be pointed out that experience in the field has shown that Gram Sabhas have not been able to perform the required functions effectively due to their large size, unorganized membership and high degree of heterogeneity.

A Gram Panchayat may comprise one, two or three villages. Each village and its attendant hamlets may normally have a population of between 1,500 and 3,000 persons (though the population of a particular village may go even upto 15,000. The Gram Sabha's/Gram Panchayat's average population in most states would be between 2,000 and 6,000 though in one state the average is about 21,000). Thus, the Gram Panchayat cannot be considered to be the grass roots in today's India; instead, it would be a hamlet, or a ward, or a single watershed/group of 2–3 contiguous watersheds, which would be the real grass roots.

Also, the Gram Panchayats are territorial units and not ecological units. Thus, a watershed may cut across boundaries of Gram Panchayats or a Gram Panchayat may cut across watershed boundaries. Where the watershed area is coterminous with the Gram Panchayat, the Gram Sabha could function as the WA. However, if there are several watersheds within the area of a Gram Panchayat, then each such watershed area, and the people depending upon the resources of the watershed, should have their own WA.

There is need for an executive body elected from the UGs and SHGs to manage the watershed programme on day-to-day basis. The Gram Panchayat cannot entirely replace the WC in its roles and responsibilities as it takes away decision-making from the direct stakeholders. This is particularly so if the watershed area is only a part of the entire village. Of course, if the Sarpanch of the Gram Panchayat is a member of a UG/SHG, then he/she could also be elected as chairperson of the WC. One option could be that the WC could also be considered as a standing committee of the Gram Panchayat for purposes of managing the watershed programme.

It is unfortunate that the Haryali Guidelines have reduced the percentage of budgets available for community organization and for training and capacity building.

We, as informed observers, are clear in our mind that the prime objective of all watershed efforts has to be improved, land-water management and rural livelihoods including the generation of incomes and optimal use of natural resources, and not the strengthening of any governmental institution like the panchayats, for which other steps could be undertaken.

Similarly, it does not make sense to let the capabilities for watershed work that CBOs, NGOs, GOs, and other agencies working as PIAs have built up over time go waste by divorcing them from watershed activities. Since both PRIs and CBOs lack in technical expertise, the role of district and lower level staff of state government departments and of experienced NGOs having professional staff in providing technical inputs either as PIAs or through other coordinating mechanisms, should not be underemphasized.

Thus, all things considered, it appears that the Haryali Guidelines would have done well to have retained provisions for WCs, WAs, and effective watershed users groups as well as NGOs etc., working in coordination with panchayat bodies. This would not only enable the achievement of natural resource related land-water management goals, but also result in the greater importance of panchayat bodies. Accordingly, appropriate mechanisms and procedures for promoting harmonious relations between participatory watershed groups (which are community-based organizations) and Gram Panchayats need to be innovated with and put into practice.

As stated at the outset, PRIs constitute the third tier of Indian federalism. Watershed bodies working in parallel to, or at levels lower than, panchayat bodies comprise (in a manner similar to the case of water users associations in the irrigation sector) part of a fourth tier whose importance is gradually being understood. Neither needs to replace the other, both can co-exist and reinforce each other, as also coordinate and interact with functionaries of the state government (second tier of Indian federalism) for performing the complex tasks of watershed development and management.

References

Chandrudu, M.V. Rama, 2003(a). "Historical Transact of Watershed Policies in India: Shifts in Content and Philosophy and Their Implications". Paper circulated at Orientation and Training Workshop on Watershed Development and Management, organized by Indian Society of Ecological Economics and Gujarat Institute of Development Research at Ahmedabad from 16 to 19 October, 2003.

Chandrudu, M.V. Rama, 2003(b). "Haryali and Other Guidelines: Issues, Concerns and Gaps" in *Haryali Guidelines: Issues and Concerns,* WASSAN and APRLP, Hyderabad.

Hooja, Meenakshi and Hooja, Rakesh, 2001. "Institutions of Self-Government or Agencies for Development: Panchayats in India", *South Asian Journal of Socio-Politics Studies*, Vol. 2, No. 1, January-June 2001.

Hooja, Rakesh, 1985. "People's Participation in Comprehensive Watershed Area Development" in Hoshiar Singh (ed.), *Rural Development in India,* Printwell, Jaipur, reprinted in Rakesh Hooja, *Administrative Interventions in Rural Development,* Rawat Publications, Jaipur, 1987.

———, 2003. "Below the Third Tier: Water Users Associations in India" in on-line research library on federalism of Forum of Federations—an international network on federalism based in Ottawa Canada *(www.forumfed.org),* revised version published in *The Indian Journal of Federal Studies,* No. 1, March 2004.

———, 2004. "Water Users Associations as the Fourth Tier of Indian Federalism", *South Asian Journal of Socio-Political Studies,* Vol. 4, No. 2, June 2004.

———, 2006. *The Administration of Water for Agriculture: Essays in Management of Irrigation, Watersheds and Drainage,* Rawat Publications, Jaipur.

Hooja, Rakesh, and Pangare, Ganesh, 2002. "Some Reflections on Software Aspects of Water Policy: CAD, PIM, Watershed Development and Management and Water Harvesting". Paper presented at a Round Table in Water Policy organized by INSEE at New Delhi, May 10, 2002. Its revised version printed as India—NPIM Working Paper No. 13, New Delhi, January 2003.

Hooja, Rakesh, and Hooja, Rakshat, 2003. "The Changing Role of Panchayat Bodies in Watershed Development". Paper presented at National Seminar on Panchayats at Madhya Pradesh Institute of Social Science Research, Ujjain, in December 2003 and being published in the forthcoming seminar volume, *A Decade of Panchayati Raj in India,* edited by D.C. Sah and Y.K. Sisodia, Rawat Publications, Jaipur. (This paper was also invited for presentation at the IWMI-Tata Partnership Annual Researchers Meet on Water, at Anand from 17 to 19 February 2004).

Hooja, Rakshat, 2004. "Why Only Panchayats?, Other Local Associations Can Also Manage Watersheds Effectively", *Down To Earth,* Vol. 12, No. 18, February 15, 2004.

Indian Network on Participatory Irrigation Management, 2002. Land-Water Management and Johads: Process Documentation of the Activities and Approach of Tarun Bharat Sangh – an unpublished report by Ganesh Pangare, Talha Jamal and Rakshat Hooja written for Ford Foundation.

Jamal, Talha, Hooja, Rakshat and Pangare, Ganesh, 2004. " Johad Versus Watershed: A Case Study of Tarun Bharat Sangh's Approach to Water Harvesting and Conservation for Drought Mitigation" in Jasveen Jairath, Vishva Ballabh, and Khalid Hussain (eds.), *Drought and Integrated Water Resources Management in South Asia: Issues, Alternatives and Futures,* Sage, New Delhi (publication sponsored by SaciWATERs, Hyderabad).

Ministry of Agriculture, Government of India, (2000). *Guidelines for National Watershed Development for Rainfed Areas,* New Delhi.

Ministry of Rural Development, Government of India, (1994). *Guidelines for Watershed Development,* New Delhi.

———, (2001). *Guidelines for Watershed Development* (Revised 2001), New Delhi.

———, (2003). *Guidelines for Haryali,* New Delhi.

OIKOS 2000. *Social and Institutional Issues in Watershed Management in India,* Oikos, New Delhi and IIRR, Philippines.

WASSAN and APRLP, 2003. *Haryali Guidelines: Issues and Concerns, Suggestions and Recommendations of Consultations and National Workshop,* Hyderabad.

7 Participatory Approach for Sustainable Agricultural Technology Transfer

Sujit Kumar Paul

The term 'sustainable development' was coined by World Commission on Environment headed by Gro Harlem Brundtland in the report, *Our Common Future* (London, 1984). The Commission defined sustainable development as "development that meets the needs of the present without compromising the ability of the future generation to meet their own needs". Towards sustainable development, the most important is sustainable agricultural development. For the first time, the population supporting capacity of the land over a long time was being questioned. In 1987, the World Commission on Environment and Development highlighted this issue. Consequently, in 1988, the Technical Advisory Committee to the Commission gave the definition of sustainable agriculture as follows: "Sustainable agriculture should involve the successful management of resources to satisfy changing human needs while maintaining or enhancing the quality of environment and conserving the natural resources".

Agricultural sustainability and ecosystem protection have recently taken centre stage in international aid and development programme. Agricultural sustainability refers to maintenance and enhancement of productivity on a long-term basis and should use improved and friendly technologies for economic development of agricultural sector. Even the solution to providing food, economic and healthy security to meet the growing demand of teeming population with limited land resources lay in the adoption of a holistic approach for achieving environment friendly sustainable development.

As a result of continued mining of soil and overexploitation of water resources, we have reached a stage where any further neglect and slackness in using soil and water resources in a sustainable manner will not only restrict our ability to feed the increasing population, but also result in adverse environmental consequences which would not be easily retrieved. Of all the undesired consequences of large-scale irrigation development, salinity and waterlogging are most frequently mentioned in the context of irrigation sustainability. In this context, the emphasis on farm development has to be shifted to the sustainability of entire farming system and spectrum of farming practices which provides farmers with economically viable and environmentally sound alternatives in developing their farming system.

The improvement in the productivity of agricultural crops is nowadays viewed from their sustainable in the fields. As farmers are switching over from the modern, intensive to ecologically protective agricultural practices, the scope of organic farming bio-fertilizers in enhancing bio-productivity of the soil is bright. The latter being a major resource, the management of soil fertility and integrated nutrient supply are important prerequisites for sustainable agriculture. Attaining sustainable agricultural development is now one of the major thrusts in many developed and developing nations. Use of environment-friendly and appropriate technologies are the key components in achieving this. In this present study, attempts have been made to pinpoint the farmer's preference, acceptance and achievement in relation to sustainable agricultural development.

For the purpose of the study a remote village Kaipara of Purulia district of West Bengal has been taken into account that is the working area of the Kribhco Indo British Rainfed Farming Project (KRIBP-E).

The Development Agency

Krishak Bharti Cooperative Ltd. (KRIBHCO), the world's premier fertilizer producing cooperative, has an outstanding truck record to its credit in all spheres of activities. It was incorporated on 17 April 1980 as a national level cooperative society. The society has set up huge Ammonia-Urea Complex at Hazira near Surat in Gujarat, based on natural gas from Bombay High/South basin, with an annual capacity of 14.25 lakh MT of urea. During 1998-99, KRIBHCO produced

15.40 lakh MT of urea with the utilization of 106.1 per cent of its rated capacity, Besides manufacturing and marketing of fertilizer, seeds and other agricultural inputs, KRIBHCO continues to provide excellent services to farming community through various promotional, educational and rural development activities, aimed at uplifting the livelihood status of the rural community.

The Project

The irrigated area in our country is very less, so rainfed farming is the prime concern. Keeping this is mind, KRIBHCO, with the financial and technical assistance from Overseas Development Administration (ODA), UK, now Department for International Development (DFID), started a rainfed farming project, called Kribhco Indo-British Rainfed Farming Project (East)—KRIBP(E), in three contiguous states of Rajasthan, Madhya Pradesh and Gujarat in Western India. With the success of this project, Government of India and DFID, handed over another project for Eastern Plateau region covering 110 villages in eight districts of Bihar, Orissa and West Bengal for a period of five years from April, 1995.

Objective of the Project

To improve the livelihood of the resource-poor community, emphasizing integrated farming system development through:

1. participatory approaches,
2. use of low cost technology,
3. renewable of natural resources,
4. institution building (development of groups),
5. gender focused (stressing women participation), and
6. sustainability.

Socio-Economic Profile of the Area

Kaipara village is in the KRIBE (E) cluster of Kaipara in Barabazar block Purulia district in West Bengal. The village is situated 35 km south from Purulia town and 25 km north-east from the block headquarters (Barabazar). The village is 15 km away from the barabazar-Purulia metal road. The village is very remote and interior of the district. According to the study of KRIBHCO (1998), the village Kaipara had a total population of 1,142 persons. Out of these, 586 were male and 556 were female population comprising 196 households. The rate of literacy for males was 34 per cent and for female it was 12 per cent that accounted for an average literacy rate of 23 per cent for the total village. In terms of economic classification out of the total households 75 per cent households are deficit (D), i.e., the households who do not get full meals throughout the year. About 2.2 per cent households are self-sufficient (SS), i.e., households just get full meals throughout the year and 3 per cent households are surplus (S), i.e., getting full meals throughout the year, these households can think for other conspicuous consumption expenditures also.

Kaipara Village at a Glance

1. 15 km away from metal road, 25 km from block office, 35 km from Purulia town
2. Three tolas (hamlets): (a) Khamartarn, (b) Basti, (c) Gussaipua
3. No. of households: 196
4. Social classification: (a) Mahato (OBC)-75, (b) Oraon (ST)-53, (c) Ruhidas (SC)-20, (d) Others-48.
5. Economic classification: (a) Deficit-75 per cent, (b) SS-22 per cent, (c) surplus
6. Population: 1,142.
7. Literacy: Mate-34 per cent, female-12 per cent, Average-23%
8. Migration (seasonal)-52 per cent
9. Rainfall–1,200 mm/year
10. Undulated sloppy land with red laterite soil
11. Ponds (suitable for aquaculture): 15 (8+7), (P+S)
12. Irrigated area: 4.86 acres
13. Cropped area: 376 acres
14. Forest land: Nil
15. Household using HYV paddy: 2.55 per cent
16. Household using chemical fertilizers: 2.04 per cent
17. Livestock position: (a) Goat-286, (b) Sheep-125, (c) Pig-45, (d) Poultry-563, (e) Cattle-309 and (f) Buffalo-113.

Kharif (acres)		*Rabi (acres)*		*Summer Paddy (acres)*
Local paddy	300	Vegetables	08	1.5
HYV paddy	27	Wheat	01	
Maize	10	Potato	01	
Blackgram	10	Others	05	
P. Pea	05			
Vegetables	10			
Others	14			
Total	376	Total	09	

Village Kaipara, which has been adopted for project activities, is very remote and interior, climate is very dry, the natural forests have been overused, vegetation is nil and the villagers are very poor. The soil has become open, highly eroded, barren and undergone massive degradation with hardly any humus. The average annual rainfall is about 1,200 mm. and restricted in between July to mid-September. The topography of the village is undulated and upland covers 65–70 per cent. The upland soils are of higher textures with low water retention capacity. The entire area is monocropped and the single crop is paddy. The cropping intensity is 96 per cent. Though the forest area in Purulia district is 13.98 per cent, but in fact in the village the forest area is nil.

Occupational Status and Landholdings

Agriculture is the main source of livelihood of the villagers. Over 89 per cent of the total population is dependent on agriculture but those actually employed as agricultural workers are 48.74 per cent. This indicates that there exist surplus non-worker labour forces, which remain as a disguised agricultural labour. Most of the scheduled caste population (specially Ruhidas community) used to go to nearby states for shoe-making work. Almost all the landless households used to migrate to nearby districts for agricultural wage labour. Majority of the villagers have less than 2.51 acres of land and there are also landless labourers.

Table 1

Distribution of Households According to Landholdings

Landholdings (in acres)	*General Caste*	*Scheduled Caste*	*Scheduled Tribe*
Landless	19 (15.45)	14 (70.00)	22 (41.51)
0.10–2.50	43 (34.96)	6 (30.00)	31 (58.49)
2.51–500	36 (29.26)		
Above 5	8 (6.50)		

Percentage to total are given in the parentheses.

From Table 1, it is implicit that land concentration mostly occurred among the general castes. All the scheduled caste and scheduled tribe farmers have less than 2.51 acres of land, which implies that they mostly belong to the marginal and small farmers. But the landless farmers are also not negligible for all the ethnic groups and this is highest among the scheduled castes. Though the general caste people have some quantity of land but the land situation is not suitable for good crop cultivation. Most of the land of this area is unbunded upland. Soil erosion is a major problem. The farming system depends almost entirely on rainfall during the kharif season concentrating on rice based cropping system. Water is the major constraint to crop production.

Participatory Approaches

The Kribhco Rainfed Farming Project aims to improve the livelihoods of poor farmers through a participatory approach. The approach has been used for participatory planning of natural resources. The project strategy oriented towards the goal of improving the livelihoods of poor farming communities, involves an extended process of participatory planning in order to generate location-specific natural resource development plans. Programme activities cover a range of farming system areas; crop development, agro-forestry, SWC, wasteland development, minor irrigation, horticulture, livestock development and savings and credit management. The sustainability of benefits beyond the life of the project depends upon continued involvement of communities in resource management, often through village-based groups. The project aims to achieve sustainable farming system improvements though enhancing the capabilities of the villagers in local resource management and in gaining access to external resources, including those provided through government programmes.

The agricultural development participatory approach involves the following steps: (1) village entry, (2) rapport building, (3) PRA exercise, (4) CPA exercise, (5) IFPRA, (6) identification and prioritization of development options, (7) work plan design, (8) training, exposure visit, selection *of jankar*, (9) implementation, (10) evaluation, and (11) feedback analysis of the problems.

The process of participatory approaches, which has followed in project villages, has been narrated in Figure 1.

Village Entry

In the process of village entry the project staff should:

- Clearly know about the project activity, purpose of the project and their own identity.
- Learn as quickly as possible about local pattern and style of leadership.

Figure 1

Village entry

Rapport building

g
r
o
u
p
f
o
r
m
a
t
i
o
n

PRA exercise

CPA exercise

Small-scale activities

IFPRA

Identification and prioritization of developmental options

Work plan design

Training, exposure visit, selection of jankar

Monitoring

Implementation

Evaluation

Feedback analysis of the problems

— Develop a good understanding of local issues and recent development experiences.
— Stress the project interest in natural resource development, poverty reduction and the aim of working with men and women.
— Communicate in appropriate ways.
— Discus development possibilities with the villagers.

Rapport-Building

In entering the village the project staff should make a series of informal contacts and meetings and the rapport-building should involve:

- Identification of influential persons of the village and contact with them.
- Understanding the socio-economic condition of the villagers.
- Meeting and discussion with a wide cross-section of the community, both men and women through individual contact.
- Establishing friendly relations with all the village people.
- Learning to understand and respect their culture and participate in their social events and gatherings.
- Participating in village events and taking interest in ongoing activities.

Participatory Rural Appraisal

Participatory rural appraisal (PRA) is a set of highly participatory techniques and exercises that involves the community fully in discussing the needs and problems and in identifying the causal factors for them. PRA avoids the chance of any bias of prejudice of the facilitators to affect the process. On the other hand, the process is not for merely data collection and information gathering, but also considers the views, opinions and perception of the target communities. Since the techniques are interesting, participatory and in an environment wherein the community participants feel comfortable, there is a likelihood of participants owing the process right from the beginning. The participatory and stimulating environment also forms the foundation for initiating community organization attempt.

Each PRA session had a definite set of exercises. Certain exercises were conducted specifically with specific group, i.e., either with men or women or youth. All the exercises that formed part of PRA are listed below:

1. Expectation of participants.
2. Mapping of village.
3. Skill inventory.
4. Preferred enterprises and their feasibility.
5. Seasonality, availability of labour.
6. Daily schedule.
7. Resources inventory.
8. Industrial climate in the region.
9. Educational profile of the concerned.
10. Potential for cooperatives.
11. Motivations of achievers.

Community Problem Analysis

The community problem analysis (CPA) starts with a series of informal individual and group meetings with men and women from all sections of the community. This will result in a brief report that critically reviews the main problems identified and deals with the following points:

1. A listing of main problems identified and for each problem a discussion of:
   - Whose problem and who mentioned and when?
   - How many different individuals/groups mentioned the problem as area of concern and how frequently was it raised in the village?
   - Whether the problem is a real problem.
2. A grouping of the main problems into:
   - Simple problems that can immediately be tackled as a way of consolidating rapport.
   - Complex and interrelated problems related of farming systems development.
3. Analysis of key farming system problems with men and women from different groups in the community:
   - Better understanding the interrelated nature of these problems.
   - Develop the skills and understanding of the local community so that they can be active participants in planning in future development options.
4. In understanding the CPA, a variety of methods, including group discussions, role playing, other PRA techniques etc. should be followed.

IFPRA

Issue-focused PRA should be undertaken on the following topics with the community to gain a better understanding of:

- Wealth ranking and livelihood analysis.
- Women's knowledge and perspectives.
- Existing forms of community organization.
- Cropping systems and land types.
- Trees and use of forests.

— Soil and water conservation (SWC).
— Livestock.

Identification and Prioritization of Development Options

After conducting PRA and IFPRA, activities should be identified and priority should be given in the specific projects during the first year. In the following years, the types of projects undertaken in first year are likely to continue. New projects should start in consultation with local communities and an attempt should be made to ensure that project schemes benefit members of all socio-economic groups.

Development of Village Work Plan

The development of village work plan (VWP) should involve the activity-focused groups in the community to complete the following tasks:

— collection of information for detailed planning
— awareness building
— planning for scheme management
— skill training
— group strengthening
— documentation of resolution
— development schemes
— village organization development
— further planning activities
— a budget

Training, Exposure Visit, Selection of Jankars

Training and exposure visit may be done on individual and community basis. In this period, *jankars* should be selected for monitoring and implementation of the group works.

Area of Intervention and Achievements

After the intervention of the project it has been found that the agricultural development has been done through participatory approaches. From the project side, attempts have been made to explore the possibilities for better utilization of available natural resources both in off-farm and on-farm activities though active participation of the community. Since, the project is based on participatory approaches the community is involved in all stages right from identification of options, prioritization and planning to execution with close facilitation by project staff. Moreover, monitoring and evaluation are also done with active participation of the community.

After entering and rapport-building in the village, the project staff concentrated to form groups with active participation with the community. At present, there are four functional groups at Kaipara village. These are:

1. Kaipara Naba Yuba Sangha (male members—60)
2. Kaipara Mohila Samiti (female members—40)
3. Khamartarn Naba Tarun Sangha (male members—28)
4. Khamartanr Mohila Samiti (female members—25)

Table 2

Socio-economic Status of the Groups

Economic Status			*Social Status*		
D	*SS*	*S*	*ST*	*SC*	*OTH*
58	2	—	—	20	40
39	1	—	—	15	25
25	2	1	8	to	10
23	1	1	7	8	10

D: Deficit, SS: Self-Sufficient, S: Surplus, ST: Scheduled Tribe, SC: Scheduled Caste, OTH: Others.

Crop Production

The economy of the village mainly revolves round the crop activities. So, the main focus was given to identification of new crop varieties based on the need of the community. Under this intervention, seed multiplication programme, introduction of new crop varieties and improved vegetable cultivation have been taken for getting the maximum benefit. Much of the attention has been given in cropping system through improvement to the productivity of the kharif production and expansion of rabi/summer production. The development of improved cropping system is considered to be an interactive process extending over the whole project period. So far the cultivation of HYV is concerned, during kharif (mainly paddy) has been increased by 14 per cent, whereas the rabi cropping has been increased by 12.5 per cent in 1998–99 compared to the previous year, mainly due to the introduction of short duration varieties and by increasing the irrigation potentialities. Besides HYV kharif paddy cultivation, the farmers of this village cultivate wheat, mustard, vegetable, summer paddy and so on. Cropping pattern and cropping intensity has increased. Upto March 1999, total area introduced for HYV paddy was 60 acres, vegetable cultivation 15 acres, rabi crop 40 acres, high value crop 45 acres. Improved agricultural implements, HYV seed etc., were provided from the project site for agricultural development. One vermicompost pit also been started for vermicomposting which is effective for sustainable agricultural development. Initiative was also taken for seed multiplication programme. A good quality seed was proved for better yield. After harvesting, the farmers were suggested to keep the seeds for next crop. Not only this, the farmers were also advised to sell the seeds to farmers of other villages.

Soil and Water Conservation

About 50–60 per cent of the uplands are unbunded, which encounters for loss of top soil through erosion every year, resulting in the loss of nutrient/humus affecting the crop yield which reduces drastically. Besides that, the slope of upper ecology does not leave a scope for water retention; resultant water run off is high avoiding the infiltration of rainwater. The alarming rate of land degradation has stressed the need for efficient management technique for sustainability of land use system. High priority is, therefore, given to the construction of SWC structures and incorporation of vegetative measures to check the soil and water loss. In this village, rabi cropping has also been undertaken on SWC treated areas. A total of 32 hectares of area has been treated effectively through stone and soil building upto March, 1999. Migration has also been checked due to the employment and earning opportunities from SWC work.

Agro-forestry

In the SWC treated area, suitable emphasis was given for development of agro-forestry, horticultural crops, pulses production and social forestry within the farming system with close participation of the community. Fuelwood, fodder, timber, vegetables and pulses are required to be produced in the village itself for making them self-sufficient for their daily needs. In the tree programme, much more emphasis was given to agro-forestry system. Total area covered for agro-forestry is 59 hectares of the village. It has become possible due the agro-forestry system. Several grain crops, vegetables, fruit crops, grafts and sabui grasses have been inter-cropped with forest tree species. Vision of the project is to provide an opportunity to the farmers for short-term as well as long-term benefit.

Attempts have been made for better plants in nursery and tree plantation and agro-forestry programme by keeping in view the following:

1. To maximize the growth in short rainy period.
2. Production of healthy seedling pre-dig pits.
3. Planting in pre-dig pits.
4. Protection from free grazing.
5. Utilization of barren land with field crop, fodder, subui grass etc.
6. Self-sufficient lent in fodder, pulses and timber.
7. Effective soil conservation.

Water Resource Development

The farmers of the village are resource-poor. The area of the village is almost dry. The irrigated area is very negligible. Only 4.86 acres of land of the village is irrigated. The villagers totally depend on monsoon. The average annual rainfall is about 1,200 mm and restricted in between July to mid-September. The topography of the area is undulated and upland covers 70 per cent. The entire area is monocropped. So, without irrigation facility, agricultural development cannot be possible in the rain-fed condition.

After the intervention of the project, from the above point of view, much emphasis has been given for water resource development. Total four tanks have been re-excavated and two pumpsets supplied. Now, the irrigated area has been increased upto 47.87 acres. After the construction of check dams and river lift irrigation, about 70 per cent area will be under irrigation facility and the economic condition of the villagers will improve.

Human Resource Development

Human resource is the most important asset in the country because all other natural resources can be better utilized by motivating and active participation of human resources only. Thus, there is a need to invest time, money and efforts in their development. The investment of time, money and effort in it provides fruitful results as the human resource can be developed to an unlimited extent because every human being has endless potentials. Most of the villagers of the village are illiterate. They have no technical knowledge. All the project activities are participatory, sustainable, pro-poor and gender-sensitive. The project had achieved its objectives by using participatory tools with the strategy of bottom up, village based development programme planning and mobilizing the self-help groups to undertake the development initiatives. *Jankar* training, community training, workshop and exposure visits are the most effective implementation of all such programmes with effective people's participation. The training and exposure visits become the most important for human resource development.

Training and exposure visits ensure sustainability of development programmes and enhance skill and knowledge of the jankars and community. The outcomes of these training programmes and exposure visits for the *jankar* and community on regular basis are as follows:

- Confidence-building through seeing and believing concept and open LIP ways for community interactions.
- Effective facilitation by involving community in decision-making during the group meetings.
- To facilitate and coordinate the activities in the village.
- To build and strengthen the knowledge and skill of the community of efficient implementation and management of programme in groups.
- Raise the awareness level of the community
- Promotes an open discussion on the possible benefit of project interventions.
- To accelerate the adoption of sustainable farming system.

Without human resource development, any activity particularly agricultural activity cannot be successful. After getting training and exposure visit, awareness among the community has developed and the utilization of HYV seeds, chemical fertilizers, pesticides, improved agricultural implements and so on. Irrigation system has also developed. Regarding human resource development, total 25 *jankar* trainings, 32 community trainings, four exposure visits, eight awareness building camps conducted and 286 persons (134 male and 152 female) have been participated. Through these training and exposure visits agricultural development is taking place in this village.

Table 3
Activities at Kaipara for Agricultural Development

Activities		*Achievement*	
		1999–2000	*2000–2001*
Crop production	HYV introduction (acres)	10	50
	Vegetable cultivation (acres)	10	15
	Rabi (acres)	20	30
SWC/WRD	High value crop (acres)	15	30
	Bunding etc. (acres)	14	66
	Re-excavation of ponds (nos.)	—	2
	Check dam (nos.)	—	—
	Excavation of pond (nos.)	—	1
	Supply of pumpset (nos.)	—	1
Agro-forestry	Area covered under plantation (acres)	12	68
	Fruit plants grown (nos.)	—	600
HRD	Training of *jankar* (nos.)	10	16
	Training of community (persons)	100	186
	Exposure visit (persons)	20	50
	Awareness building camp (nos.)	6	
	Adult literacy centre (nos.)	1	1
	Health camp (nos.)	2	2
	Drinking water (tubewell nos.)	1	1

Conclusion

A certain reorientation is needed in agricultural education, research, development and extension of the developed technology, strategy and methodology to achieve this goal of sustainability. Both in agriculture and industry, the concept of sustainability has so far been considered predominantly at the level of economics. For example, farmers generally take decisions about the technology to be adopted on the basis of risk and cost-benefit ratio. Social sustainability also plays an important role since farmers of different regions have different dietary habits. Therefore, farmers grow those crops, which are desired for their home consumption ignoring the ecological consideration. In order to attain sustainability, plans and programmes must be framed to focus on the principle of ecology, economic and equity.

The findings lead us to conclude that farmers' education, their participation in different organizations, the environmental problems they encounter and their thinking towards sustainability issues through 'System approaches' are closely linked. The basic point is thus to increase the literacy level among farmers. This would be useful in increasing farmers' active participation and knowledge towards achieving sustainable agricultural development.

References

Dasgupta, D. and P. Pal, 1997. "Indigenous Knowledge Base and Agriculture Research Paradigm", *Journal of Interacademicia,* Vol. 1, No. 4 (special), December 1997.

KRIBHCO 1995. *Village Profile of Kaipara Cluster,* Kribhco Indo-British Rainfed Farming Project (E), Purulia.

Maitri, 1998. *A Quarterly Newsletter of Kribhco Indo-British Rainfed Farming Project (E),* Vol. III, No. 2 and 3.

Mukherjee, N., 1997. *Participatory Rural Appraisal: Methodologies and Applications,* Concept Publishing Company, New Delhi.

Rahman, M.Z., M.A. Kashem and H. Mikuni, 1997. "Farmers' Communication Behaviour for Technological Intervention: A Japan, Bangladesh Cross-Cultural Study", *Journal of Interacademicia,* Vol. 1, No. 4 (special), December 1997.

Singh, V., 1998. *A Systems Approach in Increasing Bio-mass Production in Red and Laterite Soils of Purulia and Midnapore,* Paper presented in the National Seminar on Strategy of Minimisation of Forage Production by 2000 AD, held on May 5 to 7, 1998.

Shah, A.K., 1998. "Environmental Protection and Sustainable Agriculture", *Employment News,* Vol. XXIII, No. 22.

8 Beyond Farmers' Participation in Irrigation

Participatory Irrigation Management Approaches in India

Rakesh Hooja

There used to be a time when farmers' participation in irrigation management was treated as a major means for improving the performance of irrigation in the country. However, it is now considered inadequate and now it is Participatory Irrigation Management (PIM) which is advocated as the means to irrigation reforms and efficient irrigation. The difference between farmers' or beneficiary participation and PIM lies in the extent, nature and style of participation involved as well as the role played in the management of irrigation and the irrigation system.

Participation can be passive or active. It can be token or nominal or partial. Or it can be wholehearted participation in all aspects of the planning, management and implementation. PIM, however, refers to a particular model of participatory beneficiary management as shall be described later in the paper.

Types of Participation in Water Resource Management and Irrigation

Before turning to a discussion of PIM, it would be appropriate to briefly look at some views on the type and nature of participation in irrigation or water resource management.

Mary R. Hollensteiner had in 1978 set forth six modes of people's participation in human settlement planning in the Philippines. T.K. Jayaraman (1980) found this relevant in the context of watershed management programmes in India as the following extract from a paper by him reveals:

> Mary R. Hollensteiner cites six modes of people's participation. The first mode involves only the educated and moneyed people in the community without the participation of the 'grassroots' or the beneficiaries. The second mode is one in which the people or beneficiaries are asked to legitimize or ratify projects identified and formulated by the government. In the third mode of participation, the people are consulted about the project but they do not actually participate in the planning and management of the project. In the fourth mode, the people are consulted from the very start and they actively participate in the planning and management of projects. In the fifth mode, the people or the beneficiaries are represented in the highest policy making body of the agency. Finally in the sixth mode, the representatives of the people control the highest policy making body of the agency.

Similarly, a typology of participation in watershed projects evolved by Pimbert and Pretty (1997) was adapted and presented in the well-known book edited by Farrington, Turton and James titled *Participatory Watershed Development: Challenges in the Twenty First Century* (OUP, 1999). This typology is reproduced below:

Typology	*Components of Each Type*
Passive participation	People participate by being told what is going to happen or has already happened.
Participation in information giving	People participate by giving answers to questions posed by extractive researchers and project managers.
Participation by consultation	People participate by being consulted and external agencies listen to their views. External agencies define both problems and solutions.
Participation for material resources	People participate by providing resources, for example labour, in return for cash and food.
Functional participation	People participate by forming groups to meet predetermined objectives relating to the project, which can involve the development or promotion of externally initiated social organization.
Interactive participation	People participate in joint analysis, which leads to joint action plans and formation of new groups and strengthening of old ones.
Self-mobilization	People participate by taking initiatives independent of external change systems.

In both Hollensteiner's modes of participation and the Pimbert-Pretty typology, it is the later modes or types involving greater degree of participation verging upon the taking over of management and the developing on the part of the users group of a sense of ownership (and more particularly Hollensteiners fourth mode and Pimbert and Pretty's 'functional participation' and 'self-mobilization') that approximate the most to the PIM approaches being propogated these days.

Turning from watersheds to canal irrigation, we find Meinzen-Dick et al. (1994) setting forth a four-by-six matrix of joint management options with differing control on the part of the governmental irrigation agency and of water users' association (WUA), where it is situations of WUA ownership with agency regulation or of full WUA control, which correspond to PIM. The Meinzen-Dick et al., matrix is being reproduced as Table 1.

Table 1

	Full agency control	*Agency O&M (user input)*	*Shared management*	*WUA O&M*	*WUA ownership agency regulation*	*Full WUA control*
Regulation	Agency	Agency	Agency	Agency	Agency	WUA
Ownership of structures	Agency	Agency	Agency	Agency	WUA	WUA
O and M responsibility	Agency	Agency	Both	WUA	WUA	WUA
User representation	Agency	WUA	WUA	WUA	WUA	WUA

What is PIM?

As the preceding section indicates Participatory Irrigation Management (PIM) is more than 'just farmers' participation in irrigation management.

PIM is the taking over of at least one level of irrigation channels/canals above the outlet, i.e., taking over at least a minor canal by a Water Users Association (WUA) who take over the management of both the operation and maintenance of that canal. In addition, the WUA and the irrigation agency (Irrigation/Command Area Development (CAD)/Water Resources Department) associate with each other in a joint partnership at managing the entire irrigation system. Thus, the PIM approach is based upon integrated and joint management of irrigation with the community (in the form of the WUA) and government agencies working together for equitable, rational, timely and convenient allocation of water and increase of efficiencies both in canal management and on-field water application.

Accordingly, PIM involves a redefinition of the government's role in irrigation and not a reduction, nor a downsizing of the irrigation agency.

The PIM approach which can be applied to major, medium and minor canal irrigation systems and even to large tank, or lift irrigation systems, allows for flexibility from region to region, irrigation system to irrigation system and even WUA to WUA.

Once WUAs adopt PIM they become part of the community-based organizations (CBOs) that constitute the fourth tier of Indian federalism, acting independently of, yet in coordination with, Panchayati Raj Institutions (PRIs, third tier) and state government (second tier). WUAs need to be separate from PRIs as they need to follow hydrological boundaries while PRI boundaries have evolved due to historical or administrative reasons. Also, PRIs meet periodically, while WUA members need to interact on a daily basis especially during the cropping and watering season. All members of WUAs are water users unlike in the case of PRIs and accordingly PRIs have many concerns and objectives which do not relate to water, while WUAs and its members and office bearers are focussed on irrigated agriculture and water management.

PIM-related Developments in Various Indian States

Andhra Pradesh (1997), Rajasthan (2000), Tamil Nadu (2000), Madhya Pradesh (2002) and Maharashtra (2005) have enacted Farmers Management of Irrigation System Acts, which are similar in many respects having drawn inspiration from the Andhra Act (APFMIS, or Andhra Pradesh Farmers Management of Irrigation Systems Act, 1997). Bihar has provided for government distributaries and minors etc., to be handed over to WUAs as per Bihar Irrigation Act, 1997 and this now also applies to Jharkhand.

Earlier, Gujarat, Maharashtra, Orissa, Uttar Pradesh, Tamil Nadu, Karnataka and Rajasthan had made use of either the concerned state-level Societies Registration Act or the Cooperative Societies Act to constitute and register Water User Associations. Karnataka Irrigation and Certain Other Laws (Amendment) Act, 2000 has provided for WUAs and federations of WUAs to be registered under the Cooperative Societies Act and specified the functions for WUAs to perform. Orissa has a Pani Panchayat legislation.

Both Andhra Pradesh and Madhya Pradesh have gone through the first round of elections to WUAs/Distributary Committees etc., as per their FMIS Acts. Based on their experience, both Andhra and Madhya Pradesh have amended their Acts. Andhra Pradesh went through its second round of elections to WUAs starting from October, 2003.

Andhra Pradesh has 10,755 WUAs, Madhya Pradesh (including what is now Chattisgarh) has 2,416 WUAs. These are the states where state-wise introduction of PIM has been completed. Some other states have either a few pilot PIM projects or have managed to introduce PIM only in some regions/irrigation projects. States reporting significant number of WUAs formed include Tamil Nadu, Maharashtra, Gujarat, Karnataka and Rajasthan.

Two Approaches to Spread of PIM

One approach, also called 'big-bang approach', initially tried out in Mexico, has been adopted in Andhra Pradesh, Madhya Pradesh etc. The big-bang approach involves simultaneous, uniform adoption of PIM throughout one region or state usually based upon legislation or government orders.

The second approach is a bottom-up, slow and steady, flexible 'cafeteria' approach where only if water users so decide, do they set up a WUA and wherein each individual WUA itself decides about its internal structure and working practices as well as what functions it wants to take up initially. The WUA may subsequently add on more functions as it gains experience and finds itself facing many irrigation-related problems. This is different from the big-bang approach where a uniform structure and uniform working practices as well as a uniform set of functions are prescribed for all WUAs. In the 'cafeteria' approach, a network of WUAs adopting PIM gradually spreads throughout the irrigation system and the region or state.

It is theoretically possible for legislation to provide for flexible, bottom-up, 'cafeteria' approach, though presently the various state-level Farmers Management of Irrigation Systems Acts in India have all followed the uniform big-bang approach.

WUA Functions

There is difference of opinion whether WUAs should only perform irrigation and canal management activities which they take over from the irrigation agency, or whether they should also perform other tasks related to irrigated agriculture.

The Andhra Pradesh Farmers Management of Irrigation Systems Act provides for the following functions for WUAs: preparing and implementing 'warabandi' (or water distribution schedule based on 'turns' for receiving water) schedules; planning and implementing the maintenance of the irrigation system; regulating the use of water amongst various outlets; promoting economy in the use of the allocated water; monitoring flows of water; water budgeting; and resolving disputes between members and water users in its area of operations (besides functions related to maintaining records and the internal administration of the WUA). The Tamil Nadu legislation has followed suit. Rajasthan has added the task of preparation of demand for and collection of water charges, as has Madhya Pradesh (for Lift Irrigation Schemes only), and (though they have gone in for a different pattern of WUAs in their legislation) Karnataka. The Orissa Pani Panchayat Bill, however, enables the WUAs to also perform agriculture-related functions.

By and large, PIM legislation in India has followed the views of those who feel that the functions of WUAs should be limited to only irrigation department-related functions, viz., maintenance of the canal and its structures, distribution of water, resolving disputes related to water distribution and collection of irrigation charges.

Many experts, however, feel that WUAs can achieve institutional sustainability and both economic and institutional viability only if they undertake various irrigated agriculture-related tasks including even input management and post-harvest activities, in addition to canal management.

We tend to agree with the view that WUAs should undertake a broader set of functions. What it means is that there should be two sets of tasks enumerated: one a core or compulsory group of tasks related to the management and maintenance of the canal (or lift) system which is the bare minimum that a WUA has to take up as part of PIM and, the second, a list of additional and optional agriculture and land-water management related tasks which the WUA could adopt either at its inception or gradually add on as time passes.

The core or compulsory activities could be as follows:

— Acting as an interface between the farmers and the main system management of the irrigation project as well as other concerned government agencies (Command Area Development/Rural Development/Agricultural Ground Water/Cooperative Development/(land) Revenue and Irrigation Departments).

- Water distribution; irrigation scheduling including both rotational running of canals and warabandi ensuring that water reaches to all members (as also non-members) as per their due shares.
- Operation and maintenance of the irrigation and drainage system.
- Collection (and assessment) of water charges and other user charges or special charges that the WUAs may levy.
- Resolution of local disputes amongst members; if necessary, the setting up of an internal system of penalties and other incentives or disincentives.
- Conflict resolution between members and non-members.
- Drainage-related activities.
- Provision of drinking water from canals.
- Design and construction of new works (irrigation works, OFD works, drainage works) as well as rehabilitation of canals and structures (deferred maintenance works).
- Maintenance of commercial, financial and water accounting records.
- Cooperating with other WUAs to form federations of WUAs to take over larger canal sub-systems.

The additional and optional tasks could be as follows:

- Agriculture extension and farmers' training.
- Recommending of cropping patterns and package of agricultural practices suitable for the WUA's farmers.
- Helping to arrange for other inputs besides water and for credit supply to members for undertaking irrigated agriculture.
- Irrigation extension and propagation of better on-farm water application and better intra-outlet command water management.
- Encouraging and taking up of conjunctive water use, or community lift irrigation.
- Post-harvest practices (grading, packaging, storage, marketing).
- Any other task as mutually agreed upon by the members (e.g., canal side plantation, construction/maintenance of farm tracks,

providing of matching funds on behalf of the command area to the District Rural Development Agency, or to Zila Parishad/Panchayat Samiti for taking up of rural development work).

A WUA's functions would differ depending upon whether the WUA is for a canal system, or for a largish tank scheme, or for a community lift, as also upon whether it gets constituted before the irrigation system is constructed or afterwards when actual irrigation precedes the constitution of the WUA.

Government's Role in PIM

As WUAs take over many functions (including the management of canals) the Government CAD (or Irrigation) Department would have to gear itself to look more to construction and management of dams and the main canal system or drainage works, providing technical advice, training, introduction of new technologies, major repairs, creation of an organization for interfacing with WUAs and other government departments, and for motivating and catalyzing the formation of WUAs, as also undertaking long-term water resource planning.

The government has to create an enabling environment through (a) policy resolutions, (b) providing intellectual, administrative and implementational leadership, (c) putting into place legal and administrative provisions and procedures including Acts, rules, government orders, (d) specific programmes, projects and activities to be implemented or sponsored by government, (e) undertaking mass awareness building and promotional efforts, (f) providing technical advice and technical back-up as well as funds to WUAs for selective activities while continuing to perform many tasks on its own and initiating newer tasks which were not being undertaken earlier in the pre-PIM era by government agencies, (g) ensuring attitudinal and behavioural change amongst employees of all government departments directly or indirectly concerned with canal (and community lift) irrigation, (h) enabling the taking up of pilot PIM projects and PIM demonstration projects, (i) creating nodal points for PIM in all concerned government departments at both the Central Government and State Government levels with a multidisciplinary PIM unit supported by an advisory group of experts being located in the Water Resources or Irrigation/Command Area Development Department, (j) creating multidisciplinary mobile PIM propagation teams to move from project to project, motivate as well as orient and train farmers and field/project level government staff, obtain feedback about administrative as well as policy changes required at the government level, and generally take steps to ensure that PIM takes off and functions properly, (k) preparing guidelines and field manuals, (l) arranging for various sorts of PIM-related training (m) helping WUAs to rehabilitate old irrigation systems to bring them up to at least a minimum operational level, (n) involving NGOs and community organizers, (o) providing incentives, monetary, or otherwise, for (i) farmers to undertake PIM, and (ii) government staff to facilitate it, (p) helping WUAs in conflict resolution with other agencies, as also by (q) putting into place transparent provisions for interaction or arbitration between WUAs and government agencies.

The duties of government regarding PIM and responsibilities towards WUAs would need to be spelt out not only in legislation or in government orders, but also in Memorandum of Understanding (MoU) between the concerned government agency and each specific WUA.

The government needs to decree that a part of the water or irrigation charges recovered shall be the share of the WUA depending upon the number of activities it takes over from the government as well as the level of irrigation system (minor, branch-canal, distributary, main canal, drains, headworks and dam) whose management is taken over by the WUA.

A system of payments, incentives, disincentives, subsidies and grants would need to be devised which encourages WUAs to raise their own resources.

Training for PIM

PIM training has to be planned and conceptualized in its broadest sense to include mass awareness building and attitudinal change in addition to imparting of skills and knowledge related to irrigation, participation, group dynamics and conflict resolution, irrigation laws etc.

The PIM-related training would need to:

1. Create a favourable climate within the country in general for the propagation of PIM.
2. Prepare water users to undertake PIM through Water Users Associations (WUAs).

3. Enable the government departments and agencies related to water resources and irrigated agriculture to re-orient and re-invent themselves and to adopt new roles, organizational structures, processes and ways of functioning so that they can play a facilitative role for furthering PIM and joint farmer-government agency partnerships.
4. Change the orientations and knowledge base of water professionals and policy makers in the water sector.
5. Equip lower-level functionaries of government, employees of NGOs and others to facilitate PIM and thus to ensure better water management.

Training and orientation programmes need to be planned and organized for a variety of categories of people. Such categories of trainees would include: (1) politicians (at central, state and various sub-state-local-self-government/Panchayati Raj/cooperative etc., levels), (2) farmers, (3) WUA personnel (elected office bearers as well as WUA employees), (4) NGOs, (5) community organizers, (6) senior officers (In central and state government as well as Divisional Commissioners and District Collectors), (7) middle-level officers (both generalists as well as specialists from agriculture, irrigation, CAD, groundwater, rural development and panchayats, cooperatives etc., departments and from the district administration), (8) junior-level officers (especially those related to irrigation, CAD and agriculture, and such others with whom the WUAs are likely to have regular interaction), (9) officers of registering authorities (since, in many states of India, the WUAs are being registered under either Cooperative Societies Act or the Registration of Societies Act or by the CAD authority/irrigation department), (10) trainers (from WALMIs/IMTIs WALAMTARIs or other training institutes related to agriculture, irrigation, rural development and panchayats, cooperative etc., or trainers picked up from amongst government department's implementing PIM, or WUA chairpersons, or NGOs etc.), and (11) mass media professionals and the general public (including students).

PIM training is too important to be left entirely to training experts. Those involved in implementing PIM as also those involved in formulating PIM-related policies and strategies, both need to be intimately associated and involved in delivering PIM training.

Central and state governments, research and training institutes and NGOs should prepare training manuals on various aspects of PIM.

There should, both at the national and state levels, be PIM Documentation Centres and Information Clearing Houses on PIM manned by NGOs which provide both policy-oriented and training-related back-up and support to all concerned at various levels.

At the state level, each state should prepare a perspective plan on PIM training, orientation and capacity building and ensure that the training becomes a two-way flow of knowledge (technical and policy-oriented) to the field and of feedback from water users and PIM implementers to the government and thus can positively influence implementation of PIM. PIM training action plans and PIM training advisory groups would also be desirable.

Contents of a Model State Level PIM Act in the Indian Context

PIM legislation should specify that regardless of whether the source is lift irrigation (from rivers, water bodies or community tubewells), or a tank system, or a conventional irrigation system based upon storage and water distribution through canals, wherever water is to be distributed among 30 or more farmers, the PIM and WUA approach should be mandatory.

As long as water rights continue to be linked to land ownership (as is the case in India) each landholder drawing water from the canal minor (or from the river lift irrigation schemes, community tubewell or the channel of a tank scheme) would be a member of the WUA.

The legislation should specify the rights and duties of both members and non-members within the command area.

The provisions regarding internal organization of WUAs should provide for some flexibility from WUA to WUA.

As regards functions to be performed by WUAs, the legislation should provide for both core or compulsory tasks and additional or optional tasks.

The PIM Act should contain provision for each WUA to sign two sets of MoUs: one related to core and compulsory tasks with representatives of Irrigation/CAD/Water Resources/Ground Water Department, and the second related to additional optional tasks with representatives of Agriculture/CAD/Rural Development/Panchayats Department. There should be scope for mutually agreed modifications of the MoUs as both WUAs and government agencies come to face what we may call second generation problems of PIM.

A suggestive list of functions that government agencies would need to perform to make PIM effective, as well as an indication of the type of enabling or facilitating role that government should play regarding PIM, and of the types of changes required within government agencies should form part of PIM legislation.

PIM legislation should specify that it is aimed at participatory, multidisciplinary and integrated management of irrigated agriculture and of irrigation systems and, accordingly, the concerned government agencies need to function in support of PIM-related activities.

The PIM Act should clarify that WUAs functioning before the enactment of the legislation do not get derailed due to the provisions of the new Act and ensure that there is a transitional period allowed, and sufficient flexibility is provided for, so as to enable the existing WUAs to continue functioning.

Each government department having some bearing or influence on PIM should be mandated to designate a nodal officer for PIM. The main department responsible for PIM should constitute a multidisciplinary PIM cell at the department level to manage all PIM-related work.

Multidisciplinary PIM propagation teams should be constituted to move from project to project to take all the required steps for the propagation of PIM and to obtain feedback for use in refining various policies and strategies pertaining to PIM.

A state-level PIM support group at the state secretariat level, a state-level Water Users Council for coordination of PIM, a committee of experts on PIM to help arbitrate disputes/differences of opinion and a PIM training and advocacy advisory group are some of the types of bodies that a PIM legislation could describe and empower.

Conclusions

Farmers' willingness to undertake PIM is dependent upon whether the returns from PIM provide them enough of an incentive to offset the cost, monetary or otherwise, of participating and undertaking managerial and implementational responsibilities.

The goal of PIM is not the mere transfer or 'turnover' of irrigation systems or sub-systems to WUAs—such transfer is only a means and not an end. Nor is the goal merely to ensure deferred maintenance or rehabilitation of canal systems. The saving of government funds is also not a goal of PIM. Nor should PIM be viewed merely as a mechanism to pass on governmental responsibilities to WUAs, or to make the WUAs agents for implementing government schemes.

The goal of PIM is improved and integrated management of water and irrigated agriculture through a joint partnership of WUAs at various levels with the concerned governmental agencies.

However, it needs to be borne in mind that PIM is not a panacea for all the difficulties being faced by irrigation systems. Many issues have purely technical solutions. Others would require government action. However, the technical fixes or government action by themselves may not suffice without PIM.

With competition amongst different uses and different regions for water increasing day by day, as is the demand for water due to growing population and changing lifestyles, PIM needs to be introduced in all water/irrigation projects. Thus, there is a need for the universalization of PIM throughout all irrigation or water resource projects in India.

References

Farrington, J., C. Turton and A.J. James, 1999. *Participatory Watershed Development: Challenges for the Twenty First Century,* Oxford University Press, New Delhi.

Greenfield, D., 1998 and earlier editions. *Handbook on Participatory Irrigation Management,* The Economic Development Institute of the World Bank, Washington DC.

Greenfield, D. and Mark Svendson (eds.), 2000. *Case Studies in Participatory Irrigation Management*, Economic Development Institute, Washington DC.

Goldensohn, M. also often referred to as ISPAN, 1994. *Participation and Empowerment: An Assessment of Water Users Associations in Asia and Egypt,* Irrigation Support Project for Asia and the Near-East (ISPAN), Washington DC.

Gulati, A., R. Meinzen-Dick and K.V. Raju, 2005. *Institutional Reforms in Indian Irrigation*, Sage, New Delhi.

Hollensteiner, Mary R., 1978. "People Power: Community Participation in the Planning and Implementation of Human Settlements", *Philippine Studies*, 1978, pp. 5–36.

Hooja, Rakesh, 1996. "Objective of PIM", *INPIM Newsletter*, No. 2, March 1996.

———, 1997(a). "Promoting Water Users Associations in Participatory Irrigation Management: Some Reflections", *Indian Journal of Public Administration*, Vol. 43, No. 4, October-December 1997.

———, 1997(b). "Participatory Irrigation Management: A Report", *Prashasnika*, Vol. 24, No. 2, July-December 1997.

———, 1997(c). "PIM Efforts in Rajasthan" in Ramesh K. Arora and P.C. Mathur, (eds.), *Administrative System of Rajasthan*, Aalekh, Jaipur.

———, 1998(a). "Command Area Development in India: Water Resources Based Development of Irrigated Areas" in T.N. Chaturvedi (ed.), *Fifty Years of Indian Administration: Retrospect and Prospects,* Indian Institute of Public Administration, New Delhi, earlier published in *Indian Journal of Public Administration,* Vol. 43, No. 3, July-September 1997.

———, 1998(b). "Propagating Participatory Irrigation Management: A Strategy in the Indian Context", *Administrative Change*, Vol. 25, No. 2 and Vol. 26, No. 1, January-December 1998.

———, 2000. "Administering Water in India in 2050 AD", *Water and Energy International*, Vol. 46, No. 2, April-June 2000.

———, 2001(a). Multidisciplinary and Participatory Water Management for Irrigation Command Areas, *IndiaNPIM Working Paper/Monograph,* No. 2, New Delhi.

———, 2001(b). "Guest Editorial", *Water and Energy International,* Vol. 58, No. 2, April-June 2001.

———, 2003(a). "Two Approaches to Participatory Irrigation Management: Reforming Irrigation in India" in S.N. Mishra, A.D. Mishra and Shweta Mishra, (eds.), *Public Governance and Decentralization,* Mittal Publication, New Delhi.

———, 2003(b). "Revisiting Participatory Irrigation Management in India", *Indian Journal of Public Administration*, Vol. 49, No. 3, September 2003.

———, 2004(a). "Ten Questions Regarding the Participatory Irrigation Management Approach in the Indian Context", *Political Economy Journal of India,* Vol. 13, No. 3 and 4, July-December 2004.

———, 2004(b). "State level PIM Legislation: Some Reflections", *Prashasnika,* Vol. 31, No. 1, January-June 2004.

———, 2004(c). "Water Users Associations as part of the Fourth Tier of Indian Federalism" in *South Asian Journal of Socio-Political Studies,* Vol. 4, No. 2, June 2004.

———, 2005. "Training for Participatory Irrigation Management in India", *ASTI Journal of Training and Development*, Vol. 6, No. 1, January-June 2005.

———, 2006. *Management of Water for Agriculture: Irrigation, Watersheds and Drainage*, Rawat Publications, Jaipur.

Hooja, Rakesh, R.C. Bower and S.N. Mundhra, (eds.), 1997. *Irrigation Agriculture Anti-Social Development*, Himanshu Publication, Udaipur.

Hooja, Rakesh, and G. Pangare 2002. "Some Reflections on Software Aspects of Water Policy: CAD, PIM, Watershed Development and Management and Water Harvesting", paper presented at Round Table on Water Policy organized by Indian Society of Ecological Economics at India International Centre, New Delhi on 10 May 2002, revised version published as *India NPIM Working Paper*, No. 13, January 2003.

Hooja, Rakesh, G. Pangare and K.V. Raju (eds.), 2002. *Users in Water Management: The Andhra Model and Its Repliciability in India,* Rawat Publications, Jaipur.

IndiaNPIM, 2000. Attitude and Behavioral Change for PIM: 4 Workshop Report.

IndiaNPIM, 2001. *Irrigation Management Transfer: Sharing Lessons from Global Experience* (reprinted from INPIM, FAO International Conference on Irrigation Management Transfer), supplement to *Indian NPIM Newsletter,* No. 11 and 12, July 2001.

IndiaNPIM, 2002. *Proceedings of National Workshop on PIM—FOT Experiences in Tamil Nadu,* August 6 to 8, 2001, Madurai, *Comparing PIM Legislation in Various States,* India NPIM Working Paper, No. 11, New Delhi.

———, 2003. *National Experience Sharing Workshop on PIM: Report of Workshop,* organized at Pune, 25–27 June, 2002.

Jayaraman, T.K., 1980. "Strategy for Mass Mobilization and People's Participation in the Implementation of Watershed Management Programme", paper presented at Seminar on Strategy for Mass Mobilization and People's Participation in the Implementation of Watershed Management Programme, Central Board of Irrigation and Power, New Delhi, October 1980.

Joshi, L.K. and Rakesh Hooja, (eds.), 2000. *Participatory Irrigation Management: Paradigm for 21st Century* (2 Volumes), Rawat Publications, Jaipur.

Maloney, C. and K.V. Raju, 1994. *Managing Irrigation Together: Practice and Policy in India,* Sage, New Delhi.

Meinzen-Dick, R., 1997. "Farmer Participation in Irrigation: 20 Years of Experience and Lessons for the Future", *Irrigation and Drainage Systems,* Vol. 11, 1997.

Meinzen-Dick, R., M. Mendoza, C. Sadoulet, G. Abiad Shields, and A. Subramanian, 1994. "Sustainable Water User Associations: Lessons from a Literature Review". Presented at Water Resources Seminar Landsdowne, Virginia USA and reprinted in A. Subramanian, N.V. Jagannathan and R. Meinzen-Dick, (eds.), *Users Organizations for Sustainable Water Services,* World Bank Technical Paper, No. 354, Washington DC.

Meinzen-Dick R., R. Reidinger and A. Monzardo, 1995. *Participation in Irrigation,* Environmental Department Participation Papers Series, World Bank, Washington DC.

Ministry of Water Resources, India, 2003. *Vision for Integrated Water Resources Development and Management,* New Delhi.

Ostrom, E., 1992. *Crafting Institutions for Self-governing Irrigation Systems,* Institute for Contemporary Studies, San Francisco, California.

Oblitas, K. and J.R. Peter, 1999. *Transferring Irrigation Management to Framers in Andhra Pradesh,* World Bank Technical Paper 339, Washington DC.

Parlin, B.W. and M.W. Lusk, (eds.), 1991. *Farmer's Participation and Irrigation Organization*, Westview Press, Colorado.

Pimbert, M. and J. Pretty, 1997. "Diversity and Sustainability in Community Based Conservation", paper presented at UNESCO IIPA Regional Workshop on Community Based Conservation, India, 9–12 February, 1997.

Planning Commission, India, 2001. *Report of the Working Group on Command Area Development Programme (CADP) for 10th Five-Year Plan 2002–2007*, New Delhi, September 2001.

Raju, K.V. and J. Brewer, 1996. "Types of Irrigation Management Transfer Models in India", paper presented at International Association for the Study of Common Property Resources Meeting, Berkeley, California, June 1996.

Sampath, R.K. and R.A. Young, (eds.), 1990. *Social, Economic and Institutional Issues in Third World Irrigation Management*, Westview Press, Boulder, Colorado.

Sinha, P.K., 2002. The WUA Approach to Improved System Performance in India, India NPIM Working Paper, No. 12.

Sivamohan, M.V.K. and C.A. Scott, (eds.), 1994. *India: Irrigation Management Partnerships*, Booklinks, Hyderabad.

Tang, S.Y. and E. Ostrom, 1993. *The Governance and Management of Irrigation Systems: An Institutional Perspective*, ODI, Irrigation Management Network (Network Paper 23), London.

Uphoff, N., R. Meinzen-Dick and N. St. Julien, 1985. *Improving Policies and Programmes for Farmer Organization and Participation in Irrigation Water Management*, Water Management Synthesis Paper 1, Cornell University.

9 Governance, Advocacy Planning and Community Participation

A Study of Community Development Workers in South Africa

John J. Williams

The formal introduction of democracy in South Africa has been a major success story of the latter part of the 20th century. Even so, throughout South Africa, many communities, especially poor communities, must yet experience, the democratic dividend of a better life for all, of this democratic 'miracle'. Apart from this introductory section, clarifying the research problematique of this paper, the following sections constitute the remainder of this presentation:

- Advocacy planning and democratic practice;
- Community participation as advocacy planning;
- Some examples of community participation, 1994–2004;
- Towards a theoretical framework to understand community development planners as advocacy planners;
- Theoretical implications of this research; and
- Specific recommendations.

Major Research Argument

The local state is the site of democratic practice for ordinary people. Whilst the 'state' is a highly contested concept, for the purposes of this paper, however, it is defined as an ensemble of relations of power, socially, economically, politically, and ideologically, operating not merely locally but also nationally or globally. Most importantly, perhaps, the state is not reducible to the government, although a particular government, in terms of its specific institutional arrangements, and bureaucratic procedures would have a profound impact on the ensemble of power relations, interests, motivations, strategic dilemmas informing the state.

Keeping the local state accountable, i.e., answerable to ordinary people by responding to their rights and basic needs, occurs when the substantive features of democracy are entrenched and practised through various forms of citizenship, contestation, access and a sense of belonging to the community and the country at large. Amongst other interpretations, this specifically means that:

- Accountability, even in a 'democratic state' does not roll in under the wheels of inevitability; on the contrary, we must plan for it, struggle for it conceptually, theoretically, organizationally, institutionally and empirically. Hence, the import of keeping the local state accountable; and.
- Constitutionally-driven rights, as in the case post-apartheid South Africa, can only be realized if they are deliberately and systematically incorporated into the planning programmes and practices of local authorities such as municipalities. Hence, the import of advocacy planning a la community development workers (CDWs).

Research question: Can CDWs keep the local state accountable? Using a range of methodological techniques the problematic of service delivery and the resultant challenges for development workers can be disclosed, viz.,

- Evaluation research: policy design, implementation. monitoring, evaluation in terms of key performance indicators (kpi's);
- base line indicators (existing situation);
- input indicators (amounts and resources spent on specific sectors);
- output indicators (number and types of services rendered: effective, equitable, economic);
- impact indicators (do these services provided make a difference in the actual lives of people on a daily basis?).

- gap analysis: difference between policy statements, goals, intentions, practices and the experiences of ordinary citizens with regard to these policy statements, goals and intentions.
- participant observation: drawn on experiences as planning practitioner, City of Cape Town.
- autobiographical narratives (subaltern speak in own voice interviews.
- content analysis: of formal Integrated Development Plans (IDPs).
- literature review (case studies: discourses of affirmation/disconfirmation of rights).

Based on a combination of the aforementioned methodologies, the following socio-economic conditions of Metropolitan Cape Town emerge:

First, profound racial-cum-ethnic faultlines of differentiated characterize access to basic services/rights continue to characterize citizenship.

Second, though there have been some material improvements in the lives of some ordinary people since the abolition of apartheid—such as access to water, health services and housing, however, these improvements at grass-roots level, almost pale into insignificance in relation to the institutional neglect and bureaucratic incompetence that seem to deprive ordinary citizens of their constitutional rights;

Already three years ago, the South African Human Rights Commission (*Cape Times*, 23 April 2003), pointed out that while there is a huge housing backlog, the housing department has underspent by about Rs 100 million approximately US $ 12 million) in the 2001–02 financial year. The critical shortage of houses has been proved by the mushrooming of more than 1,088 informal settlements throughout the country:

- Less than 50 per cent of poor people are getting the free water promised by the government before the local election of 2000 (ibid.):
- Thousands of pensioners, who are entitled to social grants are not getting their money (ibid.);
- In the Limpopo Province alone, 92,000 welfare recipients of pension and disability grants had them unfairly terminated by the province's welfare department (ibid.);

- In the Province of the Eastern Cape, applications for social assistance were often lost and pensioners waited more than a year before they could receive financial assistance from the government (ibid.);
- Of the 1.2 million people identified by the Department of Social Development as deserving disability grants, only 7,14,000 were actually receiving them (ibid.);
- Only 2 per cent of land has been redistributed; 80 per cent of the land is still owned by white commercial farmers depriving between 13 and 14 million people of access to land, thus deepening rural poverty amongst the historically marginalized and excluded poor black people of South Africa (ibid.); and
- Not only do the historically marginalized continue to suffer in rural South Africa; indeed, they continue to suffer also in urban South Africa such as on the Cape Flats where they constitute upto 80 per cent of the populace of Metropolitan Cape Town (i.e., 2.4 million of the approximately 3.2 million inhabitants) (Provincial Development Council of the Western Cape, 2002).

Not only are ordinary South Africans subject to bureaucratic incompetence, and neglect, they are, like the majority of people in the world, systemically subject to an economic system that is profit-driven, using any means necessary. Thus, for example, in 2002, in South Africa, as a whole, unemployment was more than 40 per cent and the economy has lost more than one million jobs since 1995, affecting mostly lower skilled black employees. About 45 per cent of South Africans live in poor households, i.e., earning less than the household subsistence level of Rs 1,000 (i.e., approximately US $ 125) per month with adults earning Rs 35,353 (approximately US $ 44) a month on average. In rural areas, the poverty levels increase to more than 50 per cent of the population. Sixty-one per cent of the Africans are poor, compared with 1 per cent whites. The largest proportion of those in the top income quinthe are white (65% of white households) and Indian (45%), with only 17 per cent so-called coloured and 10 per cent African. Three million households are without houses, 7.5 million lack access to running water and 21 million are without sanitation. Five million South Africans have HIV/AIDS whilst the crime rate in South Africa is among the highest in the world (*Sunday Times*, 27 April 2003). This means that since the birth of democratic South Africa in 1994 unemployment has increased, While 2.5 million young people have entered the potential labour market and have been unable to attain permanent jobs. The poorest 50 per cent of South Africans, almost entirely black, are almost completely marginalized from the economy (*Sunday Times*, 20 April 2003).

The preceding statistics suggest the continued absence of an integrated, humane, responsive and effective service delivery programme within and across national and provincial spheres of government.

Indeed, according to a report in the *Cape Times* (1 May 2003), on the Cape Flats, predominantly black residential areas, 70 per cent of the people have problems feeding their children; unemployment for males is 32 per cent and for females 53 per cent; there are 5 persons per household; 82 per cent have less than grade 12 education. In the meanwhile, the wealthy in the Cape Town owe the municipality upto Rand 1.75 billion, i.e., 70 per cent of debt (arrears for electricity rates)—yet their services are not discontinued at gunpoint as in the case of the poorest 30–35 per cent of people on the Cape Flats who owe Council R 750 million for services (ibid.). Moreover, in these racial ghettos of Cape Town, hundreds of poor people still use the bucket system to remove sewage and in some areas refuse has not been collected for two years (*Mail* and *Guardian*, 16–122 May 2003).

Table 1 illustrates the comparative spatial differences of access to services in Metropolitan Cape Town. More specifically, these statistics reinforce the glaring reality of black marginalization, exclusion and deprivation and largely white privilege and affluence and access to adequate and effective services, even in post-apartheid South Africa and more than ten years since the first democratic elections in the country's history.

In view of the overriding continuities of racism, exclusion and discriminatory practices, especially in relation to the historically marginalized, the South African president introduced Community Development Workers (hence, CDWs) in the early 21st century to fill the gap between government services and the poor. CDWs are supposed to make the poor aware of their constitutional rights such as their right to basic services including social grants, housing support and so forth. In this regard, CDWs are specially meant to act as change agents. This means, CDWs are thus officially mandated to 'develop' and 'transform' communities, amongst other activities:

Table 1

Comparative Racial Access to Services in Cape Town

Development indicator	*Black residential area WALLACEDENE*		*White residential area CONSTANTIA*		*White residential area CLIFTON*		*White residential area SEA POINT*	
	No	*%*	*No*	*%*	*No*	*%*	*No*	*%*
Employed	5520	40.89	5956	60.84	263	64.20	5702	57.32
Unemployed	7979	59.11	3834	39.16	147	35.80	4246	42.68
Total	13499	100.00	9790	100.00	410	100.00	9948	100.00
Household Subsistence Level < R 1000 per month	6755	78.02	1320	34.26	51	16.50	1944	22.98
Household Subsistence Level > R 1000 per month	1903	21.98	2534	65.74	258	83.50	6516	77.02
Total	8658	100.00	3854	100.00	309	100.00	8460	100.00
Fuel: Candies and Kerosene(Paraffin)	2876	52.37	36	0.90	0	0.00	16	0.26
Proper fuel	2616	47.63	3980	99.10	221	100.00	6176	99.74
Total	5492	100.00	4016	100.00	221	100.00	6192	100.00
Outside water only	4949	90.11	66	1.64	0	0.00	268	4.32
Access to water inside dwelling	543	9.89	3950	98.36	221	100.00	5924	95.68
Total	5492	100.00	4016	100.00	221	106.00	6192	100.00
Overall physical infrastructure	Very Poor		Excellent		Excellent		Excellent	

Source: Author's own calculations based on statistics provided by the Urban Policy Unit. City of Cape Town: 2003.

Special Note: Percentages of unemployment, below Household Subsistence Levels, the use of candies and kerosene as fuel, access to outside water only, in historically white areas of Constantia, Clifton and Sea Point, reflect the conditions of mostly black domestic and farm workers in these areas.

- Inform and assist communities with access to the services provided by the government,
- Determine the needs of communities and communicate these to government;
- Promote networks between community workers and projects to improve service delivery; and
- Compile reports and documents about progress and local issues.

Thus, it is expected that CDWs must become advocacy planners, i.e., they must act as advocates of development and transformation and toil in a specific community vis-à-vis especially in relation to Integrated Development Planning (IDP).

Advocacy Planning and Democratic Practice

The question thus arises: what is advocacy planning, and how could it be mobilized in the interests of the poor and marginalized? The next section seeks to provide a preliminary response: In his seminal article on advocacy planning, Paul Davidoff, suggests that this mode of planning is significant for participatory governance for at least two reasons, as under:

- *First*, advocacy planning emphasizes partisanship, i.e., the idea of winning a specific battle and identifying with the plight of a group that is in a position of power/resource disadvantage, and
- *Second,* advocacy planning emphasizes politics, i.e., the concept of rigorous, even aggressive negotiation with opponents or manipulating the environment to obtain a desired end on behalf of a client population.

For the sake of conceptual clarity, it is necessary to briefly illuminate the theoretical dimensions of advocacy planning and then to investigate to what extent community participation at grass-roots level since the birth of democracy in South Africa has subscribed to this transformative mode of planning.

Here, it is important to point out that the model advocacy planner begins with a critique of the present situation. Such a critique is not merely normative, on the contrary, it contains a strong analytical element which allows one to interpret, understand and explain why things are as they are. The model grass roots planner helps in the mobilization of radical practice by providing a critical account of the situation to be changed. Once one is aware that things are not as they might be, a transformation model is conceived. The idea of a grassroots advocate planner is to help communities and groups that are already mobilized to search for practical realistic/winnable solutions to the problems they experience. To this search, professional planners bring a strong analytical ability. A sense of what is likely to work and what is not, a knowledge of what has worked or failed elsewhere, and an ability to assess and evaluate alternative solutions.

Devising an appropriate strategy, which is the next step in grass roots planning practice and requires timely, accurate, and richly textured information ('intelligence'); correct interpretations of this 'Intelligence'; a careful assessment of actual options; and the continuous monitoring of grass roots activities, action results, and the changing context of collective action. In this respect, grass-roots planners can provide mobilized groups with the 'intelligence' they need for devising a successful strategy of action.

Usually, most solutions to deep-seated problems, even radical transformative solutions have technical aspects that must be considered: questions of design, of cost, of location, and so forth. In these areas grass-roots planners can help mobilize groups and refine the technical aspects of transformative solutions.

Active participation by neighbourhood residents in the identification and solution of local problems can be enhanced by using the 'social learning model'—a model which highlights the fact that learning itself is an interactive, dialogical, iterative and recursive process: it feeds on its underlying pedagogical tenets and is the dominant as well as desired social practices. But, learning is never direct; it must be passed through a theoretical and ideological filter where experience is sifted for what it has to teach us. It becomes available to us only in the 'filtered' form. Grassroots planners can make conscious use of a social learning model by devising group process methods of 'filtering' so that the group itself may learn from its own experience. These methods may involve open discussion, self-criticism, role-playing, maintaining a collective memory, and related devices suitable for this purpose. What has been learned from practice constitutes valuable knowledge, especially if the knowledge is also used to expand and revise theoretical and ideological components of transformative practice. Experiential knowledge is ephemeral, embodied in particular individuals who possess 'know-how', but it tends not to be articulated, to become generally available.

Yet, when the goal is emancipation, it is important that learning takes place collectively. This requires abstraction from experience, which may be called 'generalizing the solution' and the dissemination of newly-acquired knowledge in ways appropriate to the project: using video, film, in ways appropriate and writing: sharing experience by word-mouth, arranging for exchange visits with other mobilized groups who may be interested in the experience and so forth. In this way, the experiential fund for radical practice is enriched. In this respect, it must be emphasized that in the social learning model all the members within the group are considered potential teachers. This means that the group approaches education as a non-hierarchical and essentially non-discriminatory process. Expertise is no longer derived merely from textualized abstractions but is conceived, analyzed and explicated in the totality of human experiences irrespective of the formal or non-formal exposure to education. In the social learning model, human beings enter the pedagogical realm both as learners on the one hand and as teachers on the other, minimizing, as far as possible the distinction between sacrosanct theories and the prevailing social reality. This implies that grass-roots planning adopts a dialectical view on education where social practice informs theoretical perspectives and theoretical perspectives serve to explicate social reality.

Advocacy planning at the grass-roots level is oppositional. Sooner or later, it will run up against the state and its regulatory and repressive agencies. What happens then will be guided by the strategy that the mobilized group has adopted. In most cases, the encounter will be peaceful, and the group may even seek the active collaboration of the state, albeit under carefully controlled conditions. In this respect, grass-roots planners can mediate these encounters with the technocracy by adopting the latter's jargon and presenting the group's demands in ways that are likely to meet with the approval of the state. In doing this work of mediation, planners are usually not autonomous agents but have to act as representatives or delegates of the group for which they speak. This implies that grassroots planners must be ideologically committed to the transformative project of the group. They must see themselves as agents of collective struggle.

Advocacy planning is furthermore characterized by group processes that are difficult to manage, and the tendency to concentrate information, knowledge, decision-making in the small leadership elite is very common, especially as decision time is always pressing and usually in short supply, so that only the most committed are prepared to make the necessary time available. Thus, in any group process, there is an oligarchical tendency. Ideally, grassroots planners should ensure the effective participation of all members of the group during the entire process involving the four related phases of social planning, viz., vision, theory, strategy and action.

The meanings articulated by ideology do not remain constant but must continuously be tested in practice. Yet, the process of devising a democratically-conceived ideology, through a collective enterprise rather than through work of an individual or group, requires attitudinal skills like patience and empathy. Ideological statements must be persuasive not only to the membership of the mobilized group, but to other groups as well. They must at the same time be coherent, intellectually sophisticated, morally persuasive and simple in expression. Their function is to legitimate emancipatory practice in adversity, and to disarm and de-legitimize the opposition. Advocacy planners who become integrally a part of mobilized groups may have the necessary skills to put together statements and strategies that will serve these several purposes. Hence, grass-roots planners must never be far removed from the action itself.

Most importantly, the linkage of knowledge to action in social transformation must be accomplished through neighbourhood participants themselves. Thus, the question arises: does community participation, as practiced since the birth of democracy in 1994, adhere to the conceptual principles informing advocacy planning? This is the central question that will be considered in this paper.

Community participation, that is, the direct involvement/ engagement of ordinary people in the affairs of planning, governance and overall development programmes at local or grass-roots level, has become an integral part of democratic practice in recent years. In the case of post-apartheid South Africa, community participation has literally become synonymous with legitimate governance. In this regard, for example, the Municipal Structures Act, Chapter 4, states that "[t]he participation of citizens in the structures will ... revolutionize the way that local governance happens at the metropolitan level. Individual Municipalities will be empowered to decide what is best for their situation, with the guidance of national legislation that permits a variety of forms of local participation" (RSA, 1998). In practice, this means:

- People should have a say in decisions about actions which affect their lives.

- Public participation includes the promise that the public's contribution will influence the decision.
- The public participation process communicates the interests and meets the process needs of all participants.
- The public participation process seeks out and facilitates the involvement of those potentially affected.
- The public participation process involves participants in defining how they participate.
- The public participation process communicates to participants how their input was, or was not, utilized.
- The public participation process provides participants with the information they need to participate in a meaningful way.

Despite the preceding legal provisions, it would seem that most community participation exercises in post-apartheid South Africa are largely spectator politics, where ordinary people have mostly become endorsees of pre-designed planning programmes, often the objects of administrative manipulation and a miracle of reconciliation in the international arena of consensus politics whilst state functionaries of both the pre- and post-apartheid eras ensconce themselves as bureaucratic experts summoned to "ensure a better life for all".

Informed discussions and rational debates on the merits and demerits of specific planning programmes are literally non-existent, even though 'community participation' features as a key component of planning programmes at local level. In short, it would seem that the bureaucratic elites of officials and councilors are determined to impose their own truncated version and understanding of 'community participation' on particular communities. This highly atrophied form of 'participation' seems to be working precisely because in the South African version of democracy, the party is everything and the constituency is nothing (except every four years when it is required to vote for a specific party). Even so, such a limited form of democracy gives rise to an administered society, not a democratic society, as the consent for governance is not earned through rigorous policy debates of the merits and demerits of specific social programmes, but political acquiescence is manufactured through the skilful manipulation by a host of think tanks, self-styled experts, opinion polls and media pundits. Indeed, often community participation is managed by a host of consulting agencies on behalf of pre-designed, party-directed planning programmes and is quite clearly not fostered to empower local communities. Hence, the largely nebulous forms of community participation in one of the largest municipalities in South Africa, the City of Cape Town. This paper reviews community participation in Cape Town with the view to advance specific strategies to effect more meaningful forms of engagement, dialogue and empowerment at grass-roots level.

Community Participation as Advocacy Planning

The history of the struggle against apartheid in Cape Town indicates that community participation depends to a great extent on the nature of organization and mobilization at grass-roots level as well as the programmatic purpose of such participation (Williams, 1989). Defined in such terms, community participation is quite clearly not an unproblematic engagement of contestatory power relations. On the contrary, community participation is often driven by specific socio-economic goals that seek to ensure a 'better life for all', especially for those who have been historically marginalized during the successive colonial-cum-apartheid regimes in South Africa. Indeed, South Africa, especially as a post-apartheid constitutional state, has adopted a policy nomenclature that is replete with notions of public participation, grass-roots driven development and participatory governance (cf e.g., RSA, 1993; 1995, 1996, a,b,c; 1997, 1981 b; 1999, 2000). Even so, extant literature suggests that the very notion of participation assumes a wide range of discourses, meanings and applications within and across different contexts. More importantly perhaps, it would seem that participatory modes of governance and decision-making are profoundly influenced, if not shaped, by the contradictions, tensions, conflicts and struggles straddling not merely the political relations of power but also the economic and ideological apparatus at local level.

Local government in South Africa had until the early 1990s no constitutional safeguard, as it was perceived as a structural extension of the state and a function of provincial government. In terms of community participation, South African history reflects very little opportunity for community participation. The fact that most of the population had no political rights until 1994 demonstrates the total absence of participation of any sort. Instead, the method of government was highly centralized, deeply authoritarian and secretive, which ensured that fundamental public services were not accessible to black people (Williams, 2000).

Indeed, in the wake of the abolition of Apartheid in 1990, local government assumed an important role vis-à-vis institutional transformation. Hence public policies were formulated to create 'people centred development', predicated, amongst others, on democratic practices such as equity, transparency, accountability and respect for the rights of citizens, especially ordinary people: the poor, homeless and destitute (ANC, 1994; RSA, 1995: 1, 1999, 2000).

With a view to ensure bottom-up, people-centred, integrated development planning at grass-roots level, the South African Constitution, in sub-section 152e) states that "[t]he objective of local government is to encourage the involvement of communities and community organizations in the matters of local government" (RSA, 1996a). Whilst, as a broad theoretical statement of intent, this constitutional provision for community participation in the affairs of local government, appears to be quite a radical posture insofar it ensconces of the right of citizens to contribute towards the form, substance and overall dimensions of their respective communities, in practice, however, this constitutional right encounters profound structural limitations in the midst of bureaucratic institutions where uneven relations of power militate severely against such a constitutionally-driven community participatory model of development planning at grass-roots level.

Extant literature suggests community-oriented development plans presuppose the existence of community forums and related contractual relations through which communities can express their specific concerns and priorities to a particular local authority. This also means that communities are sufficiently conscious of their rights and obligations as citizens at grass-roots level vis-à-vis a specific municipality, i.e., effective municipal governance at local level is often the outcome of the quality of deliberative skills and civic commitment in local communities, ensuring that tensions and contradictions in development plans are resolved through the rigorous interaction between municipal councilors, officials and community organizations as borne out by the ensuing literature review. Indeed, current research in the province of Kwazulu-Natal indicates, Tables 2–5, that both citizens and councillors agree that citizen participation is useful, if not necessary instrument, to ensure effective local governance and to improve the living conditions of ordinary people at grass-roots level.

Table 2

Respondents' Perception of the Effect of Citizens' Participation in Supporting the Role of Ward Committees

Perception on the effects of citizens' participation	*%age*
It will help in the work of ward committees	80
It will make no difference	15
It will duplicate the work of the ward committee	0
Not sure	5
Total	100

Source: Jayanathan Govender, January 2006.

Table 3

Respondents' Perception on Promoting Political Party Through Citizens' Participation

Perception on promoting political party through citizens' participation	*%age*
It will help in the work of my political party	60
It will make no difference	35
It will duplicate the work of the political party	0
Not sure	5
Total	100

Source: Jayanathan Govender, January 2006.

Table 4

Respondents' Perception on Ways of Empowering Civic and Ratepayers' Organizations in Participating in the Budget Planning Processes

Ways to empower civic and ratepayers' organizations to participate in budget in planning processes	*%age*
Their organization must train interested individuals themselves	0
The municipality must train interested individuals	5
Municipality in partnership with civic and ratepayers' organizations must train interested individuals	35
Another institution must be commissioned to train interested individuals	0
No response	60
Total	100

Source: Jayanathan Govender, January 2006.

Table 5
Distribution of Respondents Rating of Issues that would be Addressed by Citizens' Participation

Municipal services	*Very important*	*Somewhat important*	*Least important*
Rent	95%	5%	0%
Rates	100%	0%	0%
Water	100%	0%	0%
Electricity	100%	0%	0%
Roads and pavements	80%	15%	5%
Sewerage	75%	20%	5%
Refuse removal	75%	15%	10%
Cleaning and grass cutting	85%	10%	5%
Municipal newspapers	45%	45%	10%
Job creation	95%	5%	0%
Local economic development	95%	5%	0%
Poverty alleviation	95%	5%	0%
Safety and security	100%	0%	0%

Source: Jayanathan Govender, January 2006.

Most researchers agree that there are various factors that contribute towards meaningful community participation at grass-roots level vis-à-vis a particular local authority (Municipality), such as the existence of community fora to (re)present the concerns and interests of a specific community to a specific planning authority, reliable and reciprocal contractual relations between the voters and their elected representatives and the political will (commitment) from councilors and officials in a specific municipality to ensure effective, efficient and sustainable community participation in development planning programmes. Since ten years of democratic rule has just been celebrated in South Africa, the question arises, what is the status of these theoretical assumptions and experiential insights on community participation at local level in South Africa?

With a view to reflect on these theoretical perspectives, the ensuing section considers briefly some examples of community participation in one of the biggest municipalities in South Africa, the much-vaunted and self-avowed liberal City of Cape Town, 1994–2004.

Some Examples of Community Participation, 1994–2005

In the City of Cape Town, where the author worked from 1990 till 2004 as a Principal Urban and Regional Planner (Policy and Research), there were various attempts at encouraging community participation in the development programmes of local government, ranging from critiquing local area planning in 1989, the definition of a metropolitan spatial development framework in 1991 to the revision and elaboration of various drafts of service delivery programmes, eventually resulting in a number of integrated development plans for the City of Cape Town.

Williams (2003–1; 2004a; 2004b) examined Area Co-ordinating Teams (ACTS) as a mode of engagement by the City of Cape Town to 'foster' Community participation in development planning at grass-roots level in the historically neglected areas of Hanover Park. Heideveld, Manenberg, Langa and Guguletu. He used both open-ended interviews and structured questionnaires to ascertain the levels of understanding, co-operation and commitment to community participation in the design, implementation, monitoring and evaluation of integrated development planning projects and programmes in Metropolitan Cape Town.

Theoretically, any public policy which encourages transparency, constructively engages and involve citizens in the functions of a local government and which seeks to facilitate an ongoing dialogue between citizens and the elected representatives is good public policy. In this regard, area coordinating teams constitute good public policy—on paper. By creating institutional space and opportunities where individuals, community organizations, council administration and elected representatives can sit and discuss issues affecting their lives, whether it be improvement of infrastructure, housing, health, or any other services which are provided by the local government, should be encouraged and sustained. In practice, though, ACTs are a structural failure. Not only are the issues raised at the ACTs completely non-binding, as the council is not obliged to follow through on any issue raised through ACTs. Also, often individual officials and councilors who are supposed to be participating in ACTs are not obligated to attend the scheduled meetings. Thus, for ACTs to become effective instruments of fundamental social change, council must support ACTs, both by passing appropriate by-laws to institutionalize them officially and to draw up a code of conduct that compels officials and councilors to attend and take seriously scheduled meetings and related development planning initiatives. In their present format, therefore, it can be concluded that ACTs have been implemented mostly for their symbolic value rather than to empower communities and to transform the unequal relations of socio-economic power in the City of Cape Town.

This means that it is not so much the presence or absence of community organizations at grass-roots level that determines the nature and impact of community participation on local government development programmes, but, whether or not their ideas and proposals with regard to development strategies are taken seriously by a specific local authority and incorporated into their specific Integrated Development Plans (IDPs). For example, in the case of Cape Town, Mackay (2004)11 indicates that whilst community organizations, in the form of development forums, are well organized in the Khayelitsha Sub-Councils and in the Mitchell's Plain Sub-Council areas, this does not mean that their development proposals enjoy the necessary consideration by the Planning Department of Cape Town. Here, one can readily refer to the various clusters 01' meetings held in these areas for 2004–2005, to allow community representatives to influence the annual budgetary process by making specific recommendations on particular service delivery programmes to the planning authorities in the Municipality of Cape Town. Yet, institutionally, the City of Cape Town does not seem to have the necessary structural and logistical support base (in place) to collate, analyze and integrate the various proposals into their planning programmes as community participation is not driven or facilitated by the IDP Directorate but by the largely dysfunctional Transformation Directorate, the nebulous Social Development Directorate and the nominal Sub-Councils Directorate. Whilst the IDP Directorate, in terms of the Municipal Systems Act, Act No. 32 of 2000 is supposed to ensure effective community participation in the planning programme of a particular municipality, yet, in the case of Cape Town, for example, the specific directorate in question, does not seem to have either the logistic capacity nor the human resources to comply with this statutory requirement. Consequently, community participation in relation to the IDP is largely a ceremonial exercise and not a systematic engagement of communities that are structurally aligned to the Development and Service Delivery Programmes of the City of Cape Town. Equally important, in Cape Town, there are no real institutional structures to coordinate, evaluate and monitor community participation in the formulation, implementation and evaluation of the Integrated Development Planning.

Hence, the institutional conflicts that seem to exist in Cape Town in relation to community participation. In this regard, Mae Kay's research (2004: 60–108) is quite revealing: For example, whilst in Cape Town, the Transformation Office claims responsibility and accountability for community participation, yet it lacks the requisite facilitation or coordination infrastructure and skills to execute this statutory task. In fact, the two public participation practitioners are unskilled, lacking the required training and knowledge base in public and development management methodologies to function optimally. Hence, the obvious lack of communication and co-ordination of logistics during the IDP's participation sessions from 2001 till 2004.

Community participation processes, for example, were arranged at the Mayoral Office, yet not a single community organization or individual member of the community was actively involved in arranging meetings or making input as to how the IDP should be conducted. Also, not a single community organization or NGO participated in the assessment of the form of public participation, the community needs analysis or the way forward regarding budgetary alignments. Whilst popular participation was supposed to be the main planning approach, yet the City of Cape Town simply expected communities to support pre-designed IDP programmes without explaining to them the substantive processes informing such programmes. For example, right from the inception of the post-apartheid municipal government in Cape Town after December 2000, and especially during the Mayor's listening campaigns in historically neglected areas, councilors and officials failed to explain the current state of service delivery to communities or the purpose of the IDP; how the IDP would evolve, the benefits the IDP offered for communities and the consequences if they did not to participate in statutory planning process. Consequently, communities attend these supposedly participatory meetings (Mayor's Listening Campaigns) as ill-informed or non-informed spectators. Hence, there is a notable decrease in attendance by communities at the public participation meetings since 2001, perhaps because they do not trust the council. Such distrust could very well be related to the fact that, institutionally, the public participation process does not seem to receive the necessary co-operation from council officials. For example, in the case of the communities of Mitchell's plain and Kraaifontein serious questions were raised about the scrapping of rent arrears and problems pertaining to service payments, yet these questions were not answered by City of Cape Town Finance Department. Also, feedback is seldom, if at all given to communities after the workshops such as the Mayor's Listening Campaign of June 2003.

In Cape Town, in 2004, ten years since the birth of democracy in South Africa, communities still do not receive equal electricity services (Williams, 1998, 1999a). Largely black communities, residing in areas maintained by ESKOM, do not receive the minimum government contribution of 60 kW like those largely white communities who reside in municipal areas. Indeed, generally, services are still delivered on the same racial basis as they were delivered prior to the birth of the non-racial Uni-city in December 2000.

In fact, racial boundaries in service delivery still exist and attitudes of management have still not changed (Williams, 2000). For example, in Cape Town, the method of waste removal is disproportionate because solid waste, trashed in standard black bins on wheels, in white areas, is removed on a weekly basis while big dumping waste bins (a hygiene threat) in black areas such as Wallacedene and Scottsdene are only removed when the need arises—i.e., they are removed on an irregular basis. In plain language, this means that whites are still the privileged group in post-apartheid Cape Town. In view of this skewed form of service delivery, the Mayor's so-called Listening Campaign remains largely an expedient, public relations exercise, and cannot be considered as an appropriate conduit for effective community participation in the development and service delivery programmes of Cape Town.

Towards a Theoretical Framework to Understand Community Development Workers as Advocacy Planners

Ontologically and hermeneutically, policy initiation, design, implementation and monitoring vis-à-vis all attempts at structural change seem to occur through the racialized, gendered, ethnicized, class-based, relations of power (economically, ideologically, politically). Hence, it is the spatialization and the concomitant geographical embeddedness of such uneven power relations that characterizes the South African social formation at the beginning of the 21st century—a veritable challenge for community development workers as they seek to give material content to the basic rights of ordinary people in South Africa.

Preliminary research on CDWs suggests that they can keep the local state accountable by linking the temporal (history), spatial (geographical embeddeness of place) and constitutional features (idealized reality) of the South African context, Here, the work of

Herbert Marcuse (1964), *One-Dimensional Man (ODM),* provides a theoretical anchor as the South African democratic project also seems to be a quest for modernity as the telos and singular defining referent. Indeed, it would seem that in the case of the CDWs mandate, 'development' has come to be a totalizing, often unproblematic mantra, filtering/directing all official policies and planning frameworks. Accordingly, this research specifically seeks to detotalize this 'development' discourse by problematizing the deepening of democracy a la CDWs (in the Western Cape, South Africa). Worcester is chosen as it is a peri-urban area within a distinctly agriculture hinterland, approximately 90 km to the north east of Cape Town where historically disadvantaged communities are as yet, not able to access and satisfy their constitutionally guaranteed rights in relation to basic service delivery. Indeed, in the case of Worcester, CDWs appear to reflect Marcuse's triad of dialogical relations vis-à-vis the temporal, spatial and constitutional features of South Africa and quite clearly are not monolithic as their foundational mandates would seem to suggest.

On the contrary, CDWs seem to be conducting their dialogue on democratic practice along the three distinct lines of social change, viz.,

- Dominant neo-liberal (status quo mode);
- Residual revolutionary (liberation mode); and
- Pragmatic (mixed mode)

It is here hypothesized that CDWs choose any of the aforementioned ideological modes of dialogues in their contact with communities and that specific community issues trigger the conceptual/theoretical frame of specific dialogues.

Dialogues are important for the deepening of democracy as they:

- Allow assumptions to be brought out into the open and encourage participants to suspend judgement in order to foster understanding and break down obstacles;
- Seek to create equality among participants. Certain conditions can be created to even out the playing field for participants with various levels of information about the issue, experience in public forums, real or perceived positions of power or authority and help build trust and a climate of safety for deep dialogue; and
- Aim for a greater understanding of others' viewpoints through empathy. In dialogue, multiple perspectives are invited to the table and encouraged to be voiced. The import of dialogue thus suggests that deepening democracy depends to a great extent on

the ideological significance CDWs attach to their work in communities, through a range of coding, viz.,

— Open coding by generating distinct categories of meanings vis-à-vis development (cf e.g., Straus and Corbin, 1990: 116–120)
— Axial coding by invoking related categories of meanings to core concepts vis-à-vis development (Straus and Corbin, 1990: 74, 102); and
— Selective coding by integrating and refining specific categories of meaning vis-à-vis development (Straus and Corbin, 1990: 116–121; Glaser, 1998: 143).

These differential codings allow the researcher to establish whether or not CDWs:

- Note differences (in terms of the meaning and practice of 'democracy');
- Accommodate differences (in terms of the meaning and practice of democracy);
- Identify procedures, principles and discourses to resolve specific community issues; and
- Establish pathways to participatory democracy (e.g., through dialogues, debates, discussions, establishing platforms, promoting council elections, and so forth).

Theoretical Implications of Research

- Theoretical carnival of conceptual hybridity, centring voices of the 'Other', the marginalized, the excluded, the subaltern,
- Epistemologically: foregrounding subjugated knowledges, valorizing and validating orality, the traditional as change-inducing, transformative, empowering consciousness and intentionality/practices (Edmund Husserl), for example;
- umntu ngamuntu ngubantu: I am a person through my linkage to and in solidarity with my fellow human beings—divorced from this ensemble of social relations I have a very limited/slanted/distorted concept and understanding of self and potentiality as a human being;
- Batho pele principles: people first (into service delivery);
- Masakhane campaign: building each other (community welfare);
- Tirisano initiatives: working together (within and across sectors) Ontologically: deconstruct concepts of planning (e.g., validating notion of para-planning);

- Heuristically: interrogate validity of colonical-cum-apartheid planning ordinances: residual/bureaucratic practices in 'new South Africa';
- Hermeneutically: allow for open-ended, flexible interpretations of changing relations of power e.g., new elite as opposed to historical notion of 'people': no such monolithic references, rather configuration of power relations translating into different concepts/understanding/versions of citizenship/citizenry—differentiated experiences of service delivery in post-apartheid South Africa,
- Axiologically: determine shortcoming/weakness of current suite of service delivery programmes, e.g., RDP as opposed to GEAR
- Deontologically: establish spaces of hope that reinforce the tenets of democratic governance and experiential nature of citizenship at grass-roots level, i.e., the ought-to-be rights-based injunctions/imperatives of the post-apartheid constitution;
- Eschatologically: Accent the historically-notion, that driven perspective, that change is the only constant and that there is a dialectical nexus between the past, present and future. Hence, the future derives from within the cumulative contradictions, tensions, fissures, conflicts of the ensemble of social relations that connect temporal/spatial practices e.g.: Henri Lefbevre: production of space (perceived, conceived, lived space) Pierre Bourdieu: habitus; Ludwig Wittgenstein: game theory; Anthony Giddens: space/place distanciation—structuration theory; Louis Althusser: notion of interpellation; Michel Foucault: micro-politics; Edmund Husserl: concept of intentionality; Frederick Nietszche: will to power; David Harvey: theory of instantiation (of hope and possibility of change commensurate with the interests of the marginalized, the poor, the other) and Alain Badiou: transformative thought must be revolting, logical, universal and risky; Discourse is shaped by particular context; context shapes discourse; Context, text and sub-text of planning and citizenship rights: profoundly influenced by configuration of power relations; Towards theoretical hybridity? Pluralization of the other, difference, naturalizing poverty? Homelessness? Squalor? Yet, the goal of CDWs is affirmation of context as locus of life-enhancing change/possibilities.

Based on the experience of community participation in Cape Town, it is clear that often the non-existence of community organizations undermines community participation.

It is, therefore, necessary that communities organize themselves into civic bodies that can represent their interests at local government level. More importantly, perhaps, in historically marginalized sections of society, communities should revisit their richly-textured experiences of organization and mobilization against the apartheid state, and adapt such strategic forms of engagement and dialogue to empower citizens at grass-roots level. In short, the birth of democratic South Africa does not mean the realization of a more equitable socio-economic dispensation. This specifically means communities should not cease to organize, on the contrary, they should refocus their organizational and mobilization energies and goals to ensure socio-economic development programmes commensurate with their enshrined constitutional rights, such as the right to life and overall human dignity (Williams, 1999b; 2000a,b,c). Local government planning programmes can only contribute towards these citizen rights if communities are aware of their rights and specifically their right to participate in local government planning programmes.

Hence, in this regard, it would perhaps be useful to review and adapt those models of mobilization that communities used to plunge the Apartheid State into systemic crisis and resulted in birth of a democratic South Africa on 27 April 2004 (Williams, 1989). These community forms of struggle include issue-based protests and mass demonstrations against poor services. It is only when communities realize that, unless they are informed citizens claiming their constitutional rights through effective community participation in local planning programmes, only then they can ensure a more equitable socio-economic dispensation in historically marginalized sections of the post-apartheid society (Williams, 2003, 2004a, b.). Relying on the good intentions of the bureaucratic elite of local government, as borne out by their highly questionable record since 1994, quite obviously does not take them to the promised land of 'a better life for all'. This, however, does not mean that the bureaucratic elite of councilors and planning officials have no role to play. On the contrary, they can make a very important contribution to effective community participation by, amongst other practical steps, acquiring the requisite skills and knowledge of public participation, civil society, local government; promoting education and literacy skills in historically neglected communities; and understanding community views on participation.

Specific Recommendations

Attitudes of municipal officials and councilors influence both the form and dimensions of participation, hence, the following specific and general recommendations to foster meaningful dialogue, engagement and empowerment at grass-roots level:

- Recognize that community participation is not a neutral endeavour;
- Encourage voluntary participation;
- Ensure that the public's contribution will influence planning decisions;
- Ensure equal opportunities for participation;
- Seek out and facilitate the involvement of those potentially affected;
- Communicate to participants how their input affected the decision;
- Provide participants with the information they need to participate in a meaningful way;
- General concerns that need to be borne in mind during planning programmes are the following interrelated elements, viz.,

  intervention: who makes the decision(s) with regard to specific issues e.g., legislative, civil society—mandatory or voluntary;

  initiation of specific steps to change existing situation on the ground e.g., in terms of Reconstruction and Development Programme (RDP): origin and development of policies.

  identification e.g., who identifies specific policy issues: delineation of factors impacting on particular service delivery;

  orientation: e.g., whose voices are heard, what are the overriding perspectives, ideals, frame of reference, intended beneficiaries?; and

  authentication: e.g., are their instances of co-determination of service-related issues, i.e., partnerships?

References

African National Congress (ANC), (1994). *The Reconstruction and Development Programme,* Johannesburg: Umanyano Publishers.

Cape Town City Council, (1989–1990). *Annual Report of the City Planner: Review of Local Area Planning,* Cape Town, Planning Department.

Cape Town City Council, (1 June 1993). *A Vision for the Future of Metropolitan Cape Town: A City of Opportunity, Equity and Sustainability,* Cape Town, Planning Department.

City of Cape Town, (1 April 2002). *Summary Report on Public Hearings of the IDP,* Cape Town.

———, (9 May 2002). *IDP Portfolio Committee Report, Report on Public Hearings,* Cape Town.

———, (14 May 2002). *Report on Public Hearings on IDP and Budget 2002,* Cape Town.

———, (May 2002). *Draft IDP Document 2002–2003,* City of Cape Town.

———, (May 2003). *IDP Review 2003–2004,* Cape Town.

———, (2003). *Mid-term Report: June 2003-December 2003*, Cape Town.

———, (July 2003). *Annual Budget 2003–2004,* Cape Town.

———, (August 2003). *Strategic Information on Census 2001, Directorate Strategic Services,* Cape Town.

———, (2004). *Refinement of Revised IDP/Budget 2004–2005 Timelines,* Cape Town.

———, (June 2004). *Integrated Development Framework 2004–2007,* Cape Town.

Friedmann, John, (1992). *Empowerment: The Politics of Alternative Development,* London, Blackwell.

Govender, Jayanathan, (2006). *Citizen Participation in the Budget Process in Local Government: A Case Study of the Thikwini Municipality in the Province of Kwazulu-Natal, South Africa,* Unpublished Masters of Public Administration Thesis, School of Government, University of the Western Cape.

Mac Kay, Johny, (2004). *Public Participation in the Integrated Development Planning Process of the City of Cape Town,* Unpublished mini-thesis submitted in partial fulfilment of the requirements for the degree of *Magister Administrations* in the School of Government, University of the Western Cape.

Republic of South Africa, (1993). *Local Government Transitional Act,* No. 209 of 1993, Pretoria, Government Printers.

———, (1995). *Remaking the Urban Sector. The Government of National Unity's Strategy for South Africa's Cities, Towns and Neighbourhoods,* Pretoria, Government Printers.

———, (1996a). *Constitution of the Republic of South Africa,* Act 108 of 1996, Pretoria, Government Printers.

———, (1996b). *Local Government Transitional Act: Second Amendment Act,* No. 12 of 1996, Pretoria, Government Printers.

———, (1996c). "Batho Pete", *White Paper on Transforming Public Service and Administration,* Pretoria, Government Printers, http://www.gov.za/structure/local-gov.htm 4/2–2001, 12:00.

———, (1997). *Urban Development Framework,* Department of Housing, Pretoria, Government Printers.

———, (1998a). *White Paper on Local Government,* Pretoria, Government Printers.

———, (1998b). *Local Government, Municipal Demarcation Act,* Act No. 27 of 1998, Pretoria, Government Printers.

———, (1998c). *Municipal Structures Act 117,* Pretoria, Government Publishers.

———, (1999). *Green Paper on Development and Planning, Government Notice,* No. 626, Pretoria, Government Printers.

———, (2000). *Local Government Municipal Systems Act,* No. 32 of 2000, Pretoria, Government Printers.

Williams, John J., (1989). *Urban Social Movements in Metropolitan Cape Town, South Africa,* Unpublished Ph.D. thesis, University of Illinois at Urbana-Champaign.

———, (1998). "Institutional Racism: The Case of Cape Town City Council", *South African Labour Bulletin,* April 1998, 22(2), pp. 68–69.

———, (1999a). World Bank Scenarios: Why They Should be Rejected?, *South African Labour Bulletin,* 23(1), pp. 60–64.

———, (1999b). *Planning the Multi-cultural City in Post-Apartheid South Africa: An Appraisal of 'Overcoming the Group Areas Act: Social Movements in Westville', South Africa,* by Keyan Tomaseli, Occasional Paper No. 3, published by the Centre for Cultural and Media Studies, University of Natal, Durban. Also: www.und.ac.za/und/ccms.

———, (2000a). "South Africa: Urban Transformation", *Cities,* 17(3), pp. 167–183.

———, (2000b). "Transformation: Challenges for South Africa (Book Review Essay: MOKOKO: The Makgoba Affair: A Reflection on Transformation", by Prof M.W. Makgoba, Vivlia Publishers, Johannesburg), Critical Arts, Ethnicity and Identity, 14(1), pp. 73–95, 2000.

———, (2000c). "Truth and Reconciliation—Beyond the TRC", *Ecquid Novi: Journal for Journalism in Southern Africa,* 21(2), pp. 207–219,

———, (2001b). Human Rights and Citizenship in Post-Apartheid South Africa, Critical Arts, 15 (1 and 2), pp. 24–49.

———, (2003). "Community Participation: Constructing the Post-Apartheid City—Case Study of the Areas Co-ordinating Teams, Cape Town, South Africa", *Citizenship, Participation and Accountability Series, 3* (research commissioned by the University of Sussex UK, in partnership with the School of Government, University of the Western Cape), Bellville, South Africa, Centre for Southern African Studies, School of Government, University of the Western Cape.

———, (2004a). Citizenship, Community Participation and Social Change: The Case of Cape Town South Africa, *Institute of Development Studies (IDS), Bulletin,* 35(2).

———, (2004b). "Cape Town's Area Coordinating Committees-bottom up Participatory Planning at Work", *Society and Economy, ID21.*

10 Women's Participation in Local Government

The Bangladesh Experience

Pranab Kumar Pandey

Women are an inseparable part of the development process of any country. Nearly half of the total population of Bangladesh is comprised of women. With the advancement of the time, the contribution of women to family, society and nation has been recognized and is immensely increasing all over the world. The fact has now been realized with predominant importance that without ensuring women development, the national development cannot be achieved.[1] This paper is an attempt to explore the extent of women empowerment in politics and their participation in development at the local governance, particularly in Union Parishad, in Bangladesh.[2]

Concept of Participation

The study of participation has gained paramount importance in recent times. Virtually, all major states and non-governmental nation-building initiatives in the Third World have people's participation as a priority objective. However, despite the ceaseless experimentation with participation and the ushering of voluminous literature, it nevertheless remains to be one of the most controversial areas of study in development management.[3]

There are divergent opinions as to what participation means? Mumtaz Soysal defines participation as all forms of action by which citizens 'take part' in the operation of administration. The 'taking part' refers to any level from macro to micro region or it may be of any type, e.g., advisory in nature or in participation, in decision-making or in implementation etc. People can participate through public or private bodies or other organizations.[4]

In the context of developing countries, people's participation is a crucial variable for plan formulation and implementation at the local level where vast majority of people live. This is more required for attaining growth with justice. It is also through participation that people begin to learn responsibility or mechanism of holding those accountable who are entrusted with the task of development or who carry the brunt of development activities.[5]

Local Government in Bangladesh

In any democratic polity, local government is given legal recognition either by an Act of Parliament or by incorporation of relevant provisions in the Constitution.[6] The Constitution of Bangladesh 1972 clearly spells out the legal basis and responsibilities of local government. Article 59 of the Constitution states that "local government in every administrative unit of the Republic shall be entrusted to bodies composed of persons elected in accordance with law."[7] Similarly, Article 60 states that for the purpose of giving full effect to the provision of Article 59, parliament shall, by law, confer powers on the local government bodies referred to in that Article including power to prepare their budgets and to maintain funds.

The institution of local government in Bangladesh has a long history. Its origin can be traced back to the demand for self-government in British India. Initially, local government was developed by British to maintain law and order in rural areas with the help of local elite backed by local police.[8] The local elites were to be nominated in the local government institutions from amongst those who were trusted by the colonial authority. The British rulers institutionalized this system to perpetuate their political, economic and administrative ends and domination as well as colonial extortion.[9] In 1870, they introduced 'Choukidary Panchayat' as the local government institution. Afterwards, this system was changed and renamed in different regimes from British government to present Bangladesh as three-tier Union Committee (1885), two-tier Union Board (1919), four-tier Union Council (1959) and Union Parishad (1973).[10] After 1973, the Union Parishad is acting as the lowest unit of local government in Bangladesh.

There are two distinct patterns of local government institutions now prevailing in Bangladesh: one for rural areas and another for urban areas. The local government in rural areas represents a hierarchical system comprising three tiers, viz., Union Parishad, Upzila Parishad and Zila Parishad, while the urban local government consists of Pourashavas and Municipal Corporation.[11]

Women's Participation in Local Government in Bangladesh

Government Initiatives

During the British period, local government remained almost an exclusive domain of men. Not of speak of contesting elections, women were not even allowed to cast vote in the elections to rural local bodies until 1956 when for the first time election was held based on universal adult franchise. The Act passed in 1923 gave women for the first time the right to vote in Calcutta municipal election.[12]

In Bangladesh, women never thought to become participants in the local government institutions. In order to secure a minimum representation of women in local-level government bodies, in 1976, the government promulgated the Local Government Ordinance. In this ordinance, the structure of local government underwent changes and the provision was made to select two women members in the Union Council.[13] For the first time women were considered to be included in the local government. With the passage of time, every government tried to incorporate more women in local government bodies. In 1983, the changes were brought in the structure of Union Parishad promulgating the Local Government (Union Parishad) Ordinance. The earlier system (1973) remained unchanged: one chairperson and nine members were to be elected directly, including three female members, one each from ward, has been added in the new ordinance.[14] In 1993, Local Government (Union Parishad) Amendment Act was passed in the parliament to secure the minimum representation of women in local government. According to this Act, a provision was made that each Union Parishad would be divided into nine wards. Moreover, three seats were reserved for women; accordingly, they were by elected chairperson and members of the Union Parishad.[15]

The Local Government (Union Parishad) Second Amendment Act, 1997 is a milestone in the history of women's empowerment in Bangladesh. In this Act, a provision was made for three reserved seats for women in each Union Parishad. In addition, they would be elected by direct election based on universal adult franchise. This was a major initiative by the government for ensuring women's participation in local government.[16]

The Real World Scenario

Despite legal provisions the participation of women in local government remained minimal. The number of women on elective positions of chairperson and members in the Union Parishad was absolutely low. In the Union Parishad election of 1973, only one woman was elected as chairperson out of 4,350 Union Parishads. Likewise, in the election of 1977, only four women were elected as chairperson whereas in the election of 1984, this number was only six.[16] In the election of 1988, 18,566 candidates contested for the chairpersonship of 4,401 Union Parishads. There were only 79 women contestants constituting only 0.4 per cent, and among them, only one woman was elected as chairperson.[17] Again, in 1992, available data indicate that for the position of chairpersons of 4,450 Union Parishads, women constituted only 0.6 per cent of the contesting candidates, i.e., 115 out of a total of 17,444. Among them, 24 women were elected as chairperson. For position of members, the figures for the respective elections in 1988 and 1992 were 863 out of 1,14,699 (constituting 0.7%) and 1,135 out of 1,69,643 (comprising again same 0.7%) contestants.[18]

With a view to pave the way for greater participation and political empowerment of women, the previous government of Bangladesh has managed to pass the Local Government (Union Parishad) Second Amendment Bill, 1997, introducing provision for direct election to reserve seats for women in the Union Parishad. In the election of 1997, 102 women fought directly for the post of

Table 1

Women as the Elected Chairpersons of Union Parishad

Year of Election	*Number of Union Parishads*	*Women Candidates*	*Elected Women Chairpersons*
1973	4352	—	1
1977	4352	—	4
1984	400	—	4+2=6
1988	4401	79	1
1992–93	4450	115	13+11=24
1997	—	—	20+3=23

Source: Sultana, Abeda, "The Role of Training in the Empowerment of Women in Union Parishad: An Analysis", *Lok Prasashan Samoyke,* No. 17, December 2000, p. 15.

chairperson of them 20 were elected. In general seats for members 456 women also contested, of them 110 were elected. Moreover, 44,134 women contested for reserved seats, of them 592 were elected unopposed and some 13,437 women were elected for reserved seats. Later, three women were also elected as chairperson.[19] The Table 1 shows the scenario of women participation in local government until 1997.

From the table, it is apparently clear that women's participation is increasing, but nothing very encouraging is still visible. Problem lies in every sphere of society. Women are neglected everywhere.

Obstacles

The task of integrating and involving women in local government activities was often an arduous and lengthy process. This was due to certain prevailing notions regarding women's status and also role in the family and the society. Most of the problems faced by the women in Bangladesh in their endeavour to come out of the houses and participate in the development activities were embedded in social and institutional structure of the country. Many of the problems were imposed by the society and were based on wrong interpretation of religion and women's role model in the family and the society.[20] We may identify the following problems relating to women's participation in the local government in Bangladesh:

(i) *Dependency on men:* Due to their non-wage economic activities, majority of the women are economically dependent on men. From childhood to older ages, women depend on men in various ways in Bangladesh. As they are dependent on their male counterparts, it becomes difficult for them to come out of home and involve themselves in local government activities.

(ii) *Ownership of land:* The lands owned by the households are mostly owned by men and women are deprived of this right. Land provides social status and political power as well as economic security. Women's landlessness reduced women's power in the household, even for wealthy women.

(iii) *Cultural apathy: The* culture of Bangladesh also affects women adversely. There is a myth that "a women's paradise is at the feet of her husband". Many women believe it and bear any violence hoping to attain her paradise.[21] Therefore, they do not show any interest to make them involved in any outside activities rather keep them busy in search of their paradise at the feet of their husbands.

(iv) *Purdha:* Purdha[22] prevents women to participate in social, economic and political activities to empower themselves. Men want to keep women always in purdha, so that they will lose their power.[23]

(v) *Educational backwardness:* Education is perhaps the single strongest factor influencing women's control of their own future. To make women knowledgeable, skilled and self-confident for their full participation in the ongoing development process of the country the most important means is education.[24] It creates awareness among the women. However, it is unfortunate to state that most of our women are illiterate. They are not informed about their right. That is why, they do not show interest in participating in local government activities.

(vi) *Weakness of democratic political institutions: The* weakness of democratic political institution is aggravated by the absence of a vigorous civil society. Besides, the laws regarding women's empowerment are not properly made. In the Local Government (Union Parishad) Second Amendment Act, 1997, there is hardly any clause where the powers of the women members are clearly spelt out. This type of mistake is needed to be overridden.

With a view to overcome the problems following suggestions may be taken into consideration:

(1) Governments that do not consider women's empowerment a priority will more likely channel their budget to defence and trade promotion. Yet, without adequate budget for implementation, the government-initiated policy measures to empower women will only be rhetoric. Political will must translate both policies and resources if they are to be effective at all. At the same time, government policies must address the need to give women access to career patterns to develop and strengthen their capacity as political leaders, develop media relations, and generate their own resources.[25]

(2) Educational opportunities such as formal education and training should be granted to women, as they are important preconditions for individual professional advancement in politics and for gender-balanced political representation.

(3) Priority must be given to monitoring the status, conditions and rights of women. There must be a sustained campaign for women's mobilization, regular reporting of monitoring, public information and advocacy in this realm.

(4) Social awareness should be built. Traditionally assigned gender roles limit women's choices of education and careers. Thus, initiative must also come from the women themselves to constantly challenge the patriarchal structures and beliefs and the ideological framework that perpetuates women's view of their seemingly natural subordinate position.

Conclusion

Women members of the local government are yet to draw serious attention from the researchers. It has already been stated that only a few number hold elective offices in local bodies. But it is only since 1997 that women have been able to associate themselves with local government in fairly large number. Very little is known about the impact of their presence upon the local bodies and upon the women community at large.[26] They should be studied along with the male members because their attitude and cooperation will largely determine the performance of women members. It is obvious that sometimes they may not get the required support and cooperation from the elected chairperson and members.

The 21st century is ushering in an era of new hopes and aspirations for womenfolk, as the women of Bangladesh can now look forward with pride and hope for having some outstanding and significant occasions that have taken place in the last two decades for their all-round development. It is true that the battle for women's active participation in the local government has just started. Though women representatives strive for political participation, they will have to go a long way. Variables like participation and family patronage have positive correlation with the process of women participation. Further, illiteracy and poverty will not prevent the women representatives from grasping the new opportunities offered to them through Local Government (Union Parishad) Second Amendment Act, 1997 and this will create a strong political ground for women in Bangladesh.

Notes

1. Muzibur Rahman Howlader, "Women in Bangladesh Civil Service and Their Participation in Decision-Making: An Analysis on a Historical and Comparative Perspective", *Journal of Administration and Diplomacy*, Vol. 3, January-December, 1995, p. 165.
2. Union Parishad is the lowest tier of existing local government structure.

3. Niaz Ahmed Khan, "Towards an Understanding of Participation: The Conceptual Labyrinth Revisited", *Administrative Change,* Vol. XX, No. 1–2, July 1992-June, 1993, p. 106.
4. R.K. Sapru, *Development Administration,* Deep and Deep Publications, New Delhi, 1986, p. 345
5. Ibid.
6. Mohammad Mohabbat Khan, "Urban Local Governance in Bangladesh: An Overview", *Journal of Administration and Diplomacy,* Vol. 4, No. 1, January-June, 1996, p. 1.
8. Md. Almas Ali, "Women's Participation in Local Government", *The Daily Star,* November, 27, 2001.
9. Ibid.
10. Shafi Ahmed et al., "One Decade of Bangladesh Under Women Leadership", *Alochoma Magazine,* October 2001, p. 3, (www.magazine.alochona.org.).
11. Bilquis Ara Alain, "Women's Participation in Local Government in Bangladesh", *The Journal of Local Government,* National Institute of Local Government, Dhaka, Bangladesh, Vol. 13, No. 2, July-December, 1984, p. 48.
12. Ibid., p. 47.
13. Shafi Ahmed et al., op. cit., p. 3.
14. Ibid.
15. Ibid.
16. Abeda Sultana, "The Role of Training in the Empowerment of Women in Union Parishad: An Analysis", *Lok Proshashon Samoyke,* No. 17, December, 2000, p. 14.
17. Shafi Ahmed et al., op. cit.
18. Ibid.
19. Md. Sadequl Islam, "Political Empowerment of Women in Bangladesh in World Perspective: An Analysis", *Rajshahi University Studies,* Part-C, Vol. 8, 2000, pp. 112–13.
20. S.M. Nurul Alain, NGOs Under Attack: A Study of Socio-Cultural and Political Dynamics of NGO Operations in Bangladesh, Department of Anthropology, Jahangir Nagar University, December, 1994, p. 62 (first draft).
21. Arun Kumar Goswami, "Empowerment of Women in Bangladesh", *Empowerment* (A Journal of Women for Women), Vol. 5, 1998, p. 59.
22. It is a sort of veil used by the Muslim women in Bangladesh for physical exclusion from the males.
23. Goswami, op. cit.
24. Ibid.
25. Sheila Espine Villaluz (ed.), "Women Around the World, Fact Sheet", *A Quarterly Fact Sheet of the Center for Legislative Development,* June, 2000, Vol. 1, No. 4, p. 5.
26. Bilquis Ara Alain, op. cit., p. 51.

Section II

Panchayati Raj: Structure, Process, Impact

11 Trends in the Debate on Panchayati Raj

Mats Kihlberg

Main Lines of the Debate

To understand the Indian debate on Panchayati Raj (PR) during the 1960s and 1970s, a brief historical survey is necessary. The important point to start from is the discussion in the Constituent Assembly, which completed the draft of the Constitution of India in 1949. The discussions centred around the meaning of the democracy. It was intended to create that in free India there is a clear dividing line between two points of view. On one side, there is the western and liberal view, which marked the constitution and, on other, that inspired by Gandhi with its traditional and rural basis.

Gandhi and his supporters believed that Indian democracy should be built up organically from below by means of self-governing villages where the power should be gathered as far as possible. This pronounced, almost anarchistic, decentralization was combined with a strong mistrust of urbanization, industrialization and political parties. Decisions would be arrived at by consensus in the small village communities where the people lived in an organic dependence of each other. The values of rural life were to be maintained in a unique Indian form of democracy.

In 1948, this ideology had quite a few followers among the politicians present in the constitutive body. The constitution was often criticized because it had not been drawn up in the spirit which Gandhi had given to national independence. What was missed above all was Panchayati Raj (PR), the local self-government of the villages. Not a word was said about this in the proposed constitution.

The man mainly responsible for the text of the constitution, B.R. Ambedkar, met this criticism with a sharp reply: "I hold that these village republics have been the ruination of India. I am therefore surprised that those who condemn provincialism and communalism should come forward as champions of the village. What is the village but a sink of localism, a den of ignorance, narrow mindedness and communalism? I am glad that the draft constitution has discarded the village and adopted the individual as its unit".[1]

Among the political leaders of the fight for freedom there was obviously a strong desire to give local self-government a central place in the constitution.

But when this was brought out in the debate it was too late to redraft the constitution. The only result was that article 40 was added to the constitution: "The State shall take steps to organize village panchayats and endow them with such powers and authority as may be necessary to enable them to function as units of self-government". The complete responsibility was placed on the states and during the 1950s these showed little interest in relinquishing any power or authority to the bodies elected by the people at lower levels. But, the ideology from Gandhi lived on and found new expressions when the PR programme started. At the beginning of the sixties, the All India Panchayat Parishad was formed under the leadership of J.P. Narayan. This was an organization, which assembled various interests in order to support and develop PR. Annual conferences were arranged where current problems were discussed and a kind of panchayat-ideology was formed.

Perhaps, the most important meeting took place in Udaipur in 1964 and resulted in the report, *Fundamental Problems of Panchayati Raj*. The meeting was arranged in cooperation with the Ministry for Community Development and among those taking part were key people in the administration both from Delhi and the states. Under the leadership of Narayan, it here became possible to reach agreement that PRIs should not be regarded as organs for the national agencies, but as 'units of self-government' at the respective levels. In the Indian Constitution, the powers and functions of the PR institutions should be regulated in the same way as is done in regard to the states. That is to say the federal system should be increased by a further level, that of local self-government, and this level should in fact be the primary one for the whole system. It would take time to develop PR to full self-governing units but this should now be stated as an aim in the constitution.

In his essay, "Swaraj for the People", Narayan argues for a 'participating democracy' which would give a deeper significance to Panchayati Raj. In order that PR shall become the basis of a 'participating democracy' various kinds of reforms are required. Most important are the following:

— Comprehensive education of the people
— Political parties should keep away from PR as they have a destructive effect on the local community. However, the parties can contribute to the general education of the people if this is carried out in an 'unbiased' manner.
— Gram Sabhas should form the foundations of local self-government and the village committees should be the executive organs for these general meetings where direct democracy functions most effectively.

In addition, a reform of the community's economic structure is also required, decentralization of small-scale, industry, handicrafts and rural development. Collective ownership of the land in every village is advocated which should be carried out by means of peaceful methods in accordance with Gramdan ideology. Only through land reform can true democracy be realized.

It is remarkable how Narayan, as most of those in the Sarvodaya movement, regards PR not as a part of the existing system of society but as the basis of a completely different society. They have a model of development which radically differs from the western 'modernization'.

The second historical point of departure for Panchayati Raj is India's *Community Development* (CD) Programme, the enormous programme started at the beginning of the 50s in order to develop the villages with self-help methods.

1. The villages were to be made largely independent of state support and people would be encouraged to take part in development work with mainly local resources.
2. All groups in the village should cooperate in this development work which should be to the advantage of everyone.

Towards the end of the fifties, the CD programme faced a crisis. A growing opinion considered that CD had failed in its main object to get the people to take part in the development work. There was criticism that CD had grown an enormous bureaucratic superstructure, that the work was carried on in traditional hierarchic forms and that the enthusiasm present at the beginning had disappeared. Criticism was also made against the unfair social effects of CD in the villages. The time was ripe for a re-examination and an investigation committee was appointed.

The report produced under the chairmanship of Balwant Rai Mehta, presented in 1957, was of historic importance for the development of Indian society.[2] Mehta's conclusions were briefly that CD had failed because the programme lacked a political and democratic foundation in the villages. People were not interested because they had no real influence, could not take part in decisions on development activities within the village or the region. By creating democratic bodies for local self-government both CD and rural development in its wider meaning would obtain new strength and stability. Thus, the emphasis of the Mehta report lies on development and mostly on CD.

This also became the official line which largely set its mark on the shaping of PR, public propaganda and the laws of the states. But although the development aim dominated there was at the same time the aim to extend and deepen Indian democracy. PR was to be a programme for 'democratic decentralization'. In some cases, as for example for Nehru, this could be considered as almost a purpose in itself apart from the idea of development. In general, it was assumed that the two purposes would support each other. However, between these two purposes there was an inner tension to be noticed later.

The proposals made in the report were discussed and approved by the Planning Commission and the National Development Council in 1958. The comments of the Planning Commission are of interest as they show a third approach to the question of PR. Contrary to Mehta report, it was considered that the district should be made the most important level in PR with special resources for planning. The district which had always been the most important administrative unit should steer and control the lower levels. But Mehta had chosen the block level as it was there that a more active participation of the people could be obtained. Mehta did not see PR as an administrative and planning organ, but for many administrators and planners it was natural to regard it in this way. Here we have the 'bureaucratic' point of view, there has even been talk of 'instrumentalists' as apart from 'decentralists'. The former saw PR as a state organization for various purposes at the local level, but with no, or very limited, independence; the latter proceeded from CD ideas and emphasized local self-government.[3]

Against the historic background it appears natural to consider the following three lines of thought:

1. The Sarvodaya movement and its views on PR as mainly developed by J.P. Narayan.
2. The CD movement and the officials' attitude when PR was started and built up.
3. Bureaucracy and the instrumental approach.

The above can be regarded as an initial rather rough analysis and division of opinion. Within these different lines of thought there are of course different groupings and nuances.

Support is given to this classification by analyses carried out by Indian investigators and other experts. Some of these will be discussed here as the terminology and interpretations vary a great deal.

Of interest is an important 1964 seminar report from the All India Panchayat Parishad, *Fundamental Problems of Panchayati Raj*. In the introduction to the report the, general secretary Patel gave a synopsis of four different opinions about PR. Two of these are the equivalents of 'Sarvodaya' and 'Bureaucracy' (or instrumentalism) listed above. The remaining two are the equivalent of what is called above the 'official' attitude. Patel differentiates here between those who consider PR as "only a means to achieve the end of community development" and those who see PR as "an extension of democracy up to the village". The idea of CD is presented in government reports and official speeches by members of the government while the democratic aim is emphasized by politicians of all colours. This confirms that within the official view there is a difference between those who are more oriented towards development and those with democratic leanings. But these views often combine and it is difficult to draw a line between them. It is therefore considered that this can be called a common view, which lies, so to say, at the centre of the ideologic scale.

Another important report in this connection is *Panchayati Raj, Planning and Democracy,* from a conference held in Jaipur in 1964. This conference discussed in detail the meaning of the concept of PR from various angles. Among those participating were Balwant Rai Mehta, S.K. De and other representatives of the official line, Sarvodaya supporters and administrators. The various perspectives were specially analyzed in a contribution of Iqbal Narain, "The Emerging Concept".[4]

Narain has arrived at the same four groups as Patel's. These are:

1. the bureaucratic approach
2. the approach inspired by Sarvodaya
3. CD (development)
4. local self-government (democracy)

He presents a picture with finer nuances of these groups than those usually obtained. Narain says that in the bureaucratic group there are 'extremists' who wish PR to have only an 'agency role', and 'moderates' who would give a degree of independent responsibility to PR but with definite guarantees and controls. The extremists come mostly from the technically specialized administration and the moderates from what can be called 'development departments'. The CD group, observes Narain is 'contextual' because it argues that PR should be guided by the 'context' from which it has grown. There is here a definite emphasis on development.

Finally, Narain mentions "the local government view point", of the democrats. He has found this point of view among politicians taking part in the first big investigation of PR in Rajasthan, the so-called Sadiq Ali Committee. They have spoken in favour of a high degree of autonomy for PR and at the same time that PR should be entrusted with greater tasks even beyond those areas, which were planned from the start.

Narain's personal opinion was that the different points of view, especially 3 and 4, could be combined into a synthesis as rural development consists of interacting factors of many different kinds. He also warned against an overemphasis of the idea of development that might create great expectations from development through PR. Equally important was the awakening of political consciousness and democratic education of the masses which could come about through PR. He wanted to see greater clarity on this aim.[5]

New Trends in the Debate

Upto now the state of opinion at the beginning and middle of the 60s has been discussed; for a number of reasons the position changed after this. The turning point is marked by the death of Nehru in 1964. The CD programme declines and in conjunction with it PR too. S.K. De retires in 1967 and a new generation of political leaders takes over with weaker links with the ideas of Gandhi and Nehru. The crop failures of 1967–68 lead to a strong concentration on increasing agricultural production rapidly by means of concentrated investments of technique and capital in certain districts, and finally to the 'green revolution' especially in parts of northern India. This in its turn contributes to an increased social and political difference between the poor and the rich in rural areas.

There is a general impression that during recent years opinion has changed in such a manner that the official line has moved from CD in the direction of instrumentalism. At the same time, a new and influential line of thought has developed among bureaucrats and technical experts who want to carry out decentralization without PR. Regional development programmes through district planning, the development of various 'growth centres' etc., are emphasized with other things in the current Five-Year Plan (1974–79). This can be called a 'technocratic' view of decentralization which devalues participation by the people.[6]

A more powerful opinion has also grown upto the left of CD and Sarvodaya, both marked by liberal ideas. This opinion stems in part from Marxist views and lies outside the basic reformism which earlier united almost all debate.

Changes in opinion are associated with the development of PR during the 60s. This has been called a change in character "from development to politics".[7] PR started with the object of creating new ways of village development, to strengthen the CD programme. But in practice PR has become "an arena for power politics under the oligarchic control of the elite in the rural areas". This synthesis of the transformation of PR, written by V.M. Sirsikar, is of course somewhat simplified: 'development', and 'politics' are not completely incompatible ideas, not even in Indian villages. However, it does capture something important in a process of change, which most observers would agree on.

Sirsikar says that this change often results in conflicts between administrators who still emphasize PR's developmental aims and local politicians in PR who are most interested in the aspects of power. When PR develops in accordance with the democratic model and real delegation of power takes place to the local level a departure is brought about from the original aim.[8]

Possibly in this paradox is to be found an explanation as to why interest for PR decreases in development administration and that an opinion appears which will carry out decentralization without PR. It is said that we must work on other and more direct lines to be able to reach the poor of the villages and carry out greater social reforms. Many expressions of these feelings have been reported from a meeting in 1973 with the advisory committee of the Ministry of Agriculture for CD and PR.[9]

The role of PR in the new programme for support to the neglected groups in the community was discussed in connection with the 'minimum needs programme' which is included in the Fifth Five-Year Plan (1974–79). Representatives for the states of Mysore and Haryana put forward the firm view that PR had not contributed to development in the villages and that in actual fact they had acted as "instruments of exploitation in the hands of the rural elite". Efforts for the support of the weaker groups in the villages should therefore not be entrusted to PR.

Dr B.S. Minhas from the Planning Commission argued along the same lines. Because of weaknesses in the present PR system it had been necessary to create special organizations for programmes intended to support the poor groups. As examples he gave the Small Farmers Development Agency (SFDA) and the programme for the Marginal Farmers and Agricultural Labour (MFAL). These organizations were more efficient and flexible and furthermore responsible to parliament.

Some representatives such as those from Maharashtra and Gujarat had, however, positive experiences of PR as an organ of development with support from the people. The meeting concluded with the recommendation that PR should be involved in both the planning and carrying out of the 'integrated rural development' and also in the social programmes planned for 1974–79. Although it was possible to agree on this formulation it is clear that opinion at the meeting was very divided.

The change in opinion can be illustrated by various reports and investigations from recent years. Why is interest in PR decreasing? How is PR to be developed in the future? Questions are asked in a spirit of self-critical probing and reinvestigation. Already at the all-Indian conference in Hyderabad, 1969 these feelings dominated and found expression both in the discussions and in the joint resolutions.[10]

But everyone concerned in the Indian debate is aware that PR has come to stay, that its repudiation is politically unthinkable. The important question is what politicians and other influential groups will do, or not do, in regard to these institutions. The question may be illustrated by the example of Rajasthan, where PR made its debut in 1959 with a very large commitment, which inspired other states to follow its example. Many investigations and research reports have stemmed from this programme. The most important investigations are the two set up by the government of Rajasthan, and which reported in 1964 and 1973.[11]

Both investigations speak frankly about the difficulties but also make suggestions about the reforms, which shall carry PR forward towards the goals set. It is interesting to see how mainly the same problems reappear after about ten years. Warnings uttered at the beginning of the 60's have often become manifest realities; the weak participation of the people in the panchayats at the basic level, the biased social recruitment of the local leaders, neglect of the weaker groups and favouring of, certain castes, conflicts with the administration, a weak mobilization of resources and so on.

But what was perhaps difficult to foresee was the declining interest, partly fear of PR, among politicians at a high level. There has been no election to PR since 1964. Every year the legislature has decided to extend the mandate period by a further year through special legislation. According to the High Power Committee of 1973, this is the most important reason for the growing public mistrust against PR and against the leaders controlling these institutions. The investigation emphasizes that this state of affairs cannot continue, and that a decision on what is to be done with PR must now be made. "A stage has come when it is patently clear that Panchayati Raj while standing on the crossroads has to decide now whether in future it has to take a leap forward towards its ultimate goal or the retrograde step of withering away or worse still, continue in its present state of slumber and stagnation".

Lately many states have carried out investigations of PR in the same way as in Rajasthan.[12] This chiefly applies to the states considered to be most active on the question of local self-government—Maharashtra, Gujarat and Andhra Pradesh. It still seems to be unclear what the fate of these investigations will be and if their proposals to strengthen and develop PR will lead to any results.

Panchayati Raj in a Broader Context

It would certainly be fruitful to see PR and the Indian debate in a comparative, international perspective. We should then be able to take account of different political and cultural environments, historical backgrounds etc. As far as I know, there are very few comparative studies of this kind. However, an attempt has been made in *Asian Studies* published by Cornell University and summarized in a report by Norman Uphoff and Milton Esman.[13] I would like to use the perspective and ideas of the Cornell studies and raise some questions about the performance and future role of PR.

The Context of 'Local Organization'

According to the Cornell study, there are always several organizations or organizational channels which can perform rural development functions. At least four channels exist in most cases:

— State administration
— Local government
— Associational organizations
— Private sector

I would like to take one example from the Indian part of the Cornell study to illustrate the importance of various channels. The researchers have quantified the relative importance of organizational channels for rural development in India and in Punjab. The figures indicate that in Punjab, where agriculture has been particularly dynamic, cooperative organizations have a major role to play and PR is comparatively weaker than in India as a whole. So-called associational organizations seem to be very important factors in Indian rural development. This is clear when you consider the development functions at the local level as defined by the Cornell study:

— Planning and goal-setting
— Resource mobilization
— Provision of services
— Integration of services
— Control of administration
— Making claims

There is room for several organizational channels to be able to cover these various functions and it is important to see the relations—or connections between local institutions and other organizations, which provide services, allocate resources and exert influence.

The Cornell studies demonstrate that 'more organized' rural areas generally have faster rural development than 'less organized'. But the point is that 'more organized' in this connection means much more than just effective local government; it includes all organizations and channels relevant for rural development. So one of my conclusions from these comparative studies would be that PR should be analyzed in a broad organizational context at the local level.

The Context of 'Rural Development'

The whole discussion about the impact and importance of PR depends very much on the meaning we give to the concept 'rural development'. According to the Cornell study, rural development should be defined as a process leading to improvements in (1) agricultural productivity, (2) rural incomes, and (3) rural welfare. Because data on rural incomes are hard to get the development index includes mainly 1 and 2 with some additional data on income distribution.

In the Indian debate, it is emphasized that PR has very little impact on agricultural productivity and that the main functions of PR are in the field of rural welfare. The Cornell study gives initially a broad definition of 'rural welfare' in terms of "health, nutrition, education and other features of a satisfactory life, such as security and equity". But the main indicators seem to be the status of health, nutrition and education in the rural areas where there are statistical data available. Other features of a satisfactory life are naturally more difficult to measure and quantify.

However, this approach to rural welfare seems to be somewhat irrelevant from the point of view of the Indian debate. It does not take into account the political and democratic development objectives, which are central in the Indian debate. To take democracy to the villages in order to have a broad popular participation in rural development issues was really one of the main objectives of PR from the start.

In the Cornell study, there is a brief discussion of "political-administrative participation" and an attempt is made to quantify this variable. The criteria used are electoral participation, control of bureaucracy, influence on rural development policy and on the allocation of resources etc. On the basis of the research data, the report comes to the conclusion that participation does not appear to be a necessary or sufficient condition for agricultural improvement (productivity). The correlation with rural welfare is somewhat stronger but still fairly weak.

When the report summarizes the relationship between local organization and rural development indicators the participation indicator is not included. The reason for this omission is not very clear. Popular participation should be regarded, as an objective—as is often the case in the Indian debate—and not just as a means of achieving agricultural development or social welfare. It could even be said that participation as defined above should be an important aspect of welfare and quality of life.

The weak relationship between participation and other objectives in rural development is not a valid reason for excluding participation from the development index. It is often pointed out in the Indian debate that PR should be a training ground for democratic decision-making and that this objective might sometimes conflict with the mere economic development objectives. An evaluation of PR should therefore include also the changing pattern of influence, decision-making and leadership at the local level.

This is even more important in view of the emphasis on "a new rural leadership" which is characteristic for the Indian debate. It was maintained from the beginning that PR should contribute to the formation of a new leadership, which should be more progressive and better integrated in the local community. According to this positive view of the new leaders, they should also be able to act as middlemen between the centre and the periphery of the Indian community. Others maintain that PR was taken over by privileged groups, which use local self-government to advance their group interests.

Anyhow, the Indian debate demonstrates that the issue of local leadership should not be disregarded and that the development index used in the Cornell study is not satisfactory in this respect. Granted this we come to the question what exactly should be the objectives of PR as far as local leadership is concerned? This question is part of a more general debate on development strategies and ideologies.

The Ideological Context

My last point is that different strategies for rural development result in different concepts of leadership. The levels of ambition concerning the efforts of the leaders will vary to a large extent.

In this connection, I would like to refer to a theoretical work on social change in India. Hugh Tinker has made some very useful distinctions in his essay where he discusses strategies for 'bridge building'.[14] In his view, the primary task in Indian social development is to bridge the gap between the elite and the masses. This can occur either through *modernization* when the people shall be 'raised' and integrated in the modern political and economic system, or through an improved *communication* across the gap through suitable middlemen between the traditional and modern sectors. There is also a third alternative available, the populistic *(communitarian),* which wants to abolish the modern sector and strengthen local and rural communities as independent units.

These different strategies envisage different roles for the local leaders. The modernization ideology considers that the leaders shall function as *agents of change,* and work actively in order to mobilize the people for new ideas. The second, the ideology of communication, gives the leaders the role of *intermediary,* not requiring further active steps to change or mobilize people. Politically, it is mainly a question of 'manipulation', whilst culturally it is a matter of interpretation and intermediary tasks. Often it is considered that the second strategy will also cause the gap to narrow but that the results will first appear in the long term.

The ideology of modernization as defined by CD gave the inspiration to PR at the start and it has been an important inspiration for a long time. "Modernizing forces have to enter the very heart of rural community", as R.N. Haldipur said in 1971.[15] Local leaders in PR should be dynamic agents of change.

But there are good reasons for arguing that the second strategy—the ideology of communication—is more realistic. It reflects social realities in rural India where local leaders perform more in accordance with the communication model than with the modernization model. The third approach seems to be even more remote from social and political realities.

If this analysis is correct the performance of PR should not be evaluated as an agent of modernization but less ambitiously as an instrument for communication between the elite and the rural masses. When it comes to mobilizing and organizing the rural masses for development, other instruments are needed, more dynamic than the institutions of local self-government.

Notes

1. AVARD, *Panchayati Raj as the Basis of Indian Policy*, p. 25.
2. *Report of the Study Team for the Study of CD Projects and National Extensive Service*, Planning Commission, New Delhi, 1958.
3. Rajni Kothari, *Politics in India*, p. 136. With reference to the Mehta Report and its treatment, see Henry Maddick, *Panchayati Raj*, 1970, pp. 52–64.
4. Also published in *Asian Survey*, September, 1965.
5. See also Narain's and P.C. Mathur's contributions to George Jacob (ed.), *Readings on Panchayati Raj*, 1967, p. 104 ff.
6. This is also based on verbal information from S.K. Dey and Rajni Kothari in March 1974. Cf S.K. Dey, *Power to the People*, pp. 111–120.
7. *Values, and the Active Community*, p. 177 ff. Cf Haldipur, Paramahamsa, op. cit., p. 94. "The Reality of Panchayati Raj, as it obtains today, is radically different from the perception of the elite that launched it. Conceived in political romanticism, Panchayati Raj manifests a political vigour that cannot perhaps be stemmed". Also S.P. Jain, "Panchayati Raj: An Appraisal", *Khadi Gramodyog*, November, 1973.
8. The character change of PR has been pointed out in studies from Rajasthan. See for example, M.V. Mathur et al., *Panchayati Raj in Rajasthan*, 1966, p. 280.
9. *Kurukshetra*, 1 March, 1973.
10. Haldipur, Paramahamsa, *Local Government Institutions in Rural India*, 1970.
11. *Report of the Study Team on Panchayati Raj*, 1964, Panchayati Raj and Development Department, Government of Rajasthan, Jaipur (usually

called the Sadiq Ali Report after its chairman), *Report of the High Power Committee on Panchayati Raj,* 1973, Panchayat and Development, Jaipur.

12. A good review is found in U.C. Ghildyal, "Illusions and Realities in Panchayati Raj: Some Reflections", *Behavioural Sciences and Community Development,* March, 1973.
13. Norman Uphoff and Milton Esman, *Local Organization for Rural Development: Analysis of Asian Experiences,* Special Series on Rural Local Government, No. 19, Cornell University, 1974.
14. Hugh Tinker, "Local Government and Politics: Political and Social Theory in India" in M.J. Swartz (ed.), *Local-level Politics, Social and Cultural Perspectives,* Chicago, 1968.
15. R.N. Haldipur, "On Remodelling Panchayati Raj", *Indian Journal of Public Administration,* July-September, 1971.

12 Process of Decentralized Governance and Planning

Abdul Aziz

Planning effort in India for over 45 years now to promote development has yielded mixed results—good progress in some and not so good in others. A look at the balance-sheet, especially of human development, prepared by UNDP holds a mirror to this. On the credit side, we have improved food production and elimination of famines, increased life expectancy, reduced infant mortality, improved literacy and health facility. Undernourishment among sizeable number of children, high level of poverty, inadequate health and sanitary facilities, adverse sex ratio, high drop-out rate among school children, and prevalence of child labour practices are on the debit side of the balance sheet (UNDP, June 1997: 7).

Failure in some areas as noted above is due to many factors, one of which is the plan approach followed. It is stated that too much of emphasis on macro plan was at the base of the failures of economic planning in India. The overemphasis on macro plan had the following drawbacks:

1. Backward areas and weaker sections could not be reached.
2. Inputs from people as to what they need could not be obtained. So basic needs of the people were overlooked.
3. And, as planning of this sort was not participatory, plan formulation was not people's need-oriented and that implementation was not cost effective.

Taking note of the drawbacks of macro plan approach, the planning pandits were in search of an alternative approach. It is in this background that a 'paradigm' shift took place recently in favour of decentralized planning and governance. The advantages claimed are that decentralization will meet all the drawbacks of macro planning in the sense that it will provide the basic needs by getting inputs from people, reach backward areas and weaker sections and be people-oriented and cost effective in so far as it is participatory in nature. The purpose of this brief paper is to capture the processes of governance and planning as they have developed under decentralization. While we set out with some basic principles of decentralized governance and planning, drawing from Karnataka experience, the actual position is also sketched to gauge where we stand as of now vis-à-vis what is desirable.

The Local Governance System

The Constitution of India provides for a quasi-federal governance system for the country with the union government functioning at the national level and the state government at the state level. Recently, with the amendment to the Constitution, the power of governance has been decentralized further down to districts, blocks and villages in the rural areas and to a hierarchy of towns and cities in the urban areas. Decentralized governments, of course, did exist earlier but they had no constitutional guarantee such that they could easily be superseded by the state governments. The Constitution Amendment Act, 1992 set this right and gave them permanency. Under the Acts passed by the state governments subsequently, there is a provision for holding elections once in five years to these bodies. Members of these bodies are directly elected; the executive positions like Presidents and Vice-Presidents are filled by means of 'indirect elections'. The official members appointed to administrative positions carry out day-to-day business under the supervision of the executive heads. In order to provide access to power to weaker sections like women, SCs, STs and backward classes, seats and executive positions are reserved as provided by the Constitution Amendment Act. This provision is considered to be one of the most progressive acts of the government in recent years. And, what is more, in states like Karnataka, the number of elected members of panchayats from these weaker sections is greater than the reserved quota set for them. Also, it is a matter of great satisfaction to note that many panchayats are today headed by women, SCs, STs and backward class individuals.

Pre-Conditions for Effective Governance

For these bodies to function effectively certain sets of conditions should be fulfilled. It is proposed in the following paragraphs to state these conditions and to examine how far these have been met in practice especially with reference to the rural governments, viz., Zila Panchayats (ZP), Taluka Panchayats (TP) and Gram Panchayats (GP).

Transfer of Powers and Resources

Transfer of adequate powers, functions and resources to decentralized governments is one such important condition. The basic issues that are of interest here are: what powers and resources are to be transferred and on the basis of what criteria? Is this transfer subject to zero-sum game in which case what conflicts arise between the power/resource givers and receivers? Secondly, under the three-tier system how powers and resources are to be distributed among the various bodies? What should be the interrelationship between different levels of governments? And how are they linked with each other so that they work in unison?

The theoretical guideline on the transfer of functions is that whatever could be done better at the lower level should be assigned to that level. Keeping this in view, in Karnataka three schedules showing areas of operations of different tiers were evolved and appended to the Karnataka Panchayat Act, 1993 (Government of Karnataka, 1993). In all, 29 subjects have been transferred to panchayats covering agriculture and allied activities, social and farm forestry, fisheries, horticulture, minor irrigation, Khadi and village industries, rural housing, drinking water, sanitation, rural roads, public health, markets and fairs, poverty alleviation programmes, primary and secondary education, social welfare, welfare of weaker sections, public distribution system, maintenance of community assets and so on. Across the different tiers, since there was considerable overlapping of functional areas, the state government issued an order in July 1994 clarifying the position. But notwithstanding this there is still some amount of confusion as to which function is under which panchayat. Secondly, there is a general complaint that the TP which is a recent creature got away with more powers and functions compared to ZPs and GPs. The matter has gone to such an extent that a section of political leaders hold that the earlier two-tier system with Zila Parishads and Mandal Panchayats under the 1983 Act was better and that it would be most appropriate to abolish the middle tier which has become a cog in the wheel. Though one may term this as an unjustified demand, since there appears to be a grain of truth in the complaint, this needs to be dispassionately looked into. Finally, transfer of powers from the state government to decentralized governments has been looked upon as loss of power by the state level officials and members of legislature. The configuration of interests of these two classes had resulted in clipping the wings of the panchayats under the Karnataka Panchayati Raj Act, 1993. The executive head position enjoyed by the presidents under the 1983 Act was taken away and under the new Act more powers were given to officials. When this act of the previous government drew massive protests, the new government, by an ordinance, declared the presidents and vice-presidents of panchayats to be the executive heads. The ex-officio membership with voting rights given to local MLAs and MPs under the Act with a view to accommodating their interests in local governance, however, continues to be an irritant in the panchayat circles.

On the question of organic link across the various tiers of panchayats, the mechanism evolved is to provide for ex-officio membership to a certain number of lower tier members in the immediate higher-tier. Thus, on a rotation basis, a fifth of the presidents of GPs and TPs sit as members in TPs and ZPs respectively. Though this arrangement is laudable in principle, it has degenerated itself into some kind of a contentious issue. Thus, while the ZP members demand that they be allowed to sit in the legislature on the same principle, they and their counterparts in the TPs desire to share powers on a reciprocal basis with members of their immediate lower tier panchayats. This is a clear case of indulging in competitive power grabbing in the backward and forward power channels. Such a demand from the panchayat members is primarily set off by mistakenly providing berths to MLAs and MPs in ZPs and TPs. For, as ex-officio members, MLAs and MPs in general dominate the proceedings of the panchayats and corner benefits for their supporters and preferred villages. The members of ZPs and TPs naturally entertain the hope that they could also do so if they got membership in their immediate lower tiers!

As for finances, the guideline is that whatever finances are required to perform the functions assigned should be devolved to these bodies, both by way of grants and taxation powers. In Karnataka, until recently the practice was that about 34 per cent of own non-loan state resources were devolved to decentralized governments. The recommendation of the State Finance Commission (1996) is to raise it to 36 per cent of which 85 per cent was allotted to panchayats and 15 per cent to urban bodies (Government of Karnataka, July 1996).

By way of distributing these resources, the criteria followed were population and backwardness by applying weightages of 50 per cent each. But the State Finance Commission, 1996 added an additional criterion of area of the Panchayats with a weightage of 33.3 per cent. The reduction of weightages assigned to the traditional criteria of population and backwardness from 50 per cent each to 33.33 per cent each and the introduction of area as a criterion in regard to resource allocation has triggered off criticism particularly from those panchayats whose physical area is small. The point made is that this will go against the interests of backward panchayats insofaras they stand to lose in the bargain and widen disparities across panchayats as more funds are likely to be allotted to the larger size panchayats. This argument is baseless because the panchayats which have larger areas are panchayats where villages are dispersed and population densities are lower. Incidentally, the low density panchayats are also backward in nature. Therefore, there appears to be some degree of convergence between the criteria of backwardness and larger area. Hence, area criterion indirectly also points to backwardness suggesting thereby that adding area criterion strengthens the case of backward panchayats than weakening it.

Planning Process

The second set of conditions is that these bodies should have autonomy of decision-making in respect of planning and administration. At the same time, they should be accountable and possess transparency too in their day-to-day working. They should identify people's needs and local resources, on that basis formulate projects, prioritize them, and link these projects in the integrated area development framework such that whatever projects are formulated they become economically viable.

In actual practice, the planning process begins with the meeting of the village council (Gram Sabha) where people's needs are identified and priorities are drawn up. These needs are processed at the village panchayat level, an action plan is prepared and passed onto the Taluka Panchayat which after incorporating all the GP action plans into its own plan passes it onto the ZP for transmission to the

State Planning Department. The mechanism evolved here undoubtedly appears to bestow autonomy on the governing bodies in regard to planning and implementation. But a deeper analysis suggests that the processes inherent in the mechanism produce different kinds of noises. This needs to be elaborated a bit considering the importance of the subject.

In the first place, Gram Sabha meetings are not regularly held and, if held, meetings take place in the panchayat office. Attendance of citizens in these meetings is thin. Most of those who attend these meetings are the potential beneficiaries with a desire to seek assistance under the various poverty alleviation programmes. Indeed, the Gram Sabhas are actually reduced to the status of an assembly that is merely engaged in identifying beneficiaries under various schemes of assistance. This knocks out the principles of transparency and accountability to people from the concept of decentralization. Besides, it may be desirable to add that the panchayat planners do not enjoy full autonomy in regard to plan formulation because of the following reasons:

1. The resources allocated especially to GPs are so minimal* that they hardly can exercise any choice with regard to local plan programmes.
2. The ongoing programmes are so many and the quantum of resources to be allocated to the spillover projects is so large that hardly anything is left for taking up new projects.
3. It is reported that the State Planning Department officials, overseeing the planning exercise done by the ZPs on the basis of people's needs and priorities, change allocations thereby negating the very spirit of autonomy implied in decentralized governance. Such interventions by the officials reportedly take place at the instance of heads of various state department and the district ministers who would not like to see a cut in or lower allocation going to their own departments.

Coordination of Governance

Thirdly, a high degree of coordination of governance and planning at different levels is another prerequisite for good governance. It is

* A Gram Panchayat which holds a population of five to seven thousand gets a grant of Rs 1.25 lakh per annum. It, of course, gets a JRY grant of around Rs 2 lakh from the Union government. But that is a tied grant; the panchayat does not enjoy the autonomy to allocate these funds for purposes it deems fit.

common knowledge that, as these bodies start functioning, some externalities are likely to arise. Three types of externalities can be anticipated; Thus, (a) a decision of a panchayat may affect the interests of another panchayat; (b) in respect of two neighbouring panchayats, each may look to the other to make a move; as a result none will act. Hence, opportunities for development are blocked; and (c) failure of bargaining process to determine sharing of resource and cost may impose hardships on both the panchayats. In such cases, two options are available: (a) voluntary coming together to resolve such problems; and (b) allowing to be arbitrated by an apex body. The pity is no such arrangement is made so far except proposing a District Planning Committee with the responsibility of coordinating the district level panchayat and municipalities plans. At the most, this committee may act as an agency for meshing panchayat and municipal plans. Therefore, the problem of externalities will continue to stare at our face. There is then a case for establishing a separate apex body to tackle such problems. In this context, the recommendation of the Expert Committee for establishing a panchayat council at the state level for coordinating the activities of the Panchayats (Government of Karnataka, 1996) becomes quite appropriate and urgent.

People's Participation

Finally, people's participation is another pre-requisite for good governance. People's participation in theory would imply participation of citizens, their representatives and organizations like youth clubs, Mahila Mandals, and participation of non-government organizations in the planning and governance process. For various reasons, this condition is not fulfilled because of the following reasons: Low level of awareness among citizens has led to a dismally low level of participation in the governance process. People's organizations are yet to make a mark in this respect, they are still interested in ceremonial functions and getting dignitaries to address the members. The NGOs have some psychological barriers. On the one hand, their self-righteous attitude prevents them from working with the local political leaders and panchayat members. On the other, the latter look upon NGOs as competitors; suspecting their bonafides the panchayat members hardly allow themselves to interact and work with the NGOs.

Concluding Remarks

On the whole, there is a wide gap between what is desirable and what is actual so far as decentralized governance is concerned. If this is the case with Karnataka, which has a good record of decentralization, what would be the position in other states which are yet to make a beginning in local governance. May be some concerted effort ought to be made to train the panchayat officials in the art and science of decentralized governance and planning. Wherever such attempts have been made some good results have been achieved. Training has created, particularly among the weaker sections, some degree of awareness, promoted attitudinal changes and imparted skills of governance and planning. It is hoped that with such continued effort and exposure, the official and non-official members of the panchayats will be sensitized to the principles of decentralized governance and they, in turn, will initiate processes that promote a truly participatory transparent and accountable decentralized governance system in the rural areas.

References

Government of Karnataka, (1993). *The Karnataka Panchayati Raj Act 1993*, Government of Karnataka, Bangalore.

———, (March 1996). *The Report of the Expert Committee on Karnataka Panchayati Raj Act 1993*, Government of Karnataka, Bangalore.

———, (July 1996). *Report of the State Finance Commission in Relating of Panchayati Raj Institutions,* Government of Karnataka, Bangalore.

UNDP, (June 1997). *India: The Road to Human Development,* New Delhi.

13 Local Level Planning for Integrated Rural Development

Case Studies from India and Abroad

K.V. Sundaram

India has had long years of experience in rural development and has tried a variety of approaches, with different emphasis, during the last quarter of the century or so. The following is a simple listing of these approaches:

Approach	*Emphasis*
Rural reconstruction	Village-centred movement based on principles of voluntary effort.
Community development	Rural development based on ideas of motivation, self-help and self-reliance.
Target sector	Intensive development of sector or sectors of activity with emphasis on concentrating in areas of comparative advantage.
Target groups	Growth with social justice for the weaker sections of population.
Growth centres	Spatial planning and development.
Backward area development	Reduction of regional imbalances in development.
Minimum needs	Equalization of social consumption.
Area planning with full employment	Integrated rural development in an area framed with the removal of unemployment (poverty) as an important aim.

A colossal programme of community development was launched from the First Five-Year Plan, which was designed to transform the economic and social life of the Indian villages. While this programme did build up an institutional framework with a multidisciplinary approach and facilitated the implementation of concrete development projects in respect of improved crop production, cattle breeding, transport, rural industry, public health activity and social education, it was not a complete success in decentralized planning for many reasons. Its impact on agricultural improvement was meagre, and worse still, whatever benefit it imparted was restricted to an elitist minority. The vast majority of the rural masses, who lacked the requisite resource base and were thinly employed, were bypassed and the fundamental problem of land relations and the related power structure in the villages remained the same. On the administrative front, coordination of activities of the different government departments at the block level proved to be the biggest problem. Above all, the schematic approach, which it adopted, led only to 'top-down' planning without initiating a bottom-up process in planning.

The Community Development Programme (CDP) underwent several changes in emphasis over time, which may be interpreted as the various countervailing forces or correctives applied to the planning process from time to time. However, such correctives, on the whole, led only to piecemeal and fragmented planning rather than to an integrated and comprehensive approach to rural development. The present concept of 'Integrated Rural Development and Block Level Planning', which is being pursued in the current Sixth Plan (1978–83)[1] has emerged from these experiments in the choice of planning interventions.

This programme aims at integrated rural development at the block level to secure fuller utilization of local resources, both physical and human, and to provide full employment opportunities in the area within a specific time frame.[2] It envisages integration of the programme of agriculture and allied activities, cottage and village industries, socio-economic infrastructure, including the Minimum Needs Programme (MNP) and the development of human resources. One of the components of the programme is the identification of the target groups, i.e., the beneficiaries comprising the small and marginal farmers, landless labourers and rural artisans and development of appropriate schemes for individual assistance, will generate increased income for them. In doing so, the prospective beneficiaries are to be selected starting from the poorest of the poor in an ascending scale.[3] The basic idea implied in this component of the programme, i.e., the beneficiary-oriented approach is already ingrained in the Small Farmers Development Programme[4] one of the ongoing programmes in India. The new elements are the establishment of various linkages and the task of integrating the programme in the agriculture sector with those of the other sectors.

Out of the more than 5,000 blocks in India, about 3,000 are already covered by one or more of the special area-based programmes, such as the Small Farmers Development Agency (SFDA), Drought Prone Area Programme (DPAP) and Command Area Development Programme (CADP), each one of them with their own particular emphasis. The Integrated Rural Development Programme (IRDP) of India envisages 'broadening their bases', which would not merely help solving the problems of the natural environment and resource use, but would also ensure the development of the productive, institutional and social infrastructure in their areas. For this purpose, a phased programme approach has been recommended, according to which 2,000 out of the 3,000 blocks with ongoing programme will be selected for the proposed comprehensive treatment during the Sixth Five-Year Plan period. In addition to this, the Indian programme also seeks to cover another 1,500 blocks for the five years (300 blocks each year) in areas which are not having any special programmes. In all, the target coverage during the Sixth Plan period is 3,500 out of the 5,000 blocks in the country.

The Department of Rural Development of the Ministry of Agriculture and Irrigation in the Government of India, which is administering the special area-based programmes in the country has provided some guidelines for intensive development of blocks under the Integrated Rural Development Programme. These guidelines mainly relate to the methodology for the formulation of schemes in the agriculture and allied sectors of activity. On the basis of these guidelines, the programme has been initiated in all the states of the country and has made some progress during the last two years (i.e., 1978–79 and 1979–80).

So far as the realization of the policy objective of area planning for full employment is concerned, the progress has been somewhat halting. This is attributed to the delay in the issue of guidelines for comprehensive and integrated area planning, the organizational and other bottlenecks associated with transition and the initial teething troubles that had to be encountered while administering the new programme. For spelling out the methodology of comprehensive block level plans, the Planning Commission had set up a Working Group in November 1977, under the chairmanship of Prof. M.L. Dantwala, an eminent economist, which submitted its report in May 1978. Taking into account the recommendations contained in this report, the Planning Commission has only recently (December 1979) issued the guidelines for block level planning to the state governments. This delay has led to a certain time lag between policy enunciation and programme implementation.

Any evaluation of field performance has to take note of policy pronouncements and the guidelines framed by the government to effectuate the policy into action programmes. In this context, the guidelines issued by the Planning Commission have great relevance, as these constitute a statement of intent, against which it is possible to measure the current performance in the blocks. However, a brief account of the official guidelines highlighting some points is necessary for our present discussion.

The guidelines have envisaged the block-level plan as a seven-year perspective plan (from 1981–82 to 1987–88), synchronizing with the remaining two years of India's Sixth Plan and the full five-year period of the subsequent Seventh Plan. Since the existing block-level set-up is unequal to the task of micro-level planning, both in number as well as capability, the induction of some expertise in the planning team as well as some administrative adaptations have been suggested. The existing nucleus set up for block-level development is proposed to be enlarged by the addition of three members—an economist/statistician, a credit planning officer and an industries officer for small and cottage industries. Also, all functionaries of the line departments are proposed to be brought under the control of the Chief Planning Officer, so that effective coordination would be possible at the block level. While the brunt of block level planning will be borne by the official machinery, the guidelines have also envisaged the involvement of voluntary agencies with the necessary experience and expertise, 'wherever possible' both in plan formulation as well as implementation.

The guidelines have advocated certain essential steps in local level planning process, which include undertaking a base line survey[5] assessing financial resources for the plan,[6] setting up of a planning machinery and establishing some coordinative mechanisms at higher levels to facilitate task of integration. The major components of the block level plan have been spelt out as:

1. Programmes aiming at optimizing the production potential of the area in the various sectors, e.g., agriculture, animal husbandry, forests, village and small scale industries etc.
2. Special production programmes for the target groups in the area in the light of the resource potential.
3. Manpower planning and skill development in relation to the production programmes.
4. A programme for the provision of basic minimum needs.
5. Programme for institutional support.

The guidelines have suggested that while preparing the individual sectoral plans and the final integrated plan, the major objectives of augmenting employment for increased incomes especially for the weaker sections must be kept in view. In this context, the sectoral planners have been advised to devise project/programmes, which would help augment the duration of employment of the people in their existing occupations. After exhausting all the possibilities of providing employment through production programmes, the guidelines have suggested a special public works programme (e.g., Food for Work scheme) to provide for transitory unskilled employment.

The official guidelines clearly define the aim, set out the methodology in broad terms and make some reference to the tools that are needed, administrative and financial tools, to ensure that the plans are optimally executed. Nevertheless, they do not go into all operational details. The official letter forwarding the guidelines to the states says that while the guidelines cover only "some broad and essential aspects", they may be supplemented "from time to time, as considered necessary" by the Ministry of Rural Reconstruction of Government of India and elaborated further by the state governments "by incorporating such modifications as necessary in the context of the geographical, administrative and other peculiarities of their respective States".

Indian Cases

Kazhakeotam in Trivandrum District (Kerala)

The case study area—Kazhakeotam block in Trivandrum district (Kerala) (area: 133.65 sq km; population: 15278)[7]—is bounded in the south by the city of Trivandrum.[8] It comprises seven panchayats, two of them lying along the coast. In terms of working force composition, the primary, secondary and tertiary sectors accounted for 38, 26 and 36 per cent respectively of the total number of workers in 1971. Thus, the block must be regarded as somewhat typical, in the sense that agriculture is not so dominant a source of employment and income, as in most other blocks. The hetrogeneity of the rural economy indicated by the composition of the working force may not, however, be interpreted as diversification, pointing to an affluent economy. This is because the non-agricultural enterprises are not in the organized sector, but fall wholly in the 'rural and household industry' sector characterized by low technology and low productivity, e.g., coir and coir-based industries, oil mills, weaving, bricks and tiles, rice and flour mills.

The block is well-connected by rail and road and is comparatively better endowed in terms of social provision (both education and health care). It has also achieved a fair measure of cooperativization in respect of short and medium term credit with four service cooperatives, one cooperative bank and as many as 18 branches of commercial banks. In the non-credit cooperative sector also, several cooperatives have come up, e.g., coir, fisheries, handloom and milk, though their performance has been below par.

The Scheduled Caste members account for 11.4 per cent of the total block population and they constitute an indigent group. More than 1,000 households are engaged in fishing, eking out an uncertain and meagre livelihood.

Investigations at various levels reveal that the vast majority of the people are thinly employed. A sample household survey (35 households) undertaken for the case study indicated the following range of income and employment in the area:

Family Type	*Employment (man-days)*	*Annual Income (Rs)*
A typical small nuclear family (agr.) labour	100	1550
Large, complex agricultural family with subsidiary occupations	175	2000–3000
Handloom family	250	1800
Family deriving income mainly from coir-based occupations	300	1800
Fisher folk	Data insufficient for building up any quantitative assessment of income and employment.	

The IRDP, the performance of which has been reviewed in the case study, started implementation in the block in November 1978. The study refers to the operations over a brief period of nine months only (November 1978 to July 1979). During this period, the project had identified a total number of 615 beneficiaries, one-fifth of them were belonging to SC families. The family plans of 562 beneficiaries had already been approved by the District Collector and the approvals of others were in the pipeline. The two major categories of beneficiary-oriented schemes undertaken by the project authorities were: distribution of milch cows and digging of wells. The physical achievement reported against these schemes were 117 and 53 respectively, which is rated as 'fairly good performance' as it has served to strengthen the resource base of a considerable number of indigent households in a relatively short period.

An assessment of the contribution of the scheme in the context of seven parameters viz., the identification of beneficiaries, the preparation and adoption of family plans, financial assistance, extension and supporting systems, coordination with other agencies, follow up and monitoring, and organization and machinery throws up the following conclusions:

1. The identification of the eligible beneficiary households was not systematic and exhaustive. There was also no public participation in the selection of beneficiaries. In the rush and preoccupation with financial targets, the overriding priority of implementing functionaries was on piloting a respectable number of family plans, rather than on a systematic identification of the families.
2. While the heterogenous character of the block economy with its different components like fishing, coir, hand-spinning and weaving or handloom called for a separate package of measures appropriate to each, the family plans that were formulated followed a rule of thumb approach, with a few standard schemes being designed to increase employment and income, particularly of farm families. The scheme formulation appears to have been circumscribed by the range of competence and information of the Village Extension Officer. In a process of mechanistic simplification, schemes necessitating upgradations of technology[9] or relevant in the context of diversification of the economy, were sacrificed, as the capacity to innovate was absent with the functionaries. This only serves to underline the difficult nature of the tasks involved in local level planning and implementation.

Unless the functionaries have the requisite competence to handle these problems, local level planning will be more often than not, reduced to a mechanical and often irrelevant exercise. The selection of projects was restricted to bankable schemes only and as such, they was necessarily those that did not conform to 'integrated' development. Thus, the selective approach to family plans has militated against integrated development efforts.

3. The special importance of extension and support service, in a programme designed for a group of people that needs them most, does not seem to have been grasped, as these were not simultaneously attended to. The case study notes that there is a clear need for the simultaneous strengthening of the extension machinery and toning up of the support services.
4. While coordination has been ensured, of developmental activities within the concerned departments, the coordination with other departments and agencies, which has been envisaged in the programme, has not been attempted. Coordination has also been not fully effective for district or block level organization.
5. The voluntary agencies have not yet been drawn into the exercise.
6. The study has noted the absence of an organization and machinery, adequate to cope with the tasks assigned in the context of block level planning and integrated rural development. The present organization and machinery are inadequate for these tasks. Monitoring and follow-up have not been taken up seriously.

The case study of Kazhakeotam block shows that while some intensification of agricultural development has been achieved, which has benefited individual families, integrated development in the sense in which it has been originally conceived by the planners, has not really come about. It has underscored the point that if family programmes are to continue on a self-sustaining basis, then such programmes must be closely linked with the locally available resources for which comprehensive block level planning is needed.

Uthiramerur Block in Chingleput District (Tamil Nadu)

The study area—Uthiramerur block in Chingleput district (area: 420.56 sq km; population: 1,04,200; number of households: 22,241)—comprises 127 villages, constituted into 73 villages panchayats and one town which has an urban local body called 'Town

Panchayat'. The population of the block has Scheduled Caste and Scheduled Tribe component, accounting for 26.9 per cent of the total population. Eighty-four per cent of the population is rural. The occupational classification shows cultivators (44%), agricultural labourers (37%), and the remaining 19 per cent in other non-agricultural occupations. The total cropped area of the Block is 73 per cent, of which 27 per cent is double cropped. Small holdings predominate with the marginal and small farmers holding about 91 per cent of the total number of holdings. Paddy, groundnut, sugarcane, chillies and ginger are the important crops, with paddy predominating (71%) the cultivated area. With one primary land development bank, 18 primary agricultural credit societies, eight weavers' cooperative societies and 48 milk producers' societies and four branches of nationalized commercial banks, the block has a fairly good institutional set-up for disbursing credit for agriculture and allied activities. Industrially too, it is fairly advanced with one textile mill, 54 rice mills, 14 oil mills, handloom industry supporting 3,500 persons and other cottage industries. The block is also well-endowed with infrastructure like electricity, roads and drinking water supply. The democratic institutions in the area are the village panchayats, and the Panchayat Union Council (federation of panchayats), although at the time of the visit of the ESCAP team, the Panchayat Union Council having been superseded by the government was not functioning. Development activities at the block level are coordinated by the Block Development Officer (BDO), who is assisted by Extension Officers in agriculture, animal husbandary and cooperatives. While the Extension Officers are under the administrative control of the BDO, who is assisted by Extension Officer in agriculture, animal husbandary and cooperatives, they are technically controlled by other departments from where they had been drawn. Two special programmes for rural development are operating in the district, viz., the Small Farmers' Development Agency (SFDA) Programmes and the Integrated Rural Development Programme (IRDP). The implementation of these programmes as well as their performance have been analyzed in the case study.

The SFDA project, being essentially a beneficiary-oriented project, involves the following stages in project implementation:

1. identification of the target group;
2. assessment of their requirements; and
3. linking them with the various functional institutions meant for credit, input and services.

The case study analysis has revealed that the initial identification of the eligible families has not been done systematically, that control and monitoring functions at the field level needed great improvements and that follow up contacts with the beneficiaries have been neglected. The study has traced these inadequacies to an ill-equipped departmental machinery and has emphasized the need for organizational and administrative changes in this context. The study has also drawn attention to the lack of area specificity in the schemes adopted, the failure to use resource inventory information for scheme formulation[10] and lack of efficiency in extension services.[11] A definitional ambiguity with regard to 'family' which is the unit for identifying the target group of beneficiaries and the dual control system with the SFDA on the one hand and the sectoral departments on the other are also mentioned as deficiencies in the programme.

The IRDP, which is in operation in the block from April, 1978 seems to have suffered an organizational jolt during the middle of the year. It was initially implemented by the BDO and his technical and non-technical supporting staff, but since September, 1979, the implementation of programme had been transferred to the SFDA. This inevitably impeded the project momentum.

The project started with the identification of the target group of families in the block through a survey, based on which an action programme and financial plan for a period of three years was drawn up. Based on certain assumptions, the effective target group was identified as 13,424 families and their coverage was phased out over the three years' period. The task of linking up each family in the target group with an appropriate economic activity (participation in which will help the family to earn a certain incremental income) was then taken in hand. Thus, the tasks actually accomplished in the Uthiramerur block were the identification of target families and the doling out of the benefits to them in the form of subsidy on the SFDA pattern. This achievement is very much short of that envisaged in block level planning in the comprehensive sense. The experience here clearly shows that the integration of the beneficiary-oriented scheme with infrastructure and other supporting programmes was hardly attempted. What had been reviewed here was only a programme, and not a plan. The discussion also revealed that the field functionaries were not clear as to the precise manner in which integration was to be brought about among the different components of the plan. This is indicative of the lack of adequate preparatory efforts by the authorities before operationalizing this programme. According to the case study, several operational details had been left to be decided at the local level, which in practice, has not worked to satisfaction This only points to the confused thinking at the operational level as to who should really administer the programme. The mid stream transfer slowed the pace of implementation of the action programme.

As analysis of the programme content in the plan has revealed that about 73 per cent of the outlay had been spent on purchase and supply of milch animals, plough, bullocks and sheeps. This trend had an unfavourable effect of increasing the market price of the animals, thereby decreasing the benefit to the farmers. The study has reported that "many farmers therefore are forced to sell away the animals immediately after purchase, finding it difficult to meet the loan repayment schedule". Further, the linkages with such programmes, as for example, breeding, fodder etc., were lost sight of with the result that the programme resulted in adverse impact upon the beneficiaries. Apart from the lack of an organizational pattern conducive to integration among the sectoral activities, the case study has also identified the absence of a separate planning machinery for undertaking a detailed planning exercise and the lack of a training support to enable the field functionaries to grasp the real content and spirit of the programme as other major lacunae.

Review

A review of performance at the block level in the two cases examined above shows that while block level planning on a systematic basis has not yet taken off, considerable experience has been acquired in implementing beneficiary-oriented programmes.

The process of identification of beneficiaries is carried out by Village Welfare Officers (VWO) through door-to-door visits, who collect data on family resources and felt needs of activities or materials for increased income and betterment of living conditions. On the basis of this data, a family plan is formulated by the family itself in consultation with the VWO. The sum total of family plans of the beneficiaries together with the infrastructural support plan constitutes the block development plan with its various components including agriculture and allied activities, village and cottage industries and service sectors.[12] The BDO, with the assistance of specialists from line departments and a group of village workers, plays a leading role in planning for the block level development and implementation of programmes.

A proposed activity of the family plan is funded by the government by granting subsidies amounting to 25 per cent in case of small farmers and 33.3 per cent in case of marginal farmers and the remaining portion to be financed by the commercial banks. The differential rate of interest charged to income earner less than Rs 3,500 is 4 per cent. As a rule, the individual beneficiary is given the subsidy from the government in kind only. As a follow up, the performance of the family plan is reviewed and advice is given, as needed.

The planning process described above has an in-built element of local participation, as the family actively participates in the formulation and implementation of the plan. Further, the Panchayat Samiti consisting of a body of elected representatives provides advice and assistance to the BDO and his team of VWOs in the management of block affairs. In fact, the Block Development Committee, a consultative and decision-making body, is formed with the BDO, the chairmen of the panchayats, representatives from pressure groups and voluntary organizations and district officers from the line departments. At the higher levels, the State Planning Board and District Planning Committee exist. At the state level, coordination is effected between the state/sectoral plan and the district/block development plans.

A Proto-type Block Level Plan

The plan, considered as a prototype exercise, has been framed by the National Institute of Rural Development, Hyderabad, for one of the blocks in Andhra Pradesh, the Ibrahimpatnau block in Ranga Reddy district. The plan is claimed to be based on the methodology outlined by the Working Group on Block Level Planning set up by the Planning Commission. The plan combines in a common plan frame, the merits of sectoral as well as spatial aspects of planning, purposively designed to improve production, to bring benefits of development to the rural poor and to increase employment. The plan has attempted the following tasks:

1. analysis of the existing level of development in the block area;
2. identification of the problems and constraints in the way of development;
3. identification of the centres of growth which can generate and regulate the process of developmental activities in the area;
4. assessment of the potentialities of development in the agriculture and allied sectors to propose suitable programmes and optimize growth and generation of maximum employment;

5. identification of the spatial and functional gaps and to propose infrastructure to support the developmental activities;
6. assessment of the employment potential in different sectors and to propose ways and means of creating full employment conditions in the block; and
7. integrating all sectoral development programmes into the spatial framework to attain an integrated development of the block area.

The study has started with spatial planning by identifying the existing and potential centres or focal points of development on the basis of movement pattern of the people and their activities in the area. On the basis of this exercise, the block area has been divided into micro-planning units with a central village in each, which would serve as the focal point to generate growth impulses. These micro-planning units are used in the plan as the basic spatial units where investment could be made and also to take into account the type and quantum of benefit that would accrue to the people in general and the rural poor, in particular. Within these units, the present situation and available potential for different activities have been assessed and future requirements worked out.

The study was based on both secondary and primary data. Secondary data were collected from different offices located at the block as well as the district headquarters. Primary data were collected through questionnaires exclusively designed for the study of:

1. village economy,
2. household economy,
3. artisan economy,
4. business and commerce, and
5. industry

In the village studies, the focus was on the small and marginal farmers and landless agricultural labourers in each major sector of development, e.g., agriculture, forestry, animal husbandry, fisheries, industry etc., analysis was made of the existing level of development, the potential for future development as well as the labour utilization and employment potential. Since the focus of the plan was on the development programmes for the weaker sections of rural society, to enable them to augment their family income through provision of gainful employment opportunities, alternative uses of land, water and human resources were examined and certain models evolved indicating the optimum mix of occupations which would make the household economy of the various poor categories of people viable under different assumptions.

The Ibrahimpatnau plan is a ten year perspective plan for the period from 1978 to 1988 and has not merely attempted to reconcile the needs of the area and target groups and individuals in a common plan frame, but has also outlined the organizational changes needed for implementing the plan programmes and increasing their efficiency in implementation. It has emphasized the need for integrating the programmes of the elective body (Panchayat Samiti), the government machinery and voluntary organizations. It has also noted that the task of planning operational details of the programmes and reviewing the problems in their implementation is not done and had therefore emphasized the need for involving the people in the planning function and in reviewing the implementation of programmes. For this purpose, it has suggested the setting up of panels consisting of extension officers as well as representatives of beneficiaries and voluntary agencies. The plan has also expressed itself against the adoption at local levels of uniform schemes based on model schemes evolved at district and higher levels. It was noted that all the target families to be helped for increasing their income above poverty line require training. Therefore, it has suggested the identification of the training requirements and formation of a Training Coordination Committee to coordinate the various training programmes. These various suggestions contained in the plan seem to be quite significant in the context of the realization that good plans do not by themselves guarantee anything unless appropriate ways are found to implement them.

Case Studies from Abroad

Malaysia

The Indian case studies have brought out some of the missing elements in local level planning for integrated rural development. Since what had been reviewed in those studies was only a programme and not a plan, the need for coordination of the programmes in the productive sectors of the economy and their further linking with infrastructural development and social development in a reciprocally supportive manner must be greatly emphasized. In addition, the prototype block plan, which was discussed, illustrates the technicality and complexity of the issues involved in micro-level planning. The other case studies—Malaysia and Nepal reviewed here serve to emphasize the two vital elements in the local level planning process, viz., the organizational structure and citizen participation. The need for a permeative planning mechanism in which people can genuinely participate has been emphasized in these studies.

The Malaysian case study on Muda Irrigation Project[13] indicates the methodology of integrated rural development in a selected rice-growing area in Malaysia. Initiated during the First Malaysian Plan (1966–70), it started primarily as an engineering project involving the construction of physical facilities. Although the major goal of the project was envisaged as promoting more intensive use of land resources by double-cropping and thereby increasing the level of national self-sufficiency in rice production, the concerned agencies, even during the period of physical construction, had begun to question whether the goals of income distribution and welfare were not equally legitimate. It was also realized soon that the physical infrastructure formed only a part of an overall innovative agronomic package and that a concerted and integrated approach to rural development was necessary to achieve the various goals of rural development. This eventually led to the creation of the coordinator's office for the project and the rephasing of the double-cropping programme into viable irrigation compartments, which made it possible to concentrate scarce resources in different sub-regions according to planned schedule. Inter-state problems calling coordinated planning, and inability of the State Governments to finance the project individually, led to the creation of a semi-autonomous organization—the Muda Agricultural Development Authority (MADA)—by the Federal Government in 1972. Its creation provided the administrative framework to undertake integrated rural development and to develop the structures by which local-level participation in decision-making could be initiated through the farmers' associations. The changing perspectives of Muda's role as a development agency and in relation to the farming community in general which is described in the case study, affords useful insights for local level planning and involvement by citizens. The second phase of Muda project which incorporates not only the engineering parameters but also the agricultural, social, political and economic parameters, also illustrates how agricultural facilities and several dynamic extension strategies should be formulated to ensure active farmer participation. The major extension strategies include the formation of fieldwork groups, revolving around the field neighbourhood concept, establishment or functional linkages between change agents and change recipients, organization of large scale pilot demonstration projects and the stepping up of existing extension services. The functional basis of the new institutional structure which links field work groups in irrigation blocks to small agricultural units and the area farmers associations has led to the development of a dynamic and commercialized farming community which, in turn, has further potentialities for increased involvement of farmers in local level integrated rural development planning.

The case study only critically assesses the components of a local level plan for integrated rural development. In particular, institutions emphasizing the grass-roots participation in rural development processes are required so that any new technology introduced into the area would be economically feasible, physically sound and socially acceptable. The study highlights the important ingredients for a successful implementation of the rural development plan which include (a) the formulation of an agronomic package, (b) the establishment of a semi-autonomous body to integrate the various aspects of the development process, and (c) the establishment of an institutional infrastructure consisting of farmers' associations and work groups to promote local level participation.

Nepal

Shrestha's study on local level planning in Nepal lays emphasis on the participatory process for rural development planning and the institutional arrangements that are desired to ensure the full-fledged participation of the low-income groups in the decision-making process in planning and implementation. The crucial issues in local development planning and implementation are discussed with special reference to the Raswer Niwakot Rural Development Project. This approach is designed to support His Majesty's government's development strategy, which seeks to balance economic growth with income distribution, provide for more equitable regional development and ensure productive benefit from previous road investment. For this purpose, a detailed investment plan has been drawn up and is being implemented through the sectoral agencies as well as the local panchayats. Case studies of three village panchayats have been undertaken to bring out the extent of citizen participation in planning, in implementation of projects as well as in their subsequent maintenance. The case study illustrations point to the following conclusions:

1. Given the opportunity, the village communities have the capability to plan and implement their own programmes,

mobilize their own resources and manage the project on a continuing basis. The case of reforestation project in Belkot village panchayat is an excellent example of local self-help effort of this kind. The case also emphasizes that development intervention by the government has to be judiciously identified so that it does not bring about any negative effect on the local initiative.

2. The institutionalization of the small farmers greatly helps the planning for local development, e.g., by assisting the poorer people to obtain loans on group-liability basis. The case study of Tupche village panchayat has brought out the importance of the supportive role of local panchayats in the Small Farmers' Programme as well as the effectiveness of the " 'small farmers' groups" in several areas of social development in the village, such as, promotion of family planning and avoidance of unproductive expenditure on social ceremonies. It has also revealed how the transformation of the poorer strata of the village is achieved through, 'small farmers'. The study has drawn attention to instances where the projects have failed, because of the absence of the involvement of public in the planning and development process.
3. Inter-sectoral consultation and accord are infrequent and ineffective in the planning process in the district. Therefore, there is no integrated planning at the local level. Sectoral planning which is mostly done at the national level lacks local focus. In other words, integration as a strategy for planning and implementation of sectoral plans has not been achieved in practice.
4. The existing planning procedures for the project are not based on the understanding of the critical ingredients of participation, viz., participation in decision-making, participation in implementation, including resource mobilization, participation in benefit-sharing and participation in evaluation. There is no permeative planning mechanism in which people can genuinely participate.
5. The current planning exercises are not based on an objective assessment of the existing situation. Neither officials nor the public representatives are equipped with the information necessary for it.
6. Citizen participation in the planning process is now confined to need identification only. In order to actuate integrated planning

at local level, the planning exercise at the village level has to be more than need indentification and must be a multi-sectoral endeavour encompassing all the components of planning. This would require considerable training and experience on the part of the village leadership and bureaucracy, and a sustained and integrated support, as that given to 'small farmers' groups' by the project management.

7. An important area of local planning is the creation and strengthening of institutional phenomenon which stands out in the context of Nepal is the 'user groups', which may be developed as an institution competent to plan, implement, manage and evaluate the project and to generate necessary resources for it. The Nepal case has also shown that such user groups should be promoted within the framework of village organizations. The establishment and nurturing of such an institution should be done as part of the extension and support functions to be performed at the district and service centre level and supported by necessary policy measures adopted at the national level.
8. While planning activity naturally includes review and evaluation exercises at regular intervals at each of the levels involved, it must be given a special place of importance in rural development at the national level.
9. Given the stratified nature of the village society, mere flow of resources to the local level does not necessarily result in their equitable distribution to all segments of local population. The Nepal case study amply illustrates this point.

Issues in Local Level Planning for Integrated Rural Development

The performance of local level planning for integrated rural development reviewed in the case studies can now be summarized with a view to drawing some lessons for the future. It is perhaps necessary at the outset to emphasize the point that the task of local level planning for integrated rural development is one of enormous complexity.

The case studies have provided some analysis of the constraints and potentials encountered during the process of local level planning for integrated rural development, of the mechanisms that have evolved to deal with them, and of the effectiveness of these mechanisms in improving the performance of the projects. What has been obtained from these analyses is a bundle of insights. In presenting a view of local planning for integrated rural development from these insights, it is assumed that the rural masses, especially the small farmers, tenants, landless labourers, artisans etc., will improve their productivity, income and living conditions on a sustained basis. The discussion, therefore, focuses on the following questions, which are closely interrelated:

1. A planning approach concentrating on a small geographic area seems to be the best way of local level planning for integrated rural development, as the intensive planning and implementation within a selected locality will help to identify the basic interrelations between the different components of the IRD and evolve the strategies which could be effectively replicated. Area development approach will also help to establish the cross-functional planning framework to link the micro-level planning to the macro target setting and planning. The development experience in many countries (i.e., India, Bangladesh) has demonstrated the usefulness of such an approach in coming to grips with specific problems.
2. The plan framework of area development should be both comprehensive and in line with resource and administrative capabilities. It is comprehensive in the sense that it takes into account, within the rural space, all the relevant sectors of the economy and uses the interrelationship so as to identify and exploit the linkages and external effects between those sectors. For such comprehensive planning, a method should be evolved through which the objectives can be transformed into action. The planning method should be flexible and adaptable to continuous changes. In the Indian context, the National Planning Commission has outlined such a method in its official guidelines.
3. In the orientation of the IRD there is the focus on the rural poor. The beneficiary-oriented style of planning, involving the identification of the target groups below the poverty line, preparing individual family plans for them and linking them to credit channels is an important component of the IRD programme, as operationalized in India. Planning for the target group and infrastructural development are complementary. In fact, the former can be effective only when supported by the latter and must therefore be preceded by it in the general sequence of implementation. While seeking to tackle the problem of rural poverty, the question of individual versus group approach assumes great relevance. The individual approach is more specific and effective, but time consuming and costly. In some

contexts, it may even be disliked by the people who may be averse to being identified as poor (e.g., Thailand, Sri Lanka). The group approach, on the other hand, may hasten coverage but would call for considerable effort towards institutionalization of interest groups, which, however, has a built-in risk that may lead to the monopoly of the dominant group. The decision as to the particular approach for any country will be determined by the circumstances peculiar to it and its level of development.

4. The systematic planning process at the grass-roots level implies the performance of the following technical functions:
   (i) Resource inventory and data collection including analysis of the prevailing levels of development, potential for further development and identification of constraints to development.
   (ii) Identification of priorities and selection of key programmes.
   (iii) Project/scheme formulation and the establishment of their spatial and temporal linkages within an integrated framework.
   (iv) Devising a plan for fuller utilization of manpower resource.
   (v) Assessment of availability of financial resources from various sources.
   (vi) Monitoring and concurrent evaluation or parallel audit of development plans and their modification from time to time in the light of experience.

   The successful performance of the above functions will demand the existence of a technical planning machinery. In the context of the paucity of trained personnel in the developing countries, the problem of the planning machinery has to be solved in appropriate ways. In India, the block level planning machinery is sought to be placed with the district planning organization and is thus envisaged as a peripatetic team.

5. The selection of appropriate projects/schemes is of crucial importance in local level planning for IRD. In any scientific approach to this problem, the selection should be preceded by an evaluation of all feasible projects/schemes. To be realistic, the projects/schemes must be grounded in resource inventory information. Lack of area specificity in the schemes selected and the failure to use the resources inventory information were revealed during the discussion of Indian case studies. In most exercises on local level

planning, project formulation has been reduced to a selection of limited, uniform and standardized set of schemes. Since the planning agency at the local level is not equipped to find technological solutions, there seems to be no immediate solution of this problem. In this context, the provision of better organizational support to local level planning for integrated rural develpment in terms of technical staff to perform the functions of economic programme identification, assumes great importance.

6. The concept of local level planning for IRD is wider than that of agricultural development or community development alone. It implies a consciously formulated, systematic, multi-sectoral programme to attain enhanced productivity and diminished poverty. It means *simultaneous* planning of the economy—agriculture, industry and services—at the local level where development actions are taking place. The expression 'simultaneous' must be underscored because it refers to the coordinated planning of these activities, the result of which will lead to a plan composed of concrete projects for implementation. The case studies, for instance, have revealed that increasing the resource base of the rural poor is no doubt important but not sufficient.[14] It is also necessary to follow up the whole system of income generation.
7. Local level planning for IRD is a highly coordinated exercise in two senses. Firstly, it seeks to integrate multiple objectives viz., more production, more employment and more equitable distribution of income. How to achieve such an integration is the crux of the problem. Lack of built-in mechanisms for coordination among the various sectoral departments concerned with local level planning for IRD is the greatest single problem in the rural administrative system. In the studies reviewed, coordination seems to depend purely on the personal relations of the district chief with the departmental heads. It is in this context that the role of a properly conceived micro-level plan assumes great significance. It could well become an instrument for achieving effectiveness in coordination. Thus, if a plan of action is prepared in advance, every departmental activity falls in its place and to that extent coordination is facilitated. Another way in which coordination could be facilitated is by clothing the district chief with adequate authority over the area, by bringing all the line departments effectively under him and by giving him, for

instance, the powers to allocate among the sectoral departments such as is done in Sri Lanka.

8. One of the glaring constraints on local level planning for IRD is provided by the administrative system which is usually oriented towards sectoral and departmental activities rather than geared to area development or development of certain target groups. To overcome the difficulties that arise from this conflict, other patterns of organization are thought of, e.g., establishment of special authorities for development. The unique feature of such authorities as compared with other government agencies is that their scope of activity is not vertical by function or sector, but horizontal by area. Generally, the authorities that have been established belong to development authorities responsible for planning and for coordination between the organs of implementation (e.g., SFDA in India).[15]
9. Local level planning for integrated rural development can succeed only if it is designed both for the people and with the people. The real test of local participation is in the share of actual population and especially the poorest among them. The exercise of this power is demonstrated in the process of decision-making regarding the allocation of resources, and planning of the operational details of the plan as well as involvement in reviewing problems of implementation and responsibility for the up-keep and maintenance of project etc.
10. The formulation and implementation of plans for local development require personnel who have received training beyond that of their specific disciplines. Experts in a certain field must learn how to relate the role of their disciplines as an interdependent part of a comprehensive area plan. This requires knowledge of associated fields of development and experience in a team approach to area analysis. Such training enables the planner to maximize his contribution as member of a multidisciplinary team and to coordinate integrated development activities. The training programmes should consist of short practices and action-oriented courses combining theoretical lectures with practical application and demonstrations.
11. An important aspect for consideration during the implementation process is the provision made for the regular monitoring of the programmes particularly from the point of view of the impact on the target population. In India, the arrangements made for

monitoring the family plans were quite detailed. But the arrangement for monitoring the linkages of family plans with other programmes was not adequate.

12. One of the vital issues on which clear indications were not available was relating to the question of the linkages necessary between the local plan and the higher level planning (e.g., national including sectoral, and regional planning). This has implications for sustaining the success of the family plans at the local level. While the need for multi-level planning is clear, the procedures and mechanisms for initiating iterative and transactive planning must be evolved in country specific situations. More in-depth studies are needed in this context.

In conclusion, it can be said that a fair amount of methodological progress has been achieved through the work undertaken by several national and international agencies and research institutions. There is, however, still room for considerable progress regarding the actual application of such methods in the field. In this context, there is great need for in-depth analysis of the process of local level planning in individual countries and evolving appropriate guidelines.

Notes

1. The removal of unemployment and significant underemployment, an appreciable rise in the standard of living of the poorest section of the population and provision by the State to provide basic needs to the poor people have been embodied as the primary objectives Of India's Draft Sixth Plan (1978–83). These objectives have been set out to be achieved within a period of ten years.
2. The meaning of 'full employment' in this context is neither the provision of full work to all those who are looking for jobs nor ensuring the full utilization of all available material resources in the local area. It is limited to the generation of additional employment and the raising of the income level of the identified target groups above the poverty line.
3. This approach of identifying the poorest families for individual assistance has been termed 'Antyodaya Approach' in the Indian Plan. According to the programme, about 400 families below the poverty line are to be identified in a block in a year and provided with the necessary support. According to the Planning Commission, poverty line refers to individual income of Rs 63 per month. The case studies have adopted a family income of less than Rs 400 per month for identifying the families below the poverty line.

4. 'Small Farmer' in India is one who has less than five acres of unirrigated or 2.5 acres of irrigated land. 'Marginal Farmer' is one who has less than two acres of land.
5. The baseline survey is intended to (a) facilitate an assessment of the prevailing situation, i.e., the natural resources and their level of utilization in the area, (b) identify the gaps, and (c) provide a benchmark against which further development progress can be measured. The resource inventory which is the most important aspect of baseline survey will consist of the inventory of (a) physical and biological resources, (b) human resources, and (c) infrastructure and institutions. The guidelines have also provided an illustrative list of essential information necessary for block level planning.
6. A method of assessing the financial size of a block plan has been indicated. The guidelines have suggested the placing at the disposal of the block a certain amount of 'untied grants' from the State. This will give some degree of freedom to the local level planner. Since each item in the budget is determined in advance by the concerned sectoral agencies, the normal budget structure does not provide much leeway for the dynamic process of local level planning for integrated rural development.
7. Average area and population of a block in India is 600 sq km and 80,000 to 1,00,000 respectively.
8. It is in fact a continuum of the city, "a suburb gradually merging into rural homesteads".
9. For the fishermen in the block, it is the technology, which needs to be upgraded. But the programme has not applied itself to such problems,
10. Groundwater information had pointed to the scope for digging new wells. But very little has been attempted by way of minor irrigation works.
11. Project implementation was confined to making available the subsidy for the needed inputs without any technical guidance for adopting improved agricultural practices.
12. The linkages of the family plan with the other components were weak.
13. "Local Level Planning for Integrated Rural Development: The Muda Irrigation Project" by L.J. Fredericks.
14. For example, by giving a milch animal or two, the small farmer's problem does not get solved. It is equally important to organize an efficient marketing system.
15. SFDA is only a coordinative agency, and has to rely on other agencies of government for various implementation tasks. The problems confronting a coordinative agency are complex, as it has to deal with a network of relationship, both with local agencies of the government and the various units of local government.

14 Panchayati Raj and Rural Development in India

Ramesh C. Shrivastava

When Panchayati Raj was started in India, the basic idea was that at the local level there should be certain amount of democracy which would give to people a sense of involvement, otherwise there was democracy at the state level, and democracy at the national level, i.e., election to the state legislative assemblies, election to the parliament, but at the local level there was no democracy, it was ruled by administrators. That's what was felt. If the people are to be involved they have to be given some sort of involvement in the functioning of the institutions or development programmes. This is the only way to take democracy to the masses. In fact, in a real democracy, people have an opportunity to get involved in development programmes. So the idea at that time was that decision-making level should be closer to the people.

The Panchayati Raj aims at establishing democracy at grass-roots level and providing a sense of involvement to the people at the village level. As Mahatma Gandhi said: "In a democracy, decentralization of political and economic power is essential, because a few centres of power cannot realize or fulfil the needs of vast multitudes of people. If India is to develop the power and responsibilities must be shared by all." The failure of our poverty alleviation and rural development programmes to achieve their avowed goals fully highlights this fact.

These programmes were designed by few people at the top and have been implemented without the involvement of people at grass-roots level. They do not reflect the needs and aspirations of people and thus fail to satisfy them.

Historical Background of Democratic Decentralization

When Mahatma Gandhi discovered that there was no mention of Panchayati Raj (PR) in the earlier draft of the Constitution, he insisted on its inclusion in the revised draft, because PR was an important component of his vision of future India in which economic and political power was decentralized and each village was self-reliant economically. He felt that people's voice should be reflected in our independence through panchayats, and therefore, "the greater is the power of panchayats, the better is for the people". Article 40 of the Constitution of India which was included in the chapter on Directive Principles of State Policy, said that "the state shall take steps to organize village panchayats and endow them with such powers and authority as may be necessary to enable them to function as units of self-government".

In the post-independence era, the introduction of the Community Development Programme (CDP) in 1952, with people's participation as its central concern, was perceived as a project which would transform the socio-economic life of the village community. But, the entire programme suffered due to the lack of involvement to the beneficiaries and their representatives in the planing and execution of development schemes meant for them. It was realized that CDP would be meaningless unless it becomes a people's programme with officials guiding them and supplying them with technical knowledge.

The Balwant Rai Mehta Study Team (Committee) was appointed in January 1957 to study and report on the Community Development Projects and National Extension Service. The Study Team offered two broad directional thrusts: (i) there should be administrative decentralization for effective implementation of development programmes, and (ii) the decentralized administrative system should be under the control of elected bodies.

The Committee further realized that development cannot progress without responsibility and power, community development can be real only when the community understands its problems, realizes its responsibilities and exercises the necessary powers through its chosen representatives. With this objective the Committee recommended an early establishment of statutory elective local bodies and devolution to them of necessary resources, powers and authority. The Committee therefore thought PR system as a means of involving people and their representatives in development programmes of the government. While explaining its philosophy, the Committee remarked the PR system establishes a linkage between local leadership enjoying confidence of local people and the government.

The three-tier PR system as recommended by the Mehta Team was first launched in Rajasthan and Andhra Pradesh in 1959. Almost all the states were quick to introduce the PR as per the Directive Principles of the Constitution. PRIs in different states and UTs have been set up under different legislations.

The basic theory behind the PR is to ensure people's participation in development programmes. Initially, it was intended that they will unleash the arrested process of change and growth, but after some time it was observed by several state level committees as well as by various studies that PR system was suffering from a number of weaknesses, and the other Asoka Mehta Committee was set up in 1978 to look into its working in various states and to make recommendations for strengthening it.

The Asoka Mehta Committee viewed that PR system was not only meant for decentralization of power and people's participation, but also for supporting rural development and strengthening the planning process at the micro level. The Committee, therefore, wanted PRIs to participate in development activities in the areas of agriculture, forestry, cottage industries, welfare activities etc.

With the launching of anti-poverty programmes and setting up of district rural development agencies (DRDAs) and other related organizations at lower levels, the need for integration of PR system with development programmes and administration was felt. C.H. Hanumantha Rao's Working Group on District Planning (1983) and G.V.K. Rao Committee (1985), set up to review the existing administrative arrangements for rural development and poverty alleviation programmes, have given recommendations for this purpose. The G.V.K. Rao Committee, for example, has recommended strengthening of Zila Parishads and district level planning as well as integration of block and lower level planning with lower level PRIs. In 1986–87, the Singhvi Committee had prepared the concept paper on Panchayati Raj. It recommended for Panchayats to be closely involved in planning implementation of rural development programmes at lower levels. The Singhvi Committee has recommended that Village Panchayats of groups of small villages if necessary should be made viable. It has also supported the recommendations of the G.V.K. Rao Committee for integrating administrative structures with Panchayati Raj Institutions. The Singhvi Committee as well as Asoka Mehta Committee suggested suitable constitutional amendments for the purpose.

Limitations of PRIs

Indeed, the concept of Panchayati Raj has undergone some changes over the years. Though it began as a narrow concept, it has expanded to cover the areas of rural development and economic planning to a reasonable extent. However, there are certain limitations that have been broadly identified as follows: (i) the concept is still very narrow as it does not view PRIs as institutions that can play an important role in the overall development of rural areas or in other words, the present concept does not see a PRI as a planning as well as implementation agency of various rural development programmes, and as an agency that can take care of routine administration, infrastructure and socio-economic welfare of rural population; (ii) there is no clarity about how to involve the weaker sections in the functioning of PRIs; (iii) there is, therefore, considerable confusion about the role of PRIs in rural development programmes, specially anti-poverty programmes; and (iv) there in no clear trend emerging in the context of decentralization of power. While, in the recent years, there is heavy talk about decentralization of power to district and lower level bodies, on the other hand central schemes are increasing both in number and size.

Past Experience

The past experience of PRIs had been a state of neglect and impoverishment. Even after being in existence for about four decades, PRIs could not acquire the status and dignity of a viable unit of self-government and responsive people's body. Several factors are responsible for the slow growth of PRIs; e.g., absence of regular and periodic elections within a stipulated period, prolonged supersession, variation in structure, powers and functions from state to state, insufficient representation of weaker sections including SCs, STs, OBCs and women, inadequate devolution of powers, lack of financial resources and above all lack of political will. PRIs, being the potential centres of people's power, aroused apprehensions in the minds of bureaucracy and elected representatives at the national and state level bodies so they were not quite willing to share power.

Rural Development Programmes: Historical Perspective

In free India, the Community Development Programme (CDP) was started in October 1952. This humble beginning had very ambitions objectives. The CDP was launched with the goal of transforming the outlook of the people, inculcating the spirit of self-reliance and generating the habit of cooperation through public bodies. The National Extension Service (NSS) scheme was introduced in October 1953. throughout India for assisting the process of development planning. These programmes ensured people's participation by organizing non-statutory committees at the village and block levels. Notwithstanding the many criticisms of CDP, it has made a positive contribution, howsoever small it may be, to the economic and social development of rural India.

Broad Spectrum of Activities

There are three stages of rural development. The first stage of rural development includes co-operative village management, rural extension programmes, community development, abolition of intermediaries, land reforms, democratic decentralization, additional investment in agriculture, irrigation, industry and so on. These development activities were expected to change the rural scenario, divert rural people from agriculture to other occupations and reduce the pressure of population on agriculture. But there was no spectacular change in the rural economy even though the economy as a whole made some progress.

In the second stage, new technology in agriculture was introduced. Production increased but did not improve the economic condition of rural people. From the starting of the Fourth Plan (1969–74), an attempt was made to attack poverty by poverty eradication programmes like Small Farmers Development Agency (SFDA), Marginal Farmers and Agricultural Labourers Agency (MFAL) and Drought Prone Area Programme (DPAP). In the Fifth Plan (1974–79), the Minimum Needs Programme was introduced to improve the quality of life of the poor.

Since all this did not bring about substantial improvement in rural area, a number of radical poverty eradication programmes were introduced in the Sixth Plan (1980–85), which continued during the Seventh Plan (1985–90). These programmes included:

1. Employment planning at the block level through National Rural Employment Programme (NREP) and Rural Landless Employment Guarantee Programme (RLEGP).
2. Integrated Rural Development Programme (IRDP) which extended the scope and content of SFDA, MFALA etc., and which aimed at the real integration of various programmes.
3. Revised minimum needs programmes.
4. Special area programmes for hilly and forest areas and for other backward areas.
5. Emphasized distributive justice through land reforms, extended public distribution system for mass consumption goods etc.

Another item of rural development which elicited wide public attention is the Jawahar Rozgar Yojana (JRY), a programme for providing additional gainful employment for the unemployed and underemployed persons in rural areas. Representing a merger of NREP and RLEGP, the scheme attempts to provide fuller employment opportunities to at least one member of each family below the poverty line who seeks unskilled employment.

An Employment Assurance Scheme (EAS) for providing assured employment to as many as 2,470 rural poor blocks of 261 districts was started in October 1993. The objective of the scheme was to provide about 100 days of assured casual manual labour employment during the lean agricultural season at the statutory minimum wages. Under EAS, more than 4.30 million persons have been registered and more than 4.81 crore man-days have been generated.

As regards self-employment for educated youth, both in urban and rural areas, the Prime Minister's Rozgar Yojana (PMRY) has been launched. It is meant for setting up micro-enterprises by educated unemploy youth. The earlier scheme for Self-Employment of Educated Unemployed Youth (SEEUY) has been amalgamated with PMRY.

But unfortunately, the rural development programmes failed to involve people in the planning and implementation of programmes. It was noticed that the CDP as well as other rural development programmes, instead of being people's programmes with government's assistance, were becoming more and more government's programmes with varying degree of people's participation. PRIs were also found weak and ineffective to mobilize the masses in support of the programmes.

Experience of various rural development programmes reveals that a mere project approach or a sectoral approach is not adequate to lead to an overall development of the area and distribution of benefits to local population, particularly the weaker sections of the society. The distribution of unemployment and poverty and the potential for development of agriculture and related activities vary widely from region to region and also within a region. Different areas in the country are at different levels of development and have varying degrees of potential, depending on local endowments. The efforts will now be to make the programme area-specific and utilize the local endowments for growth, social justice and full employment. It will, therefore, be necessary to plan for integration of various programmes and establish appropriate linkages for optimal utilization of local endowments consistent with the plan objectives, local needs and environmental balance.

Though development has taken place, but its gains have not yet reached every family in the rural India. There still remains a vast majority of the rural poor and the landless labourers for whom greater efforts need to be made in terms of creating employment opportunities and providing assistance in income generating with a view to enabling them to cross the poverty line. Though the government has in the past, tried to solve this gigantic problem with the help of available resources through various rural development programmes, but still the poverty of the rural areas calls for more effective and efficient rural services.

Besides, as the experience indicates though initiatives by the government to help rural poor have reduced the incidence of poverty, many of the programmes could not yield desired results, mainly due to lack of people's participation and well-organized institutional support, particularly at the grass-roots level. Therefore, a number of measures were taken to ensure that the benefits of these special schemes reach the real poor. For instance, people belonging to weaker sections were given priority in the development efforts so that the benefits of planned investment can go to the relatively backward sections of the community.

Panchayati Raj and Rural Development

PRIs have been assigned the most important task of rural development. They inevitably occupy the most prominent place in our democracy. The new PR system has two main objectives: the first is to strengthen the democratic set-up at the lowest level and the second is the socio-economic upliftment of the rural masses. The main motive is to bring about socio-economic development of villagers and to raise their standard of living by their active the willing participation. As we have seen in the past, the overall picture of the working of the PRIs has not been very impressive and satisfactory.

The 73rd Constitutional Amendment Act, 1992 has broken a distinctly new ground. The PRIs deserve to succeed as the principal vehicles for rural development. The economic development through various programmes that are to be taken up during the Eighth Plan, which has a massive provision for rural development, has to be channelized by provision of adequate funds and powers to the PRIs with the active involvement of the grass roots organizations in both planning and implementation. The quality of implementation will also improve as the PRIs are ideally suited to effective implementation of the programmes entrusted to them.

Involvement of people at the grass-roots level has been considered as the most effective means through which economic development can meet aspirations of the people and to ensure that the benefits really percolate down to the lowest strata of the society.

The Eleventh Schedule of the Constitution of India lists twenty-nine subjects which ought to provide an effective role to the PRIs in planning and implementation of works of local significance ranging from drinking water, agriculture, land and water conservation to communications, poverty alleviation programmes, family welfare, education libraries and cultural activities, maintenance of community assets etc.

The 73rd Constitutional Amendment Act has introduced a new PR system throughout the country. The primary goal has been to proceed with decentralization, dispersal and redistribution of power. It seeks to give responsibilities to the three-tier PRIs to make them the true decision-making centres with local power.

It is notable that the PRIs are the primary institutions of democracy where people from village, block and district could participate. Devolution of power has to start here and this is also where people at local levels get into the mainstream of development as well as public affairs. The PRIs, especially the 'Gram Sabha', make the concept of 'direct democracy'. The Gram Sabha has been designed to be the place where development issues should be discussed, development programmes initiated and beneficiaries of development schemes selected. It may be added that the prospects of the PRIs would be on the increase keeping in mind the pace of economic liberalization in India. In fact, they would become watchdog bodies to ensure proper implementation of the employment generation programmes. In fact, the PRIs would play an important role in accelerating socio-economic development in the rural areas.

It is hoped that administration of rural development and welfare schemes would be greatly facilitated through democratic decentralization and the three-tier structure of self-government envisaged in the 73rd Constitution Amendment Act. The question of devolving adequate powers on PRIs is being vigorously pursued by the centre with the states. Together with this, the rural development programmes have received added impetus in the wake of substantial set-up in central allocation, which have gone upto Rs 30,000 crores in the Eighth Plan from Rs 11,000 crores in the Seventh Plan.

In the Ninth Plan (1997–2002), the PRIs in rural areas will be directly involved in the development process. People's involvement through their elected representatives will be realized through genuine democratic decentralization.

References

Desai, Vasant, *Panchayati Raj,* Himalaya Publishing House, New Delhi,1990.

Gandhi, Mahatma, "India Independence Must Begin at the Bottom", *Kurukshetra,* February 1989.

Government of India, *Constitution of India,* New Delhi.

———, *First to Eighth Five Year Plans,* Planning Commission, New Delhi.

Gramin Vikas Newsletter, Ministry of Rural Development, New Delhi, May 1993 and April 1994.

Hirway, Indira, "Panchayati Raj at Grassroots", *Economic and Political Weekly,* Vol. XXV, No. 29, July 1989.

Mehta, B.R., *Committee Report on Plan Projects,* Planning Commission, New Delhi, Vol. 1, 1959.

Mishra, B.N., "Rural Development", *Kurukshetra,* March 1991.
Mishra, S.N., *New Horizons in Rural Development,* Mittal Publications, New Delhi.
Prasad, Mahesh, "Planned Development to End Inequality", *Yojana,* January 1996.
Ramanujam, K.N., "The Philosophy of Rural Development", *Kurukshetra,* January 1995.
Rao, P.V. Narasimha, "Education Expansion Will Help Strengthen Panchayati Raj", *Yojana,* Vol. 33, No. 1–2, January 1989.
Report of the Committee on Panchayati Raj Institutions, Government of India, New Delhi, 1978 (Chairman: Asoka Mehta).
Report of the Working Group on District Planning, Vol. 1–2, Planning Commission, New Delhi, 1983 (Chairman: C.H. Hanumantha Rao).
Sathe, Vasant, V., "Panchayati Raj: Its Validity", *Yojana,* Vol. 33, No. 1–2, January 1989.
73rd Constitution Amendment Act, Government of India, New Delhi.
Trivedi, Bhupat J., "What it Holds for Rural Development", *Kurukshetra,* January 1992.

15 Panchayati Raj and Poverty Alleviation

Need for New Administrative Structure

R.S. Kumat

Panchayati Raj and Local Self-Government have become inevitable with the 73rd Amendment of the Constitution of India. Most states have enacted appropriate legislation and even conducted elections but they have not yet become functional. Neither the politicians nor the bureaucrats are willing to transfer the powers, funds or subjects as envisaged in the Constitution and the State Acts. All sorts of announcements are being made from the house-tops to take credit for the elections eulogizing the Panchayati Raj Institutions (PRIs) but no effective steps are being taken to make them functional. On the contrary, excuses are being made for not doing so.

The Central Government, recently called all the elected representatives of Panchayati Raj and had a big mela addressed by the Prime Minister. Some announcements were made to strengthen the Panchayati Raj. But it appears that things are being thrust upon the states which seem to be unwilling to initiate the process of decentralization and democratization at the village and district levels. Bureaucrats are infamous for not having faith among the elected representatives but it appears that even the elected politicians at the higher levels, i.e., central and state levels, do not have faith in the politicians at the lower levels, i.e., Zila and village levels. Analysis that ensues will prove it and an attempt will also be made to show how things are moving at snail's pace to thwart the functioning of PRIs and the elected representatives are getting frustrated day by day; the potential that could be exploited with great advantage is being lost in the process. It is a moot question whether the politicians do not want it or the bureaucrats but the fact remains that the things are not moving and it appears that some Bhagirath is needed to bring the Ganges of Panchayati Raj on to the land, which has got entrapped in the jata of Shiva, in the manner it was envisioned and envisaged by the late Prime Minister, Rajiv Gandhi.

In the first place, some states have not yet conducted the elections though the last date by which the PRIs should have come into existence was one year from the date 73rd Constitutional Amendment came into force and more than a year has elapsed since then. The Central Government is threatening to stop grants for the erring states but there is reaction to that step. Is it really essential that the Central Government should use such measures? Is it not the duty of the states themselves to implement the constitutional provisions expeditiously?

Even the states, which have conducted the elections, have not yet transferred the functions and funds as envisaged in the Act and the Constitution. As per the Constitution of India 29 subjects are to be handled by the PRIs. In the Panchayat Acts of the respective states, division of functions between the state sector and the panchayat sector has been provided but the powers to execute those works have not been transferred for one reason or the other. It is said that they are awaiting the report of the State Finance Commission to decide the devaluation of funds but that should not stand in the way of transferring funds and functions designated for these institutions. In the absence of transfer of functions, no Zila Parishad can become functional except in those states where they were already functional even before the constitutional amendment.

Delay in transfer of work to the elected PRIs is causing frustration among the elected representatives and perhaps to pacify to them, the Central Government recently announced that Chairmen of the DRDAs (District Rural Development Agencies) will be the Zila Pramukhs (Chairman of the Zila Parishad) instead of the Collector of the district. Although the details of the announcement are not readily available, it is, however, learnt that the Zila Pramukh would only preside over the meeting of the Governing Council of the DRDA but the financial powers would rest with the Collector who would continue to be the Chairman of the Executive Committee of the DRDA. Before understanding the implications of the announcement, it is worthwhile to understand the full background of the DRDAs and their relationship with the PRIs.

DRDAs are the successors of SFDAs (Small Farmers Development Agencies) and MFALs (Marginal Farmers and Agricultural Labours, Agencies) constituted in pursuance of Venkatsubhaya Committee which opined that credit institutions were not providing credit to the small and marginal farmers and due to that green revolution had totally bypassed them. These agencies were set up to identify small and marginal farmers and work as a catalyst to channelize credit for them. When IRDP (Integrated Rural Development Programme) was launched in the country as a whole on October 2,1980, agencies of SFDA and MFAL renamed as DRDA were set up in all the districts of the country and major poverty alleviation programme was launched through them in the form of IRDP and NREP (National Rural Employment Programme, now renamed as Jawahar Rojgar Yojana or JRY) to provide income earning assets through banks and institutional agencies and provide employment for all people living below poverty line. In order to implement these schemes, funds were routed through the DRDA, a registered society under the Society Registration Act and the Collector was made the Chairman of the society. A senior officer was appointed as Project Director or the Chief Executive of the DRDA. All the financial and administrative powers were given to the Collector and the Project Director. All elected representatives to the State Legislature and the Parliament and the Zila Pramukhs and Pradhans were made the members of the general body of the DRDA. Even though, in some states, where the PR (Panchayati Raj) bodies were existing and functional, DRDA was kept separate and independent of the PR bodies. Zila Pramukhs or the Pradhans (Chairmen) were to attend as members in the governing councils of the DRDA presided over by the Collector. In Maharashtra and Gujarat, where Zila Parishad was an important executive body for development tasks, the chairmanship of the DRDA was entrusted to Chief Executive Officer (CEO) of the Zila Parishad rather than to the Pramukh of the Zila Parishad.

An academic question was raised at that time too that wherever PRIs were in existence and functional, the work of DRDA should be entrusted to them but this was not done on one pretext or the other. It was argued that the PRIs represented the elite and the landed aristocracy and they may not promote and/or safeguard the interests of the weaker sections of the society. It was argued that there was exploitative relationship between the landed aristocracy and the small farmers and the landless labourers and the elitist PRIs may exploit the weaker sections. It was, therefore, decided that the DRDA may be kept independent of the PRIs and the Collector and the Project Director should execute the programme strictly as per the guidelines. Since then, for last fifteen years, DRDAs have been functioning independently though most of the programmes are being executed through PRIs wherever they exist. Targets are assigned to the Block Development Officers (BDOs) and they in turn get executed through their own machinery and/or through Sarpanchas and Panchas. In many states, the administrative head at the state level both for PRIs and DRDAs is the same but in many other states, there are two separate departments, one dealing only with the administration of PRIs and the other with poverty alleviation programmes. This dyarchy resulted in non-participation of elected representatives in the programmes of development and poverty alleviation. Frustration grew wherever PRIs existed as the elected representatives were only to attend the quarterly meetings of DRDA and hear what the bureaucrats read out to seek their approval.

Let us see the administrative pattern of PRIs and their relationship with the DRDA in Rajasthan as shown in the chart below:

The chart shows the dyarchy prevalent in the administration of PRIs. All poverty alleviation programmes are run by the DRDA but the implementing agencies are the Panchayat Samitis and Panchayats. The Collector controls the officials of the Panchayat Samitis administratively, and as such he is able to co-ordinate between the DRDAs and the PRIs. As a result, all development plans and initiatives therein are dependent on the office and personality of the Collector. Elected representatives get sidelined and become dependent on the officials and specially the Collector. Why the elected bodies should not have fully independent charge of the development plans and are allowed to take initiative so that people at large participate in the development process?

Proposal of the Government of India to continue the Collector as Chairman of Executive Committee of the DRDA reflects the lurking

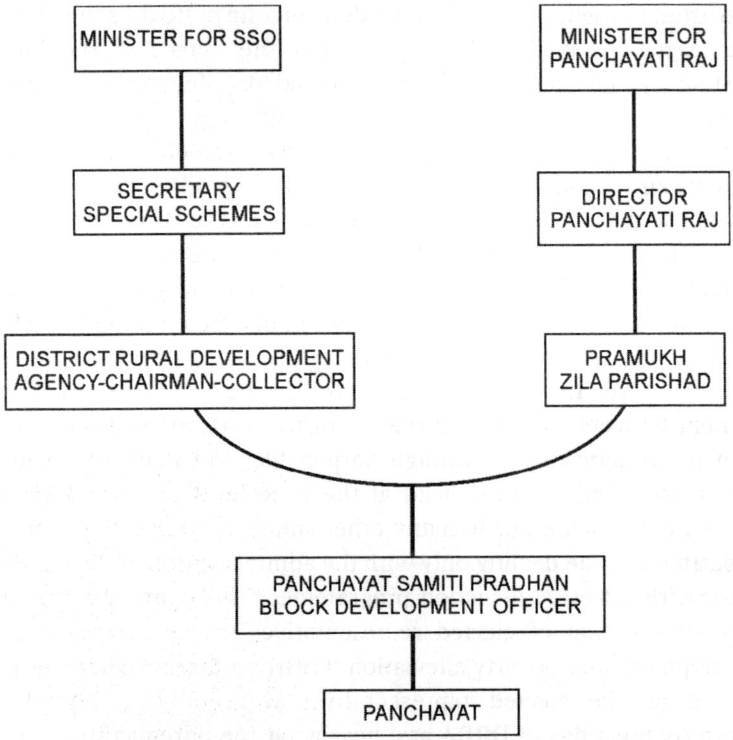

suspicion about the elected Zila Pramukhs and other elected representatives. Proposed arrangement will cause tension and confusion between the elected representatives and the Collector. There in no need to have one more hierarchy as between the Chairman and the Chief Executive of the DRDA. The line of command should be clear and direct and without dual or multiple control.

If the PRIs are directly involved, a new administrative structure will be needed and a view of same may be depicted as follows:

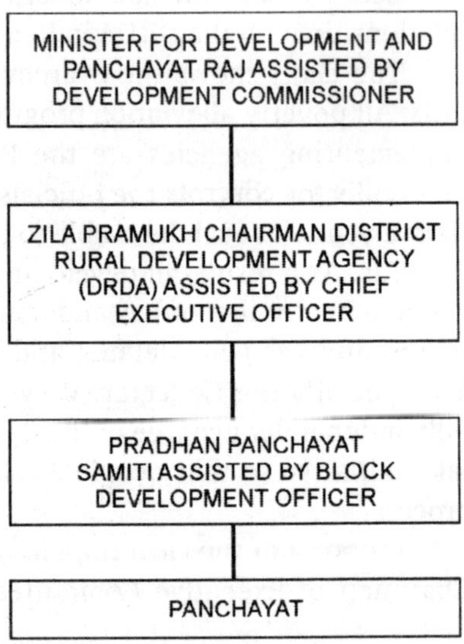

The chart clearly shows the uniform line of command

and a direct linkage among elected representatives without any dependence on or interference of officials. There is no need for the Collector to be in the picture. Let him be free to look after much-neglected subject of land revenue administration and land records management. This will also ensure reposing of full confidence in the elected representatives. Any other arrangement, wherein authority and responsibility are separated, is bound to fail and will result in dyarchy or multiple hierarchy creating confusion in the system and frustrating the very purpose for which PRIs were envisaged.

16 Finances of Panchayati Raj Institutions

A Study

A.P. Barnabas

The Panchayati Raj Institutions (PRIs) are to be seen in the context of local self-governments. Local self-government refers to where people of a locality possess certain responsibility and discretion in the administration of local public affairs and in raising the required finances to meet the expenses. The concept of local governments needs to be emphasized because the state with its multitudinous activities which affect all aspects of life tends to become monolithic and also because of its being distanced from people it tends to be impersonal. The local governments, therefore, can provide a human touch in the performance of their assigned duties. The local government is concerned with the government of specific local area constituting a political sub-unit of the state. The process of decentralization is both political and administrative. All this assumes substantial autonomy of the local self-government.

The local self-governments are expected to perform the following functions:

1. Promotion of popular participation.
2. Spurring of economic development.
3. Social transformation.
4. Equitable distribution of fruits of development.

Effective decentralization should mean that the local government is an instrument of decision-making with local autonomy, administrative capability, ability for planning and having necessary resources—human and material—to implement the decision. The structure and functions of the PRIs should be analyzed in terms of their capacity to fulfil the functions listed.

The PRIs came into existence for (i) increasing people's participation, (ii) decentralizing administration, and (iii) setting up local self-government in rural areas as a result of B.R. Mehta Committee's recommendations in 1959. However, there is a tradition of Panchayat in India. Many states in the late 1940s and early 50s had passed legislation to establish Panchayati Raj. Presently, the 73rd Amendment Act governs the PRI's structure and functions.

Among the provisions of the Act are:

1. A three-tier system except in cases where a state has a population of less than 20 lakhs.
2. Reservation of seats to SCs/STs in proportion to their population.
3. One-third of the seats reserved for women.
4. State legislatures to endow the PRIs with powers, functions and authority to levy taxes.
5. Constitution of a Finance Commission in each state to review the financial position of the PRIs.

The Study

Objective

It is essentially an extraordinary study to collect primary data with regard to the financial situation of the PRIs at the district, block and the village levels. The assumption was that such a study would provide sensitizing data to the Finance Commissions which could be used by them in making their recommendations. More specifically, the objective of the study was to collect data with regard to the income and expenditure of the PRIs at all levels for at least two to three years and to analyze resource situation with regard to the functions allocated to the PRIs.

Method

Three states were chosen in consultation with the Ministry of Rural Development, viz., Maharashtra, Gujarat and Rajasthan. Three districts in Maharashtra, two in Gujarat and two in Rajasthan were selected. Efforts were made to choose one in developed area and the other in backward area.

The attempt was also to study two Panchayat Samitis in each of the districts and two villages in each of the Panchayat Samitis. In all, seven Zila Parishads, 11 Panchayat Samitis and 24 village Panchayats were covered. The data available varied in different districts, blocks and villages. As the time available for study was limited, the data collected, although varied, were considered adequate for a sensitizing and exploratory study.

Data were collected through documents and interviews with officials at the state, district, block and village levels. Discussions were also held with the non-officials at the district, block and village levels as and when possible. In all the states the chairmen and secretaries of the Finance Commissions were also interviewed.

The Findings

The Set-up

The two states—Gujarat and Rajasthan—passed a new Act on Panchayati Raj in 1994 which included the provisions made in the 73rd Amendment Act. All the three states already had a three-tier system and as such no radical changes were required. Elections have been held in Maharashtra and Rajasthan before the passing of the new Act, whereas in Gujarat elections were due to be held.

In Maharashtra, there are 29 Zila Parishads, 298 Panchayat Samitis and 26,000 Village Panchayats. The PRIs came into existence in 1662, in accordance with the provisions of the Zila Parishad and Panchayat Samiti Act, 1961. The Zila Parishad is the pivotal unit in Maharashtra. It was felt that there was better technical and administrative competence available at the district level than at the lower levels. The number of members of the Zila Parishads elected directly varied between 50 and 75. There is also reservation for SCs/STs. There are nine committees, namely, Standing, Finance, Works, Education, Animal Husbandry, Agriculture., Water, Social Welfare and Health. There are five full-time chairmen of the sub-committee, some of whom have more than one subject to deal with. The Panchayat Samiti is the weak link. Members are elected directly. There is a Committee of Sarpanchas which is a consultative body. The Village Panchayat consists of 7 to 15 members. There is reservation for SCs/STs and women. The Sarpanch is elected from amongst the elected members. The statute provides for Gram Sabha which is to meet at least twice in a year.

Functions

There are a large number of functions assigned to the PRIs according to the Act (129 for Zila Parishads and 75 for Panchayat Samitis). However, the Zila Parishads execute and maintain works of development transferred to it by the state government, execute schemes on agency basis and undertake any other development work from its own resources. By and large, the Zila Parishad performs agency functions. The Panchayat Samiti is a sub-agent of the Zila Parishad. The Village Panchayat undertakes functions assigned to it by the Panchayat Samiti or the Zila Parishad. When it has its own funds it may take up any activity for the improvement of the village.

Administrative Set-up

The Chief Executive Officer (CEO) who is the administrative head of the Zila Parishad is from the IAS cadre. There are also two Deputy CEOs. Besides, there is a large number of Extension Officers who belong to the State Administrative Service. There is also a Finance Officer. The Block Development Officer (BDO) is the head of the block. His control over the technical officers is limited as they are accountable at the district level. The Village Development Officer is the incharge of a number of villages whereas the Gram Sewak is allocated to one village.

In Gujarat, the pattern of PRIs is more or less the same both with regard to the set-up and administration. At the village level, there is a Talaticum-Mantri and also a Gram Sewak incharge of a number of villages.

In Rajasthan, the Panchayat Samiti is the more functional unit. The BDO can be from any of the departments. There are five Extension Officers but none in agriculture and animal husbandry. The CEO, the head of the Zila Parishad administration, is from the State Administrative Service. There is also one Finance Officer.

Variation

There is great variation in income at all the three levels, both inter-state and intra-state. In Maharashtra, while one Zila Parishad had a budget of Rs 103 crores, another had Rs 40 crores although 95 per cent of the amount came as grant. In Gujarat, the variation was from Rs 107 crores to Rs 14 crores. The level of development and the population partly explains the difference. There is need for a deeper analysis of the variation and the factors contributing to it. Recommendations should have a bearing with regard to the funds available for the more backward areas. In Maharashtra and Gujarat, the Panchayat Samitis (Taluka Panchayats) acted as sub-agents of the Zila Parishads. The funds for the functions it performs come from the Zila Parishad's budget. There was some difficulty in getting the finance data at the Panchayat Samiti level in Maharashtra. In Gujarat, where information was available, the variation was from more than Rs 8 crores to Rs 2 crores in the grants received.

The budget of the Zila Parishad in Rajasthan was meagre. For Jaipur Zila Parishad it was only Rs 1.19 crores. The situation was more or less the same in other districts. The Panchayat Samiti got grants directly from the state government which also varied. Of the two Panchayat Samitis studied, one had a budget of Rs 1.08 crores and the other Rs 2.20 crores.

In Maharashtra, the income of Village Panchayat varied from Rs 17.3 lakhs to just Rs 6,922. In Gujarat, the variation was from Rs 13 lakhs to Rs 32,400. The Village Panchayats which had special advantages are those near the cities. They can collect house tax and octroi and also take donation from industries situated near or in village itself. Land royalties from minerals and sand also provide good income.

In Maharashtra, the honorarium paid to the chairman of Zila Parishad was Rs 5,000 plus other facilities like house, transport and telephone. The vice-chairman got Rs 4,000 and other facilities. In Gujarat, the honorarium paid to the chairman was Rs 1,500 and so also in Rajasthan. The backward districts in Maharashtra felt that the honorarium paid to the office-bearers of the Zila Parishad was a strain on them.

It might be of interest to note that of the nearly 5.6 lakh villages, 2.7 lakh had a population of less than 500. Another 1.4 lakh had a population between 501 and 1,000. There were about 9,000 villages with the population of more than 5,000. The situation with regard to the district was similar. There were variations at the block level from a population of 14 lakh to a little more than one lakh. (When the blocks were originally created in the early 1950s, the idea was to have a specific population, 65,000 to 70,000, and to make administrative arrangements accordingly.)

Resources

Their own resources amounted to between 3 per cent and 5 per cent of the total budget at the Zila Parishad level. This income was from cess on land revenue, share of taxes on vehicles, profession, forest and stamp duty. Some Zila Parishads had income from the land and property they own. At times there were grants for specific purposes. The income of the Panchayat Samitis was also from stamp duty, land revenue, share and grants for schemes etc. The income of the Village Panchayats included taxes, auction of fruits and grass, rents etc. A part of the land revenue collected in the village is also given back to the Village Panchayats.

Taxes

This Zila Parishads in Maharashtra and Gujarat can levy a cess on land revenue. A small percentage of the stamp duty collected by the state is also given to the Zila Parishads. So also with vehicles, professions and forest produce. There is no sharing of taxes in Rajasthan. There is, however, a land revenue grant. The Panchayat Samitis do not levy any taxes. However, the Village Panchayats, according to the Act, can levy taxes on as many as 18 items. But, they collect taxes only on three or four items.

In Maharashtra and Gujarat, for sharing of land revenue, the following formula is followed: 35 per cent is retained as collection expenditure by the revenue department and 5 per cent for District Development Fund. Of the remaining, 50 per cent to go to Village Panchayat (as per revenue earned in their jurisdiction,) 25 per cent to Panchayat Samiti and 10 per cent to Zila Parishad, 7.5 per cent to District Equalization Fund and 7.5 per cent to District Village Encouragement Fund.

The basis of sharing taxes is arbitrary and the percentage given to PRIs is different among the states.

The size of the population is taken into consideration in making grants. In Rajasthan, a per capita grant of Rs 4 is made to the Village Panchayats.

There is a need to study as to how there can be some criteria or formula (as in land revenue) with regard to sharing of all the taxes and duties collected. In Maharashtra, one per cent of the stamp duty collected in the district goes to Zila Parishads. In Gujarat, it is seven per cent.

Tax Collection

The tax at the village level is collected by the Gram Sewak or Talati-cum-Mantri. Substantial time is spent on this activity which adversely affects extension work. There is no machinery for collection of taxes at the Zila Parishad and Panchayat Samiti levels.

Funds

The District Equalization Fund is to be utilized by the Zila Parishad for reducing the socio-economic inequality among the Panchayats which fall within its jurisdiction. Further, analysis is necessary to assess the actual amount received and the manner of its expenditure.

The District Development Fund is constituted by grants from the state government and contribution by the Zila Parishads and the Village Panchayats. Loans can be taken by the PRIs for undertaking development projects. However, the utilization is very limited.

Strict Control on Grants

The Zila Parishads and Panchayat Samitis depended on about 95 per cent or more in two states and 100 per cent in one state on the grants from the state government for their activities. The concerned administrative departments continue to supervise the financial and technical matters. Further, the controlling officer makes the necessary budget provision for the transferred schemes. He also monitors the expenditure and is responsible to answer to the auditors. The role of the Zila Parishad in budgeting is, therefore, very limited. It has little power to reappropriate the funds according to the needs of the area. In Maharashtra, the BDOs complained that they were subject to five different audits in a year.

The PRIs do not have the freedom to invest their own funds except in government securities.

There is no such control on Village Panchayats as they collect their own funds and can utilize them for the welfare of the village.

Areas for Consideration

Taxes

The major share of taxes comes from land revenue and stamp duty. The income to the PRIs from vehicle, profession and forest produce is very meagre. There is some effort to increase the cess on land revenue and stamp duty. Similar action can be taken with regard to other taxes.

It is possible that Zila Parishads could be allowed to levy taxes or cess on education, cash crops, and income of factories. In Rajasthan, Rs 10 per household is collected for education. But the collection has not been good so far.

The possibility of the revenue department collecting taxes on behalf of PRIs should be explored as is being done for land revenue. May be the collection then would be more efficient. In many cases, a big gap was found between the demand and the actual collection by the Gram Sewaks.

Block Grants

Reference has been made to strict control over the grants received by the Zila Parishads. The suggestion of a block grant which the PRIs could appropriate to specific activities to meet the felt needs of the area was not generally welcomed. It was felt that the Zila Parishads did not have the capacity to plan and budget for development activities of the area. Some time ago, there used to be 'united grants'. The possibility of reviving these grants should be given due consideration. Also, a training programme for the Zila Parishad officials and non-officials to enable them to plan and implement the welfare activities of the district could be arranged.

Resources

The general feeling expressed both by the officials and non-officials was that the capacity of the PRIs to increase their own resources was limited. The potential sources of income at all the levels are development of property (shopping complexes, housing, land leased to industries and companies etc.). Wherever industries exist a cess can be levied on the taxes paid to the state by them. Utilization of land for cultivation of grass and fruit trees was another item from which income was being received. However, it is difficult to assume that the PRIs can be self-sufficient to perform the duties assigned to them. In one state it was suggested that the funds required for carrying out functions assigned to the PRIs should be fully provided for by the state as usual with necessary controls.

Funds

The District Development Fund can provide loans to the PRIs. However, there are few takers. If the loan is not repaid then that amount is recovered from the grant accrued to the PRIs. Given the reluctance to repay the loans by the villagers, the situation is understandable. (One Zila Parishad had more than Rs 1 crore in the fund but unutilized.)

People feel that any loan taken from the government is not to be repaid. Hence, the PRIs were not keen to take loans for activities for which people have to pay. One Village Panchayat which took loan for housing is finding it extremely difficult to recover it from the people.

The question of credit and credit management requires an analysis in-depth.

The Equalization Fund is to help reduce inequalities among the districts and within the districts. The utilization of fund and its impact needs to be looked at from the points of view of adequacy and efficiency.

Development Activities

There are a number of development activities which are not under the purview of the PRIs. There was negative response to the suggestion of the DRDA funds and activities being merged with the PRIs by all the officials and many of the non-officials. Although there is some coordination in the programmes, the programmes are single-line activities. There is a need to have a comprehensive view of the totality of development activities in a district and the amounts spent thereupon.

Another area that needs to be probed is the amount spent for establishment. It was mentioned that about 80 per cent of the grants go for establishment. It is difficult to define 'establishment'; generally salaries, maintenance, transport and the like are included in it. A detailed analysis of the amount spent on establishment and the amount actually spent on development schemes per se should provide insights with regard to the process of development.

Some General Issues

The financial resources of an organization are only a means to end. The PRIs were conceived as local self-government which meant planning at the local level, mobilization of adequate resources and the evoking people's participation. Judged by these criteria, the PRIs have a long way to go. The grants given to the PRIs for schemes are decided upon at the national or state level. The grants are monitored and controlled by controlling officer. At best, the role of the PRIs has been to function as an agency. Hence, the rules that are followed are those that are operational for an agency. The local government can be autonomous, partner with the state and an agency. The need is to move it from a purely agency role to that of a partner. May be this would help in moving towards autonomy. The question to be considered is to what level would be the most viable unit for local self-government to become autonomous. From various aspects, it would be seen that the district should be considered the most suitable unit. The administrative system to fulfil the functions of the PRIs is not adequate. The number of functions assigned to the PRIs is very large (e.g., 129 for Zila Parishad and 75 for Panchayat Samiti in Maharashtra). Although the administrative support is quite good in two states, in all the Zila Parishads and the Panchayat Samitis there was reference to the inadequacy of the number of personnel to implement the programmes. In Rajasthan, there is no administrative set up at the district level. At the Panchayat Samiti level, there are only five Extension Officers, none in agriculture or animal husbandry, although both these activities are listed as part of the functions of the Panchayat Samitis.

Although the functionaries belong to the State Development Cadre/Panchayat Cadre but the salaries for all come from the state. They are recruited and appointed by the state. The debate regarding centralized vertical administration versus decentralized horizontal administration is an old one. As there is no resolution of this debate, the administration tends to be mixed up. A clear analysis of the staff required to implement the schemes that have been assigned to the PRIs and their status is necessary.

Rural development connotes the overall development of rural areas' productivity, employment, infrastructure, social service and people's initiative. It is multidimensional. There is, however, ambiguity as to what constitutes rural development. Self-help, increased production, minimum needs and full employment have been the different approaches in India. The concept of integrated rural development is confined to IRDP at present which is only one activity in rural development. In the early days of community development, integrated rural development had a very different connotation.

In two states more than 50 per cent and in the third state 80 per cent of the budget of the PRIs goes to primary education. While not denying the importance of primary education, the question is whether it can be equated with rural development. The PRIs are to be instruments of rural social transformation.

If the PRIs are to be effective agents of social change, there is need for clear objectives of rural development, greater delegation of power in planning and managing the finances and an adequate administrative set-up over which it has greater control. Such an approach could provide for an effective and functional approach to integrated rural development.

Ultimately, the question is whether there is the political will to make the PRIs an effective instrument of change or are PRIs to be used only as a political rhetoric.

17 Women in Panchayati Raj Institutions

Beginning of a New Era

Pawan Kumar Banta

Panchayati Raj Institutions (PRIs) are a grass roots democracy in our country. They have provided a new dimension to rural development and democratic decentralization in direct administration. By involving PRIs for the development of the rural areas, maximum utilization of human and material resources is possible. For effective and meaningful functioning these bodies would depend on active involvement, contribution and participation of its citizens—both male and female. The participation of women in democratic process is woefully inadequate at all the levels—central, state and local. Rural women are the single largest group of backward citizens, who neither have access to power structure nor any other effective method to overcome their age-old inequality and subordination.

The provision for reservation of one-third of seats for women in PRIs as incorporated in the 73rd Amendment Act should be viewed as an attempt to improve the socio-economic status of women. A beginning to safeguard the rights to women was made by Pandit Jawahar Lal Nehru with the passing of the Hindu Code Bill. The various measures initiated by different governments were mainly directed at the improvement of women's welfare, education and health, while attempts were made to remove social disabilities of which rural women were the victims.

It is necessary for this purpose to go back into the history of efforts of free India to foster PRIs and follow their checkered course. Leaving aside the Gandhian and Sarvodaya concepts of village self-sufficiency, the cognate ideals of grass roots democracy and decentralized planning have received the overt support of many political leaders and administrators in the country. The First Five-Year Plan itself harped on this ideal in the following words:

> For democratic planning to succeed, it will have to energize the entire community. The crucial factor here is leadership, not only leadership at the top but at all levels.[1]

Elaborating on this theme, the Second Five-Year Plan observes:

> The village panchayats should be organically linked, with popular organization at a higher level, and that by stages determined in advance, democratic bodies should take over the entire general administration and development of the district or the sub-division, perhaps other than such functions as law and order, administration of justice and revenue administration.[2]

But the distressing fact is that these professions have been translated into practice. Only periodically, either with the approach of elections which require alluring slogans or with the launching of quinquennial plans which need impressive preambles paeans of praise are sung over the Panchayati Raj. Occasionally, there have been some genuine attempts at soul-searching which led to the constitution of committees to inquire into the reasons for the tardy progress of plan projects in the countryside.

One such committee was headed by Balwant Rai Mehta, whose report was published in 1957. This report begins with a sanguine motto:

> So long as we do not discover or create representative and democratic institutions ... and invest them with adequate powers and assign to them appropriate finance, we will not be able to evoke local interests or local initiative in the field of development.[3]

Reflecting on the then existing situation, the committee noted with dismay the vast gulf between the ideal and the reality. The Block Advisory Committee is generally nominated and never invested with powers of decision. We have found that often they are unrepresentative of some important sections of the local public. The District Planning Committee is perhaps even less powerful.[4]

The Balwant Rai Mehta Committee spelt out in unmistakable terms what decentralization and development of power really means. Decentralization, on the other hand, is a process whereby government divests itself completely of certain powers and responsibility and devolves them on some other. It is true that devolution of responsibility cannot be complete without a complete devolution of all the control over necessary resources. If the local bodies are to function with any vigour, initiative and success, the government will have to devolve upon it all of its own functions in these fields (like agriculture, medical, relief, education etc.) reserving to itself the functions of guidance, supervision and higher planning.[5]

But where do we stand now forty years after that report was accepted and ostensibly acted upon? The recent debate on Panchayati Raj has been revolving round the adequate participation of women in PRIs though the issue was brought in focus in Balwant Rai Mehta Committee report which recommended induction of two women members in panchayats to carry on the specific programmes for women and children. These two women members were to be co-opted in case they did not get themselves elected. Following the recommendations of this Committee women joined PRIs in many states as adopted members rather than elected ones. The principle of co-option/nomination did not produce the desired results. It resulted in sheer patronage of dominant socio-economic and political groups and co-opted women members owed allegiance to them. They were neither aware of their roles, rights and duties, nor did they know much about the functioning of PRIs. The had virtually no political experience to actively participate in proceedings of PRIs or taking up issues or specific problems of women and children. Thus, their contribution in decision-making process has been inconsequential. They have seldom been able to articulate and represent the interest of their gender. Realizing the futility of co-option/nomination, some states like Andhra Pradesh, Karnataka, Maharashtra etc., resorted to reservations to ensure adequate representation of women in PRIs. Since then, there had been persistent demand for reservation for women in adequate proportion in local bodies. Orthodox rural society, patriarchal and feudal forces, illiteracy resulting in lack of access to information and media, and poor exposure to outside world make rural women extremely weak and vulnerable than the women in urban areas. Adequate reservation quota is probably the only answer to ensure their representation in PRIs.

Following the recommendations of the Balwant Rai Mehta Committee, the three-tier system of Panchayati Raj was adopted with much fanfare in many regions of the country in the early sixties. But the enthusiasm lasted only for the first term of five years and, in the second term, the PRIs began to drag their feet. The seventies saw these institutions generally suspended all over the country. It needed a change of government to call for another introspective exercise over the dismal failure for the experiment.

The Asoka Mehta Committee, which was constituted by the Janata government, submitted its report in 1978. Besides offering several suggestions for the reorganization of the PRIs, the Committee also attempted to explain why they had failed to strike roots and develop properly in the preceding decades. The causes identified by the Committee, as one could guess, were not new. The main culprit was the continuing chasm between profession and practice, as a result of which the institutions that came into existence in the wake of the recommendations of the Balwant Rai Mehta Committee, embodied only the shell but not the substance of self-government. The PRIs were neither invested with adequate powers nor were they endowed with necessary financial autonomy. The very existence of the local bodies was dependent on the whims or conveniences of the state governments.

The rueful review given by the Asoka Mehta Committee reads as follows:

> A number of developments in the past have conspired to undermine the Panchayati Raj structure and made them ineffective. In fact, except in Maharashtra and Gujarat, the PRIs have been rarely given an opportunity to take up planning or implementation work on a sizeable scale … . The initial idea that all the developmental activities should flow only through block level organization (Panchayat Samiti) lost ground. In practice, there was a movement in the opposite direction. Some schemes were not brought within the purview of elected bodies. The planning work in some states was entrusted to a body outside the Zila Parishad under the chairmanship of a minister. The staff spared by the state to the district and lower bodies also gradually came to consist of officers who were not wanted by the state government. Financially, the quantum of resources contemplated for the Panchayat were both meagre and their potential also was not exploited by the PRIs in good measure.[6]

Moreover, there are diverse views as to what constitutes a viable basic unit for planning. For many years, a Community Development

Block with a population of one lakh or more was considered ideal for developmental administration. But some felt that it is too big for effective planning at the grass-roots level. On the other hand, an average village has been found to be too small and its resources too slender for effective planning. States like Kerala opted for a basic unit with a population of about 15,000. West Bengal and Assam too have chosen similar basic units for the Panchayati Raj. Their success in working of PRIs seems to have mainly influenced the Asoka Mehta Committee to prescribe a basic unit with about 20,000 population and an apex unit at the level of the district with an average population of one million.[7] Again, there is nothing sacrosanct about the two-tier system. The Asoka Mehta Committee itself envisages Gram Sabhas at the level of each village which are to be operational arms of the Mandal.[8] It is legitimate to ask why the Asoka Mehta Committee did not accord a statutory status to such Gram Sabhas, making for a three-tier system.

The Asoka Mehta Committee found that the PRIs have suffered a serious setback in the absence of regular elections and due to perfunctory audit. What is more, there has been an allergy to sharing authority with these nascent institutions both at official and political levels.[9] According to the Asoka Mehta Committee, the antipathy of the legislators and members of parliament towards the PRIs in which they apprehend a threat to their own positions was one of the main reasons why the PRIs were not able to develop properly.[10] The Asoka Mehta Committee also recommended the reservation of seats for various categories of the weaker sections of the rural society including the women in PRIs.

In 1987, a committee under chairmanship of L.M. Singhvi was formed to review the functioning of PRIs and to suggest measures for their revitalization. It recommended reorganization of villages to make village panchayats more viable. It suggested that they should have more financial resources and that there should be judicial tribunals in each state to adjudicate controversies about election to these local bodies their dissolution etc., including other matters relating to their functioning.[11]

It may thus be seen that women who constitute almost half of India's total population, have been given an opportunity for participation in local affairs as not less than one-third of the posts of chairpersons have been reserved in their favour. This provision would bring in a qualitative change in the composition of local bodies and make women and weaker sections equal partners in the nation's progress and development. As stated earlier, orthodox rural society, patriarchal and feudal forces, illiteracy resulting in lack of access to information and media, and poor exposure to outside world make rural women extremely weak and vulnerable than the women in urban areas. Adequate reservation is probably the only answer to ensure their representation in PRIs. The Committee on Status of Women in India (1974) not only recommended representation of women in PRIs but also establishment of statutory women panchayats at village level as a transitional measure for managing the programmes for women and children. This recommendation has never been adopted though such women panchayats have emerged in some states like Andhra Pradesh, Maharashtra and Karnataka. The U.N. Women's Decade which influenced women's thinking all over the world and forced governments to shift the emphasis of women's programmes from welfare to development. As an outcome of this shift of emphasis, the Government of India prepared a policy document, viz., the National Perspective Plan (NPP) for Women (1998–2000) on the basis of which implementation strategies to make the system more responsive to women's needs would have to be operationalized.

To secure effective participation of women in the decision-making process at national, state and local levels by the government, the NPP made several recommendations at sectoral level, of which two pertain to special measures for recruitment of women candidates to the PRIs, as under:

1. Reservation should be made of 30 per cent seats at Village Panchayat to Zila Parishad level and local municipal bodies for women. Whenever possible, higher representation of dalits/tribals women of weaker sections should be ensured.
2. Thirty per cent of executive heads of all bodies from Village Panchayat to Zila Parishad level and a certain percentage of chief executives of PRIs at lower, middle and higher levels must be reserved for women.

The Sarkaria Commission too made some far-reaching recommendations for fostering self-governance at the district level. One of the recommendations is to make consultations with the District Planning Board obligatory for formulating plans at higher level.[12] Favouring an objective mechanism for devolution of funds to the districts, the commission lays down:

> It is necessary to evolve a mechanism like Finance Commission at the state level, to enable the state government to take an objective view of the resources to be devolved or transferred to the districts.[13]

Only when the process of self-governance is strengthened at the district level and is thence carried further down to the local bodies, does Panchayati Raj acquire some content. Otherwise it remains an empty phrase.[14] According to Ram Reddy, the PRIs are viewed more as agencies of the government for the execution of its development programmes rather than as autonomous bodies.[15] Thereby, he makes it clear that the local bodies do not formulate their own plans and only implement what is planned for them at the higher echelons. Underlining the importance of block in planning and development administration, and realizing the need to preclude the possibility of the Zila Parishads overshadowing the Mandals, the Asoka Mehta Committee spelt out the interrelations between the two units in careful and cautious terms:

> With the assistance of the district planning cell, the concerned departmental functionaries stationed at the block level, will be able to build up suitable projects about various schemes and also suggest potential areas of development and the type of requirements that have to be met .... The Block Panchayats should continue to play their role in continuously articulating their interests. The planning units at the district should take note of these and incorporate them into the block plans.[16]

Rarely did the Block Parishads have a say in the matter. In spite of all the talks, the government does not seem to be prepared to set the people plan their own development with resources statutorily kept at their disposal. Why not let the people commit mistakes if it is inevitable, and learn from them as the Balwant Rai Mehta Committee report clearly enunciated? In the ultimate analysis, as the report goes on to say, "the local body must be the instrument of expression of a people's will with regard to local government".[17]

Marcus Franda, in his book, *India's Rural Development,* tries to sum up the paradox in which the country seems to be caught. He says:

> The western liberal democratic solution to India's local government problems would be simply to make each administrator feel responsible to elected politicians at every level. In most Indian states, however, a familiar argument of government leaders is that rural people need, for the time being at least, political tutelage to ensure that they act in conformity with the state and national priorities.[18]

What is the way out of this paradox? It can only be in the form of a real faith in the people and in self-governance of the PRIs, which has to be distinguished from election slogans. If any guidance should come from the top it should only be to safeguard the interests of the weaker sections. C.T. Kurian examines the nature of planning at the district level and concludes with a negative comment:

> The point to note, however, is that 80 per cent of the district plan outlays is disaggregated and apportioned among departments at the state level itself. This part, therefore, does not come under district planning in any meaningful sense. It is little more than a statement of the fact that a certain portion of total state plan funds can be shown to be spent on schemes that have a direct baring on the districts.[19]

Stressing the fact that the machinery for planning depends on the content of planning, he draws pointed attention to the narrow limits within which the planning apparatus in a district functions:

> On the content of planning at the district level, the Seventh Plan approach document is quite explicit as already pointed out: antipoverty programmes, and greater regional balances ought to be its main objectives. But, on both of these, the accent seems to be on better implementation rather than formulation of plans.[20]

Perhaps seeing no hope for district planning to come into its own under the present set-up, a former Governor of Punjab and former Cabinet Secretary has suggested that there should be a constitutional amendment to make the district level administration the third tier in the federal structure of the country after the union and the states.[21] It follows that there are more important things that ought to be considered by Constitution Amendment Bill than a directive to the states that electoral rolls should be prepared in the constituency of every Panchayat.

The Shilu Ao Committee, which examined the working of tribal development blocks, expressed the view that the size of a block should be bigger and its resources larger if it should serve as an effective base for development administration. Hence, it may be best if the states are left to choose the kind of structure that is most suited to them. Even within a state, there can be different patterns for different terrains.[22]

Panchayati Raj, as a system of governance, has got ebbs and flows in Indian policy ever since India attained independence. At present, it has gained momentum in development administration as a sequence of failures on the part of the Indian state[23] in administering development in rural areas through various approaches modelled on the west. Panchayat as a unit of administration carried out its functions within the framework established by the provisions of the Constitution of India. Success and failure of the units are attributed depending on the sway of the units over the populace. Yet the full dimension of the Panchayat has not been visualized by the administrative thinkers, though Mahatma Gandhi considered it as the vibrant thread of Indian democracy. As the Indian state is under threat, the leaders of the nation began to think of an alternative unit to bring development in rural areas, and they identified Panchayati Raj as suitable vibrating and viable unit of development administration.

India is now on the threshold of a historic transition of political power to grass roots with all the states completing the process of enacting fresh legislation for strengthening PRIs. Under the 73rd Constitutional Amendment Act of 1992, which came into effect on April 24, 1993, all the states were required to legislate afresh or amend their existing Panchayat Laws to bring them in conformity with the provision of the constitutional amendment with one year. The new Panchayati Raj system gives the country a whopping 22.5 lakh elected representatives with reserved seats for SCs/STs in proportion to their population and women who are allowed 33.3 per cent representation in all the three layers of the system. Twenty-nine areas of development have been identified in which the elected panchayats will have a free hand in planning and disbursement of funds. These include land reforms, agriculture, small-scale industry, animal husbandry, education upto the secondary level and health care. Obviously, all these are the activities in which the women have a crucial role to play despite the several handicaps they are confronted within the rural life. The objective of the enhanced representation in executive bodies of PRIs is likely to remove isolation of women from development and political process of village polity.

The 73rd Constitutional Amendment Act of 1992, which will be legislated upon in all the states, incorporates salient provisions concerning political participation of women in local government:

- In all the Panchayats, one-third of the seats will be reserved for women.
- One-third of the seats reserved for SCs and STs to be reserved for women.
- One-third offices of chairpersons of Panchayats at all levels shall be reserved for women.

— Women and child development forms part of newly added XI Schedule of the Constitution of India.

The 73rd Constitutional Amendment Act of 1992 visualizes Panchayats as vibrant and dominant vehicles for change at the grass roots level. The new Act provides for:

— preparation of area plans by Village Panchayats;
— addition of the XI Schedule of Constitution with a detailed list;
— provision of a share in finances from State Commissions to be established.

Notwithstanding the statutory provisions, past record clearly brings out the lip-service paid to panchayats in devolving powers, functions and resources. This may become a grim reality in the aftermath of the structural adjustment programme underway and concomitant cuts in governmental expenditure especially in health education, public distribution system, social welfare etc., to reduce fiscal deficit. History is witness to the fact that gradually since 1958, functions, powers and personnel were pulled out of Panchayats on one pretext or the other with a few exceptions. This is corroborated by the Asoka Mehta Committee and G.V.K. Rao Committee on administrative arrangements for rural development. In such cases, invariably, the axe fell on programmes and personnel for women development programmes.

In order to implement the new Act in letter and spirit, a strategy for human resource development needs to be evolved in order to strengthen women's role in panchayats, training is needed for leaders and workers at varied levels:

— Gram Sabha level for adult women.
— Panchayat level for members and chairpersons.
— Policy and administrative level for functionaries.

The principal components of the training should be:

— Orientation on provisions of 73rd Constitutional Amendment Act of 1992 and members' responsibilities.
— Orientation on rural development programmes.
— Management development of chairpersons/leaders.
— Gender sensitization of leaders, administrators and communities to change attitudes and beliefs.
— Training of trainers.

The existing network of village level workers, training centres, extension training units, state institutes of rural development and field training centres of non-governmental organizations could be utilized for the purpose of training. These bodies are endowed with infrastructure for training such as audio-visual aids, classrooms accommodation and faculty. Training will equip the newly elected women members to play their roles effectively and efficiently as harbingers of women's empowerment. Gender training has to remove gender stereotypes and misconceptions that women are subordinate to men. The National Perspective Plan recommended that a committee should be formed to look into the training needs of women panchayat members.

The crucial element in any decentralization would be to identify the functions, responsibilities and powers a state government decides to devolve on the local bodies and what financial resources are placed at their disposal. Consequently, the restructuring of bureaucracy would be an essential part of any process of decentralization. There would inevitably be some resistance from the bureaucracy to the attempt at restructuring. But the government cannot evade its responsibility much longer while expecting heroics from other sector. A greater degree of accountability is imperative that cannot be ignored.

In conclusion, it may be said that the Indian women today are not what they were ten years back. With the fast changing socio-economic scenario being witnessed today, coupled with the political empowerment, by the turn of the century, they are not going to be what they are today.

Notes

1. *First Five-Year Plan,* Government of India, New Delhi, 1952, p. 2.
2. *Second Five-Year Plan,* Government of India, New Delhi, 1957, p. 2.
3. Balwant Rai Mehta Committee Report (*Report to the Committee on Plan Projects*), Government of India, New Delhi, 1957, p. 7.
4. Ibid., p. 6.
5. Ibid., p. 7.
6. Asoka Mehta Committee Report (*Report of the Committee on Panchayati Raj Institutions*), Government of India, New Delhi, 1978, p. 4.
7. Ibid., p. 43.
8. Ibid., pp. 44–45.
9. Ibid., p. 5.

10. Ibid., p. 58.
11. Uma Joshi, "Women's Role Imperative for Strong PRIs", *Kurukshetra,* June 1994, pp. 19–20.
12. Sarkaria Commission Report, Recommendation No. 176.
13. Ibid., Recommendation No. 178.
14. N. Subba Reddy, "Panchayati Raj Institutions: Saga of Deceptive Slogans and Broken Pressures", *Mainstream,* Vol. XXVII, No. 27, p. 27.
15. G. Ram Reddy, *Pattern of Panchayati Raj in India,* Macmillan, 1977, p. 33.
16. *Asoka Mehta Committee Report*, p. 77.
17. *Balwant Rai Mehta Committee Report*, p. 6.
18. Marcus Franda, *India's Rural Development,* Indiana University Press, 1979, p. 123.
19. C.T. Kurian, "Decentralization Perspective in VIIth Plan" in M.S. Adiseshiah (ed.), *Seventh Plan Perspectives*, Lancer International, 1985, p. 228.
20. Ibid., p. 289.
21. Nirmal Mukherjee, "Transfer of Power", *Illustrated Weekly,* Bombay, July 2–8, 1989.
22. N. Subba Reddy, op. cit., p. 23.
23. S.N. Jha et al., *The State Political Process and Identity: Reflections of Modern India,* Sage, New Delhi, 1989, pp. 33–34.

Section III

Panchayati Raj: Cross-State Experiences

18 Dynamics of Administrative Reforms in Panchayati Raj System

A Study of Village Secretariat in Andhra Pradesh

D. Ravinder

The Government of Andhra Pradesh, as part of its administrative reforms measures in the name of 'good governance', introduced a new institution at village level known as the Village Secretariat, merging Panchayati Raj (PR) and revenue departments. The introduction of Village Secretariat system, leave alone providing good governance, brought new problems at the grass roots administration, not only within the governmental departments but also between the officials of the government and elected representatives. These new problems emerged in socio-political, administrative and financial domains. In this paper, an attempt is made at probing into these newly emerged problems to understand the underlying dynamics and nature of administrative reforms aimed at good governance in Andhra Pradesh.

Structural Innovation

The 73rd Constitutional Amendment Act has accorded an important place to local governance. The village panchayats were given prime place and called for strengthening of Panchayati Raj Institutions (PRIs). The Act emphasized the introduction of an official functionary to assist elected representatives. This official functionary was entrusted with the duties of day-to-day administrative affairs at village level and proper maintenance of accounts.[1]

In accordance with the 73rd Constitutional Amendment Act, the state of Andhra Pradesh modified its earlier legislation and brought the new Andhra Pradesh Panchayati Raj Act (Appract), 1994. Accordingly, the state government constituted a cabinet sub-committee[2] to recommed administrative reforms in PR system, as per the provisions of the new Act. It is this committee that recommended the creation of the Village Secretariat at the village level merging revenue and Panchayati Raj Departments as an experiment. This recommendation went beyond the spirit of the 73rd Amendment Act in combining the functions of that department.

On 1st January 2002, the state government, in line with the recommendations of the said committee, launched a new system of Village Secretariat, headed by Panchayat Secretary.[3] The then Chief Minister, N. Chandra Babu Naidu, explaining the objectives of the new system, said that Gram Sachivalaya (Village Secretariat) system would change the pace of development in villages and it may usher in a new work culture for the benefit of the rural people. It will provide better opportunity to villagers to get their work done. He also said that in the village administrative set-up Sarpanch would act as the key person in guiding the Village Secretary.[4]

In Andhra Pradesh, there are 21,943 Gram Panchayats. Out of these, 1,319 were notified Gram Panchayats that had the post of an Executive Officer, who used to assist the Gram Panchayat in its administration and was responsible for the maintenance of accounts and other administrative matters, prior to the introduction of present reform process. The remaining 20,264 Gram Panchayats were non-notified; in these, there was no post of an official functionary on full-time scale to assist Sarpanch in local administration.[5] With the launching of the new system of 'Village Secretariat', all the Gram Panchayats in the state have been declared as notified. Thus, the Panchayat Secretaries were appointed in all the Gram Panchayats.[6]

Before the introduction of the Village Secretariat, the government used to carry out administration at the village level through three different functionaries, viz., Executive Officers (EOs), Village Development Officers (VDOs), and Village Administrative Officers (VAOs). Of these, first two categories, i.e., EOs and VDOs belonged to the Panchayati Raj Department, and the third to the Revenue Department. The Panchayati Raj Department functionaries (EOs and VDOs) used to execute government's policies/programmes and undertake developmental works, whereas the Revenue Department functionary (VAO) used to handle land records. The introduction of the new system of Village Secretariat merged the posts and functions of two departments under one functionary of the Panchayat Secretary.

The 'job chart' of new Panchayat Secretary specified duties, covering every activity of the government, which included maintenance of land records, azmaish of crops, issuing income and caste certificates, birth and death registrations, taking precautions to meet natural disasters like cyclone, heavy rain, earthquake etc., maintenance of law and order, passing of information to the higher ups regarding murders, clashes between communities/persons, suspicious characters/strangers etc. The statutory functions assigned to Panchayat Secretaries are attending regular meetings convened by Mandal Presidents/Parishad Development Officer (MDO), Mandal Revenue Officer (MRO), district heads and implementing government schemes like Janmabhoomi, Neeru-Meeru, Clean and Green and self-help groups like the DWCRA. The job chart also included the duties to collect land revenue, house taxes etc. Besides these, an additional responsibility to inform the officers concerned on the pilferage of electricity. Thus, in a nutshell, the job chart considered that the Secretary shall act as 'friend, philosopher and guide' in all the government activities at the village level.[7]

Conflicts and Contradictions

It has to be understood that the new reforms at the grass-roots level introduced by the State Government in the name of 'good governance' have also been guided by the World Bank policies. The process of liberalization and the World Bank's slogan of 'good governance' and decentralization have structural interconnections.[8] It is a known fact that the policies and programmes of the Government of Andhra Pradesh have been influenced by the World Bank agenda in various sectors.[9] The new reforms introduced at the rural governance level are aimed at withdrawal of state from the welfare activities, privatization of natural resources and reduction of government employees. It is stated that one of the conditionalities of World Bank is to reduce the number of government employees.[10] In view of this, the decision taken by the government to merge the revenue and Panchayati Raj Departments at the village level was very much in accordance with the World Bank's conditionalities.

The cabinet sub-committee recommended the merger of the two departments at three levels. At level one, creation of the post of Village Secretary who would work under Sarpanch; at level two, revenue and development officers at the mandal level are to be merged to form a single establishment and to be working under the Mandal President; and at the third level, the power and purview of Revenue Development Officer (RDO) to be reduced to MLA constituency level and converted into new position of Constituent Development Officer (CDO), who in turn should be working under the MLA. Finally, all the development activities should come either under the District Minister or Zila Parishad Chairman.

All these reforms would result in the reduction of staff and centralization of the whole administration from state to village through the so-called e-governance process.[11] These measures, besides serving the World Bank conditionalities in terms of reduction in the size of government employees, also aim at providing an added political advantage for the ruling party. Thus, this system may be used in either ways: wherever ruling party leader is in power, the ruling party would implement programmes through their party leader, and wherever the opposition party candidate is in power at the grass-roots level, the ruling party can instruct through government channel to the officials at the grass-roots level to implement its programmes. In this way, the ruling party can take advantage in implementing its programmes and also propagation of its party activities, and very conveniently can sideline the opposition.

The government decision to merge the revenue and PR departments met with serious protests from revenue department personnel.[12] As a result, the state government limited the merger process to village level to begin with and postponed at higher level merger process indefinitely. The Revenue Services Association objected[13] to the merger of revenue and PR services on three important grounds: first, village secretaries were to be controlled by Sarpanchas who, being elected, would be subservient to political parties; second, cheque-drawing power would go from real grass-roots level workers and the workload is heavy for the secretaries as they were to handle as many as 64 subjects. The association leaders expressed their fears that the government is planning to effect similar merger at the mandal and revenue divisional levels. The association leaders are also apprehensive that the appointment of Mandal Secretaries will be done drawing the candidates from MROs and MDOs. Hence, the association demanded for the appointment of group of experts to study all the implications of the reforms. As an immediate measure, the association called for the appointment of a second village secretary for Gram Panchayat drawn from the revenue department to handle 'regulatory functions' leaving developmental functions to the first secretary already appointed from the Panchayati Raj Department.[14]

The already introduced 'reform' measures at the village level in terms of the establishment of Village Secretariat are leading to the emergence of new conflicts/contradictions. Panchayat secretaries have become the bone of contention for the Sarpanchas on the issues of developmental activities, populist programmes, and other social and political issues. On the other hand, almost all the 64 works, which comprise general, administrative, revenue etc., and assigned to the village secretary, have become unmanageable for a single person, in practice.

In an interview, the General Secretary of Panchayat Secretaries Association said that the earlier form of duties attached to 'carobars' (erstwhile village functionaries) had no 'azmoish' functions.[15] Now, the Panchayat Secretary is made responsible for 'so many duties' including political duties. The Panchayat Secretaries have become sandwiched (like *'adakatteralo pokachekka')* between politicians and officials. There is another problem with respect to the appointment of the Panchayat Secretaries. Most of them are neither qualified nor have skills and abilities to take care the enlarged duties, as envisaged by the government. Persons from hitherto cadres like bill collectors, Gram Panchayat clerks, junior assistants and others like qualified attenders, *kawalikars* and also surplus staff from the other departments[16] were appointed as Panchayat Secretaries. None of these have past experience in panchayat and revenue activities. Various higher level governmental departments send regular circulars as most urgent seeking status reports on various issues like health, education, revenue, water, agriculture, veterinary etc., at the village level, and it becomes very difficult for a single person to handle all these simultaneously. The position of Panchayat Secretary has become vulnerable due to these duties and because of a range of tax collection duties which are also assigned to them. The Secretary has to collect taxes on grazing, drinking water, property tax, land tax etc., and also user charges for different services. Failing to collect these taxes would result in the non-payment of salaries. The Secretary Association questions that how can the government expect to do the overburdened functions by a single person? In this kind of scenario one can say that the envisaged goals of good governance in the rural areas have become overburdened and thus become impractical.

Besides these, the Panchayat Secretaries Association opposed to the political involvement in their duties and categorically demanded[17] that political involvement should not be present in the revenue matters. The association apprehends that if the Sarpanchas are to be involved in the official matters, there are chances to tamper the records and they may pressurize the Panchayat Secretary to alter the records to suit their conveniences. The association is of the opinion that, since the people's representatives change periodically in every election and they do not understand the implications of non-maintenance of records and accounts. In fact, they are least bothered about all these. Usually, the problems over records and accounts arise in the later period than the actual tennurial periods of elected representatives. In this kind of scenario, only officials rather than elected representatives are held responsible and victimized.

Another issue of conflict of interest between the elected Sarpanch and the government official, i.e., the Panchayat Secretary, is over the question of cheque power. This became a issue of prestige between the two. Representatives of the both the associations, viz., the Sarpanchas and Panchayat Secretaries, have already indulged in the media war by issuing contradictory statements.[18] The Forum claims that, after the introduction of Panchayat Secretary system, nobody is listening to Sarpanchas and heeding to their orders because Secretary is a permanent employee whereas Sarpanch is a politician having no powers. The Sarpanchas Forum says that there are more demands from the public to undertake several civic amenities and other developmental works in the village. But, there are no funds. With respect to central government allocations in the schemes like JGSY, Sarpanch has a joint cheque power with a ward member. Even, with regard to Gram Panchayat funds (generated within the village), the Sarpanch has to abide by the decision of general body in allocating funds. Thus, there is no absoluteness on cheque power. In fact, the Forum says that, in several Gram Panchayats, the Sarpanchas have already handed over cheque books to Secretaries for the maintenance of records and accounts. Further, the Sarpanchas Forum argues that floating of the CBOs or parallel bodies and the appointment of Panchayat Secretaries is undermining the importance of Sarpanchas, who are elected by the people in a democratic spirit.[19]

Contrary to this argument, the Panchayat Secretaries Association says that[20] Sarpancha are always carrying cheque books and issuing cheques for their personal works and influencing us to settle the accounts finally. If any audit objections are raised, the Secretary will be held responsible, not the Sarpanch. The Secretaries Association is arguing that since other cadres of people's representatives like the MPPs and ZPPs are not vested with the cheque power, why this is being assigned to Sarpanchas? The association is of the view that prior to the introduction of the Village Secretariat system, there was no Executive Officer to perform these functions and hence Sarpanchas were given executive powers as well as cheque power. Now, in the light of the establishment of the new Village Secretariat system, there are government appointed Panchayat Secretaries to look after these functions. Therefore, the Secretaries Association argues that the cheque power should be utilized only through general body resolutions of Gram Panchayat.[21]

The government has not taken any decision over this issue. It seems to be in a fix and hence, buying some more time to settle the issue. If the government removes the cheque power from Sarpanch, it affects on electoral equations. On the other hand, the government is also heavily depending on Panchayat Secretaries for collecting various information and implementation of populist schemes. Hence, this has become problematic for the government. It has been reported that the State Government is planning to constitute a separate administrative tribunal at district level to deal with the misappropriation of funds by the people's representatives at grass-roots level.

However, the Sarpanchas Forum is very firm on the issue of cheque power. It opines that Sarpanchas have acquired the cheque power through their struggles and it is their political and democratic right and it cannot be sacrificed. If the joint cheque power is given, the Sarpanchas, the elected representatives of the people, will only become nominal in their power positions. However, the Secretaries Association is not basing its argument on these lines. It is apprehensive that the Sarpanchas, being politicians, are not accountable. In the event of Sarpanchas misusing the funds, secretaries are going to be made responsible, not the Sarpanchas. Hence, the Secretaries Association is demanding to have joint cheque power.

In the social front, the introduction of reforms for rural good governance led to few more conflicts/contradictions. Today, there are more than 50 per cent of the Sarpanchas, who belong to the reserved category (ST, SC, OBC, women), whereas the Panchayat Secretaries are drawn from (old caste-based system of Patel-Patwari-VAO-Village Secretary) upper caste background. It is pertinent to note that out of 16,000 village secretaries of the state, 95 per cent belong to upper castes.[22] This, in fact, violates statutory reservation provisions. This also is resulting in obvious social conflicts/contradictions at the grass-roots administration.

There is a woman Sarpanch, coming from OBC background, studied only upto 7th class, became Sarpanch under reserved category for a major Gram Panchayat, categorically says:[23] "It is a male-dominated society patriarchy—which is not allowing us to perform duties". She further said that their respective husbands drive women in day-to-day administrative functions. She also said that Panchayat Secretaries are also not giving proper respect to her. It was openly criticized by some women Sarpanchas[24] in an interactive meeting with the Panchayati Raj Minister that the Chandra Babu Naidu government was ignoring elected representatives and only giving importance to the government employees, In essence, the women elected representatives at grass-roots level have become what is known as 'Utsava Vigrahalu' (idols to be taken in procession ritually on certain religious festivals). Thus, the women representatives are only involved in terms of their face value to fulfil statutory obligation of the state.

A Sarpanch hailing from a scheduled tribe with minimum literacy level said that he instructed Panchayat Secretary who belonged to upper caste to conduct Gram Panchayat meeting but the Secretary ignored his order.[25] He further said that Secretary is not bringing any information to his notice and providing him rather misinformation. This kind of attitude of the Secretary is creating a lot of problems for him, he said. These Sarpanchas, elected under reservation category, feel that because they belonged lower castes and possessed illiterate background, the feudals turned Panchayat Secretaries are not in a position to digest that they are also people's representatives and they have to work under them.

It is noticed that in most of the cases, Panchayat Secretaries are overruling/ignoring the elected Sarpanchas belonged to lower castes in the villages. The Secretaries Association has in fact admitted these facts. It admitted that wherever the reserved Sarpanchas are there, they are facing problems with our colleagues.[26] It is also observed the social conflicts are also leading to the other extremes. There are also instances that the SC and ST Sarpanchas are also misusing funds and threatening the officials with dire consequences taking the advantage of SC/ST Atrocities Act.

The position of the Panchayat Secretary as per the Government Order 369 is that he/she has to work under Gram Panchayat. But, the Gram Panchayat is not a controlling authority of Panchayat Secretary, excepting for powers of leave sanctioning by the Sarpanch. Even this leave sanctioning power was not there in the beginning, came only in the later period. With respect to actual controlling authority, there were disputes between the revenue department (MRO) and the PR department (MDO). Finally, the village secretaries are brought under the control of MDO officially, but it is also ordered that they have to follow MRO's instructions. This makes the case still in contradiction and is leading to conflict of authority between MROs and MDOs. In practice, what is happening is that the secretaries are more loyal to higher officials but not to Sarpanch. And, they are not even available to people. As a result of these contradictions, the expected purpose of creating this institution is not being fulfilled.

Ramifications

The above-mentioned problems emerged due to the contradictions between the 73rd Amendment Act and the World Bank guided policies in Andhra Pradesh, which are being implemented by the state government by ignoring the local realities. The state appears to protect market interests rather than people's interests.

The study identifies three important ramifications for the local governance. Firstly, we can identify several forms of undermining of the representative local bodies like Panchayati Raj Institutions (PRIs) in the state in the context of liberalization. The Community-Based

Organizations (CBOs), for instance, being based on stakeholder approach, are promoting the parallel structures which manage the rural resources independent of PRIs and thereby leading to marginalization of these bodies.

Similarly, as it is shown in the study, it locates the tensions in the rural administration that the Village Secretariat system brought to the fore in the larger context of politics of economic reforms. The study argues for the linkages between the liberalization and the undermining process of the PRIs. Hence, in essence, the problem is not between the Sarpanch and Village Secretary, but it is due to dynamic pro-market administrative reforms initiated by state government in line with the World Bank policies.

Secondly, the study shows that the Village Secretariat not only marginalizes the Sarpancha's powers in the village administrative set-up but also undermines the representative character of the panchayats. It introduces babudom at the local level.

Lastly and more importantly, the study reveals that the Village Secretariat system reinforces upper caste hold over the rural administration and creates space for their control over the resources. As several studies have shown that social status of Sarpanchas and Mandal Parishad Presidents in the reserved posts proves to be a major impediment on their functioning. The Village Secretariat system could be seen as an important addition to this process in the state. It is ironical that the new system of Village Secretariat came into force during special 'Janmabhoomi' programme on social justice and is working against the social justice in practice.

Notes

1. Government Order No. 369, Panchayati Raj and Rural Development (MDL-II) Department, Strengthening of Local Bodies – Creation of the post of Panchayat Secretary combining the revenue and Panchayat functions in non-notified Gram Panchayats, orders issued on December 12, 2001.
2. Government of Andhra Pradesh appointed a cabinet sub committee under the chairmanship of Home Minister T. Devender Goud, and Pocharam Srinivas Reddy, Minister for Panchayati Raj, Chikkala Ramchander Rao, Minister for Cooperatives, and Dandu Shiva Rama Raju, Minister for Endowments as members to recommend administrative reforms in Panchayati Raj system.

3. Chandra Babu Naidu, Chief Minister of Andhra Pradesh inaugurated the new Village Secretariat at Adloor village in Kamareddy Mandal of Nizamabad district on 1 January 2002.
4. *The Hindu* (Hyderabad), January 2, 2002.
5. Government Order No. 369, December 12, 2001.
6. Government Order No. 4, Panchayat Raj and Rural Development (MDL-II) Department, Rules relating to the functions of Panchayat Secretary, under Section 268 read with 36(6) of Andhra Pradesh Panchayat Raj Act, 1994, orders issued on January 7, 2002.
7. *The Hindu,* December 11, 2001.
8. Supriya Roy Chowdhary, "Globalisation and Decentralisation", *The Hindu,* January 5, 2002.
9. It is reported that the Andhra Pradesh government is borrowing more amount of loans from the World Bank in India, see, *Vaartha,* February 2, 2004 and also see for the influence of World Bank policies on A.P. policies, G. Krishna Reddy, "New Populism and Liberalisation: Regime Shift under Chandrababu Naidu in A.P.", *Economic and Political Weekly,* Vol. XXXVII, No. 9, March 2–8, 2002, pp. 871–83.
10. *Vaartha,* February 19, 2002.
11. *Vaartha,* January 21, 2002.
12. Andhra Pradesh Revenue Association President K. Laxamaiah threatened the government and announced an agitation programme starting with boycott of all protocol duties by MROs, wearing black badges, lunch hour demonstration, dharnas at RDO offices and collectorates. Subsequently, organized three region-wise meetings during 28 January to 7 February 2002.
13. *The Hindu,* January 8, 2002.
14. Ibid.
15. Interview with K. Upender Reddy, Panchayat Secretary of Medipally Gram Panchayat and General Secretary of the Panchayat Secretaries Association, Ranga Reddy district, Hyderabad, January 25, 2004.
16. Government Order No. 384, Panchayat Raj and Rural Development (ESTT. IX) Public Services—Andhra Pradesh Panchayat Subordinate Services (Special) Rules, December 22, 2001.
17. Interview with K. Upender Reddy and A. Prabhakar Reddy, Executive Officer/Panchayat Secretary of Boduppal Gram Panchayat, Ranga Reddy district, Hyderabad, January 22, 2004.
18. *Vaartha,* January 24, 2002; January 1, 2002; January 28, 2002; July 7, 2002; September 9, 2002.
19. Interview with Buchaiah, Sarpanch, Bommala Ramaram Mandal in Nalgonda District, on September 22, 2002. Similar views were also expressed by Chandra Mouli, Sarpanch of Chikati Mamidi Gram Panchayat.
20. Interview with K. Upender Reddy, January 25, 2004.
21. Ibid.

22. K. Chandra Shekar Rao, President of Telangana Rashtra Samiti (TRS) said in the Assembly, *Vaartha,* December 22, 2001.
23. Interview with Laxmi Jangaiah, Sarpanch of Boduppal Gram Panchayat in Ranga Reddy district, on January 22, 2004.
24. *Vaartha,* January 28, 2004.
25. Interview with Harya Naik, Sarpanch of Bommala Ramaram Mandal in Nalgonda district on September 22, 2002.
26. Interview with K. Upender Reddy and A. Prabhakar Reddy and Vijaya Simha Reddy (President of the Panchayat Secretaries Association, Nalgonda) on January 25, 2004, January 22, 2004 and September 22, 2002 respectively.

19 The Panchayati Raj System in Goa

Sunita Kale

The Panchayati Raj system in Goa is governed by the Goa, Daman and Diu Village Panchayat Regulation Act, 1962. The Act prescribes that there shall be a Panchayat for every village as from such date as the Lieutenant Governor may, by notification, appoint with such number of members as the Lieutenant Governor may, by order, determine so far as may be in accordance with the following table:[1]

For a panchayat with population of	*Number of members*	*Class*[2]
1,500 to 2,000	5	D
2,500 to 3,500	7	C
More than 3,500	9	B
More than 8,000	11	A

The term of office of the Sarpanch was four years[3] and it could be extended for one year by the Governor. The 73rd Constitutional Amendment has now made the term for five years, extendable by six months.

Accordingly, the total number of Panchayats is 183 with 11 talukas or blocks and two districts. The number of blocks in South Goa and North Goa is six and five respectively. Each district is headed by a District Collector and each block is headed a Block Development Officer.

The grass-roots level institution of this structure is the Gram Panchayat. All the members of the Gram Panchayat are elected directly by the members of the Gram Sabha, and the adult voters of the village. The Panchas elect the Sarpanch who presides over the meetings of both the Gram Sabha and the Gram Panchayat.

Every Panchayat has a Gram Sabha. It is the general assembly made up of all adult voters in the village. It holds two meetings every year, and approves the following matters placed before it by the Gram Panchayat:[4]

1. The annual statement of accounts.
2. The report of the administration of the preceding financial year.
3. The position of proposed programmes for the current financial year.
4. The last audit report.
5. Proposals for fresh taxation.
6. Proposals for organization of community services.

Besides the Village Panchayat and Gram Sabha, there is an advisory body at the block level to advise on the matters of planning and the execution of schemes therein. This advisory body comprises political representatives from villages, government representatives, representatives from local institutions and representatives of the Scheduled Castes and the Scheduled Tribes. As it is only an advisory body, it does not have power to sanction funds.

The Programmatic Functioning of Departments

Agriculture

So far as agriculture is concerned, the state was brought into the mainstream of national development through the implementation of Five-Year Plans after liberation from Portuguese regime. Different schemes are prepared by the departments and are implemented through the BDOs, who give information to the department. There is also a Voluntary Rural Development Agency which distributes loans for industries and small businesses.

Land development is carried on by minor irrigation schemes in which funds are allocated for wells, pumps, bunds, fencing etc. Loans are also sanctioned for buying Jersy cows and buffaloes. The present area under irrigation for high-yielding varieties of paddy is 45,415 hectares and 1,897 hectares for sugarcane. The government has distributed land to the landless labourers to the extent of 260.51 hectares.[5]

Fishery

As the state has long coasts, fishery is an important industry in Goa. The beneficiaries are given subsidies for purchasing mechanized boats. Gram Sevaks, posted at Panchayat level, look after the business. They submit proposals to the BDO. Each Extension Officer scrutinizes the cases and submits the same to the BDO. Loan cases are directed to the Rural Development Agency which distributes the OBMs (Out Board Motors), testing nets and mechanized fishing vessels. The BDO sends the papers to the concerned department. The Extension Officer (Rural Works) and the Extension Officer (Development) are attached to the BDO office. The Government of Goa has distributed loans and subsidies upto the amount of Rs 60.63 lakh in 1993.[6]

The Department of Fishery sanctions funds to the fishermen and farmers through Panchayats. The BDO works for the Department of Fishery and Agriculture and also for the Rural Development Agency.

Literacy

The Ministry of Education is responsible for the implementation of the Education Policy. The BDO has nothing to do in this matter. The literacy rate was 75.51 per cent in 1993.[7] Vocational and professional education is provided in schools and colleges.

Medicare

So far as medicare is concerned, the state has 30 hospitals with 2,469 beds. There are 255 health centres and dispensaries in Goa. Health directly affects the birth rate which was 7.02 in 1993 per 1,000 population. The Ministry looks after the matters of healthcare, and the BDOs and Panchayats do not have much role to play. Family welfare programmes are carried out by Family Planning Cliniques in which programmes of immunization, tuberculosis, malaria and AIDS are also implemented. These are carried out by the Health Intelligence Bureau throughout the state.

Cottage Industry

The department has one Extension Officer (Industries) attached to the BDO. He has been entrusted with the responsibility to guide and scrutinize cases related to small-scale industries and suggest the names (to the BDO) of the people who need loans. The BDO, in turn, submits the proposals to the Directorate of Industries. He also keeps record of permanent registration of industries. The number of factories registered under the Factories Act is 466. The number of small-scale industrial units, registered under the Department of Industries was 5,201 in 1993. These units have employed 32,000 workers. Mining is also an important industry in Goa. Iron-ore, manganese-ore and fero-manganese-ore are the main resources exported to other countries. The ore exports amounted to 133.77 lakh tonnes in 1993.

It was observed during the field study that usually two schemes are sponsored in a block. First, the building of roads, and communication and health and sanitation. Grants-in-aid given for this scheme for each block is in the proportion of 25:75. The second was the village project housing scheme, which is carried out under the Twenty-Point Programme. Land is distributed free of cost and a loan of Rs 5,000 is given for building a house on the land. Besides, there are some remunerative schemes under which loans are given to the Panchayats for building markets, offices etc. These three schemes are implemented under the supervision of the District Collector through the BDOs. Under TRYSEM, vocational classes such as sewing, carpentry, fibre glass, typing, computers etc., are conducted. The instructors are given an honorarium of Rs 100 and the trainees are paid a stipend from Rs 150 to Rs 200. This money is allotted by the Rural Development Agency (RDA) and withdrawn by the BDO.

Another scheme under the RDA is the DWCRA, under which a sum of Rs 15,000 is given to a group in a village without charging any interest rate. The scheme is supervised by a Mukhya Sevika in the BDO office. The women groups manufacture products, sell them and get the profits. After having earned enough money, the sum of Rs 15,000 is returned to the government. The BDO has full control over the withdrawal of money from the bank. The groups have to maintain proper records which are subject to inspection by the RDA.

Social Welfare

This department sponsors another scheme, particularly for the OBCs, who are given Rs 5,000 for repairing the houses. Of this, Rs 3,750 are given as subsidy and Rs 1,500 as loan without interest. The Scheduled Castes and the Scheduled Tribes are given Rs 11,300 for building a house. There is also a provision for handicapped who can acquire loan-cum-subsidy. In order to give impetus to inter-caste marriages, there is a provision to pay Rs 500 to those who perform such marriages. There are other betterment schemes also which are targeted to help the poor and the needy. Besides, a sum of Rs 100 is given monthly as old age pension to help the elderly people. Proposals for the above schemes are submitted by the BDO and the loans are sanctioned by the Department of Social Welfare. Provedoria, a voluntary institution distributes Rs 100 per month to each poor in the village. A list of poor is prepared after the survey conducted for the same. Destitutes are given help under the Dayanand Niradhar Smruti Yojana. The poor families in the villages are given two electric connections. They have to acquire a certificate from Panchayat and submit the same to the BDO.

The BDO has to channelize the subsidy cases for the assistance to be given by the RDA under the Integrated Rural Development Programme (IRDP). The Jawahar Rozgar Yojana (JRY) was first taken up in Goa in 1989–90. The primary objective of this scheme was to generate gainful employment for the unemployed and underemployed. The type of work or the projects under the scheme are proposed by the Panchayats and the report is submitted to the RDA which sanctions the loan for the same. After the sanction is acquired, the Sarpanchas, under the supervision of Engineering Section of RDA, carry out the works. On completion of the project, the Sarpanchas issue completion certificates. The funds under JRY are provided by the centre and the state in the ratio of 80:20. The funds are distributed in the districts on the basis of estimated population. An account is opened in a nationalized bank which is operated by the Sarpanch and the Panchayat Secretary jointly.

A national programme of improved smokeless *chullahs* was first taken up in Goa in 1984–85 under the Twenty-Point Programme. The Sarpanchas submit a list of people to the RDA through the BDO, who wish to acquire such *chullahs*.

The BDO thus becomes a nodal agency through whom all the schemes are integrated, scrutinized and directed to the RDA and the state. The BDO is also a link between the Panchayats and the state.

Sources of Income of Panchayats

Earlier, the criterion for granting money to Panchayats was based on the proportion of 25:75 or say, Rs 25 to be contributed by the Panchayats and Rs 75 to be given by the state. This proportion did not prove fruitful and resulted in financial deficiency. Then, a modified pattern of assistance for providing matching grant to the Village

Panchayats in Goa was started on January 6, 1994. Accordingly, the Village Panchayats whose annual income is upto Rs 20,000 would get matching grant upto 200 per cent. The Village Panchayats, whose annual income is from Rs 20,000 to Rs 50,000 could get matching grant upto 100 per cent of the income.[8]

For releasing matching grants, incomes derived by the Village Panchayats by way of collection of taxes and octroi are included for the purpose of determining the eligibility for the matching grants and are excluded for the purpose of determining the quantum of matching grants. The Village Panchayats collect house tax, profession tax, and fees on drainage and hoardings. The taxes collected and matching grants to be released to six blocks in North Goa during 1994–95 were as under:

Blocks	*Taxes collected in 1993–94*	*Matching grants released in 1994–95*
Ponda	27,53,995	12,89,595
Bicholim	21,02,292	6,32,401
Tiswadi	18,35,759	6,79,786
Sattari	14,61,010	4,90,941
Pernem	2,71,628	1,76,315
Bardes	23,40,971	10,73,377

Similarly, taxes collected and matching grants given to the five blocks in South Goa during 1994–95 were as under:

Blocks	*Taxes collected in 1993–94*	*Matching grants payable in 1994–95*
Quepene	1,23,312.48	1,85,335.00
Cancone	1,10,928.03	1,92,170.67
Marmagaon/Vasco	8,96,349.88	9,40,145.00
Sanquem	25,12,916.00	1,90,520.00
Salcet	14,90,360.00	15,36,709.00

Matching grants are distributed according to the works and projects prepared by the Panchayats and the distribution of these grants is controlled by the BDOs. The project is supervised by the Extension Officer. He submits the proposals to the BDO who forwards them to the sanctioning authority, i.e., the Collector, for countersignature. The BDOs withdraw the sanctioned amount and distribute the money to the Panchayats. Finally, the auditors go and inspect the records of the Panchayats at the end of the year.

As per the annexure prepared by the office of Deputy Collector (Development), Margao, South Goa, the following funds were allocated at the disposal of the BDOs for meeting the expenditure during 1994–95 under the "Loans to Village Panchayats Under Remunerative Schemes".

	Schemes	*Heads*	*Blocks*	*Total Amount (Rs in lakhs)*	*Remarks*
1.	Allotment of house-sites	Rural housing house-sites to labourers	5	5.00	This money will have to be surrendered as sites are not available
2.	Construction assistance	Loan for housing	—	—	—
3.	Health and rural sanitation	C.D.	5	7.50	Maximum utilization
4.	Roads and communication	C.D. Rural Development	5	20.00	Fully utilized

The main sources of income for the Panchayats are house tax, vehicle tax, light, dogs, drainage and hoarding tax. Some of the taxes, e.g., the pilgrim tax, entertainment tax and tax on advertisements cannot be levied by the Panchayats due to peculiar geographical locations. Sometimes it is not profitable to levy even octroi tax as the expenses on the Nakedars are more than the amount collected. Besides, the house tax is not assessed property and so the amount collected therein is very low. Evidently, the Panchayats do not make maximum efforts to collect taxes. There are many reasons for this. First, the rural people are not habitual to pay taxes and they take these as an extra financial burden on them. The Panchayat Secretary and the Sarpanch do not insist on this matter in order to protect their own interests. Even the arrears are not collected in a regular manner. The people are reluctant to pay taxes as they are well aware that government will undertake development projects despite their reluctance to pay taxes. The modified pattern of matching grants has, to a little extent, increased the responsibility of collecting more revenue by the Panchayats. These grants depend upon the budgetary provisions of the state. The budget is usually deficit. As development depends upon the revenue collected by the Panchayats, a new Directorate of Panchayats has been set up to sanction the funds hereafter.

Control of State on Panchayats

The State Government exercises three types of control over the Gram Panchayats in Goa. Under the Goa, Daman and Diu Village Panchayats Regulation Act, 1962, not only the Panchayats are established but their size, elections and staff are also regulated. Administrative control is exercised through the rights of resolutions, inspection and suspension of the Panchayats whenever such a situation occurs. Financial control is exercised by regulating the income of the Panchayats.

The Village Panchayats are supposed to collect the revenue only from the sources listed in the Village Panchayats Act, 1962. Even the accounts have to be maintained according to the mode prescribed by the Act. Besides this, the budget estimates are also prepared according to the procedure given by the Goa, Daman and Diu Village Panchayats (Accounts and Audit and Custody of Funds) Rules, 1963.[9]

People's Participation

The Gram Sabha is the basic grass-root level institution, comprising all the voters in the village who are supposed to meet twice a year to approve the budget for various departmental schemes taken up by the Panchayat. But, in reality, the people are least bothered to attend meetings and these are held only for the sake of records. This is mainly because the people are not properly aware that they are given an opportunity to participate in these meetings. Moreover, the suggestions made by the people are not implemented as the Panchayats have not been given enough powers and funds and there is too much political interference in the working of the Panchayats. Besides this, decisions of the Gram Sabhas are not a binding on the Panchayats. This situation can show some improvement if the people assert their right to participate actively in the meetings. A significant point to be noted is that the elected representatives are usually independent candidates who are indirectly backed by the parties. Thus, the candidates cannot afford to be indifferent to the development of villages.

Relations Between Sarpanchas and the Village Panchayat Secretary

The Panchayat Secretary and the Sarpanch have to work in co-ordination with each other since they are official and non-official member of the Panchayat respectively. In a democratically elected body, the political leaders usually play an influential role over the officials. But, if the officials are educated, they sometimes assert their superiority over the non-officials. Further, the spheres and functions between the two are not clearly defined. Thus, both can interfere in each other's area. The Sarpanchas usually try to do things which are illegal on the grounds that they have the backing of the voters. On the whole, the State of Goa had only one-tier of Panchayati Raj, and so there is not much confrontation between the two, as both lack administrative and financial powers. Besides, the government directly takes up all the projects, so the officials and non-officials do not have much say in the working.

The Secretary is appointed by State Government directly. His work is to maintain the records of the Panchayats and the register of the income and expenditure. He also maintains the postage and stamp register. Therefore, the Secretary should be a person from the cadre of Upper Division Clerks, who will be capable enough to perform the jobs prescribed for him.

The BDO is obviously an official member who plays a key role in the Panchayati Raj. He is appointed by the State Government from the revenue cadre and his status is equal to that of Mamledar. The BDO is easily accessible to the villagers. He is the person through whom all papers are processed. While interviewing a BDO in a block, it was suggested that the BDO should be recruited on the basis of competitive examination, and then professionally trained for his job. He/she should be punished if found guilty of not collecting the arrears, and his/her appointment should be made on the basis of merit, since he/she has to perform a difficult job of maintaining law and order in the area.

The main grievance among the BDOs and the Gram Sevaks today is that no promotion avenues exist in their jobs which could motivate them to work more efficiently. They are just given time-bound promotional scale that too with only one increment. The BDOs and Gram Sevaks do require some incentives. There is only one Gram Sevak for four Panchayats who has to travel a distance of about 5–6 km to reach the Panchayat, but no travelling allowance is paid. This situation results in lethargy among the Gram Sevaks.

So far as the satisfaction among the people is concerned, it depends upon the performance of the Panchayats and the Sarpanchas. There is no follow up action to judge and evaluate the performance of the Panchayats. The Gram Sevaks, on the whole, feel that the pace of development shall improve only if the people are provided with a piece of land. But to utilize the land in a proper way is still more expensive.

The Block Advisory Committee (BAC) does not a play significant role in the present structure as it is only an advisory body lacking financial powers. The BAC in Goa is not functioning at present. The people are not aware of responsibility or the functions of BAC. In fact, people seem to be indifferent towards the working of Village Panchayat and the BAC.

The Goa Panchayati Raj Act, 1993

The previous structure has now been replaced with a two-tier Panchayati Raj system after the 73rd Constitutional Amendment Act. The new system shall have elected bodies at village as well as district levels. Such an amendment has been made to initiate greater participation of the people and more effective implementation of rural development programmes.

Accordingly, there will be a Gram Sabha with voters in the village. The Gram Sabha will elect members of the Panchayat, who will elect the Sarpanch. The facility of reservation for SCs/STs and women candidates will remain as such. The functions of the Panchayats will be performed as per the new Act.[10] At the district level, the new Act provides for a Zila Panchayat. It will consist of 20 elected members, MPs and members appointed by the state legislature. The functions of the Zila Panchayats would be assigned by the State Government. There shall be a Standing Committee for the Zila Panchayat. The Chief Executive Officer shall be the ex-officio Secretary of all the Standing Committees. The State Government shall appoint an officer not below the rank of the Collector of the district as Chief Executive Officer of the Zila Panchayat.[11] He shall supervise and control the execution of all the financial and administrative matters of Zila Panchayats. The Zila Panchayats are given 28 subjects for execution. This new two-tier system has started functioning from November 1995, after the term of Panchayats is over, i.e., after proper elections are held in all the Panchayats.

In Goa, the Goa Municipal (Amendment) Bill has also been adopted. It will not only weed out corrupt practices among the municipal officers but also give an opportunity to the young people to come forward and participate in the municipal elections.[12]

Conclusion

The villagers in Goa do not seem to be much interested in the 73rd Constitution Amendment Act nor are they aware of its implications. They are just busy in collecting cashew and betelnut which they had been doing since times immemorial. However, those who are little informed of the new Act feel no necessity of the two or three-tiered structure. Instead they fear that more institutions will result in more taxes, more confusion and more corruption. The smallness of Goa does not require more institutions because setting up of layers will cost the government about 80 per cent of the budgetary amount. As commented by a senior official, the status of union territory was very manageable. The reports show that progress and development in rural areas was quick and possible under the union territory administration.

The villagers do not have the tendency to pay regular taxes as a result of which the Panchayats do not have enough income. Neither they receive matching grants nor can they take up development works on their own, so the concept of decentralization remains on paper.

The political awareness among the villagers is nil, therefore sound infrastructure should be built in the beginning itself. As pointed out by the District Collector, some educated people or people having some knowledge should be posted in villages so that there is silent revolution from the grass-roots levels otherwise the system of democratic decentralization shall be a total failure in the absence of people's participation.

A peculiar thing about the people of Goa is that they are least bothered about their contribution towards the developmental process. Unless they show interest, the programme will be a sham. The villagers should be able to express their grievances, and expose the bureaucrats when their rights are encroached upon. The lethargy and indifference shown towards corruption and mismanagement would result in the failure of Panchayati Raj.

The elected leaders and the bureaucrats should try and revive the Panchayati Raj Institutions (PRIs) in Goa. Both should be committed to the idea of democratic decentralization.

The role of women in the developmental process is negligible in spite of the provision for their involvement in the Act. Illiteracy, housekeeping activities and traditional male domination do not allow them to look beyond their shells. It is hoped that the new Act will motivate them to take part in the administrative process, but time itself will tell the story.

The new Act is going to be an experiment towards more participation and involvement of both the people and the bureaucrats.

Notes

1. Government of Goa, Daman and Diu, *Village Panchayats Regulations and Rules,* Panaji, 1983, p. 4.
2. Government of Goa, *The Goa Panchayat Act,* 1993, p. 6.
3. Tanaji Halamakar, *Gram Panchayats in Goa: A Critical Study,* Rajhans, 1990, p. 35.
4. Government of Goa, Daman and Diu, *Village Panchayat Regulations and Rules,* op. cit.
5. State of Goa, *Indicators of Socio-economic Development 1993,* Directorate of Planning, Statistics and Evaluation, Government of Goa, Panaji, 1993.
6. Ibid.
7. *Health Statistics at a Glance—Goa 1993.* Issued by Health Intelligence Bureau, Directorate of Health Services, Panaji, Goa.
8. Order No. 1/15/(20)/84–F and A dated January 6, 1994 issued by the Government of Goa, Department of Community Development and Panchayats.
9. Government of Goa, Daman and Diu, *The Village Panchayats Regulations and Rules 1962*, Panaji, 1983, p. 8.
10. Government of Goa, *The Goa Panchayati Raj Act,* 1993.
11. *The Goa Panchayati Raj Act,* 1994, p. 75.
12. *The Navhind Times,* May 26, 1994.

20 Devolution of Powers and Functions to PRIs in Daman

C.P. Vithal

The Union Territory (UT) of Daman is located in Gujarat on the coast of Arabian Sea. It has a population of 62,101 as per the 1991 census. The tribal population is 20 per cent to the total population. All the villages in Daman are electrified and are connected to Daman by black top roads. All villages also have access to good health and educational facilities. They have also been connected with drinking water supply. All tanks in Daman are under the management of Tourism Department which plans to promote them as tourist resorts as the tourism is conceived as the major economic activity of the region. Daman is declared as a pollution-free zone where chemical industries are not permitted. As Daman is a tax-free zone, there is rapid industrialization and agriculture has been relegated to secondary position in the recent times. The total number of industrial units in Daman is 991. Of them, the number of small-scale units is 849 while that of medium sized is 142. The industrial estates in Daman have good physical infrastructural facilities and are located at Kachi Gaon, Somnath, Dhabey and Bhimpore. Tourism is also a major contributor to the economy of Daman. There are about 100 hotels/motels, big or small, with retail outlets of alcoholic drinks which alone contribute about Rs 200 crore per annum as excise money to the state exchequer due to the exodus of the tourists throughout the year who consider it as a holiday resort. Most of the able-bodied citizens are employed in one economic activity or the other. It is difficult to find out a person living below the poverty line (BPL) in any village of Daman. In view of the compactness of Daman, land is a scarce commodity. As a result of the overall economic growth of the region, the people could eke out a decent living.

It is against this backdrop, the present paper attempts to study the pattern of PRIs in Daman, devolution of powers and functions to PRIs, administrative arrangements at Village Panchayat level vis-à-vis functions of Panchayat Secretary, financial devolution etc.

Administrative Divisions

The Union Territory of Daman and Diu has two Collectors—one for Daman and the other for Diu. However, both Daman and Diu have one District Panchayat and one Chief Executive Officer (CEO) each. It is pertinent to mention that Daman is both a block and district unit while Diu is 200–300 km away from the main land. Perhaps, due to the compactness of the area with only eight Village Panchayats, Daman is a block as well as a district headquarters.

PRIs in Daman and Diu

Taking cues from the Constitutional (73rd Amendment) Act, the Daman and Diu Village Panchayat (Amended) Regulations, 1994 came into force in October 1994. The Union Territory of Daman and Diu had a two-tier system of Panchayati Raj: a District Panchayat at Moti Daman and 10 Village Panchayats, of which eight located in Daman and the other two in Diu. The elections to PRIs in Daman were held in September 1995 on party basis.

Powers and Functions of Village Panchayats

Under Sections 31 and 31C of Panchayat Regulations, a wide array of functions have been assigned to the Village Panchayats. These can be listed under five broad heads. They are: (i) sanitation and public health; (ii) public works; (iii) planning and development; (iv) administration; and (v) social welfare. Further, the panchayats have to perform functions connected with 29 subjects listed in the XI Schedule of the Indian Constitution.

The Village Panchayat administration is maintained by the Panchayat Secretary who has to perform multifarious functions like:

to convene the meetings of the Gram Panchayat every month and the Gram Sabha meetings twice in a year; to take note of the minutes of the meetings; to implement resolutions of the panchayat; to supervise implementation of several different kinds of developmental programmes; to collect agricultural and livestock census; to conduct below poverty line (BPL) survey; to prepare electoral rolls; to issue birth and death certificates; to collect taxes and fees; and to maintain all records and registers of the panchayat.

Besides, the Secretary has also to perform the following functions:

1. to approve building plans;
2. to issue income certificate;
3. to issue residence certificate;
4. to issue house occupancy certificate for domestic power connection;
5. to supervise JRY works;
6. to take up crop estimate survey;
7. to undertake census work; and
8. to entrust streetlight repairs.

In view of the above functions, the Panchayat Secretaries in Daman ventilated the view that they are overburdened with work. Although they are directly recruited to the present post, there seems to be a lot of stagnation in their cadre. Further, the Panchayat Secretaries in Daman are under the direct control of the Block Development Officer (BDO). There is a strong resentment on the part of Panchayat Secretaries to work under the direct control of District Panchayat for the alleged apprehension that there would be dual control of both officials and non-officials who pull them in different directions.

Devolution of Powers and Functions to Panchayats

As against 29 subjects, a very few subjects only are transferred to the Village Panchayats/District Panchayat in Daman. They pertain to agriculture, primary education and public works (village roads). So far, primary education and a wing of PWD only were transferred to the panchayats while most of the other subjects are still with different departments of district and UT administration of Daman. The modalities for the transfer of powers, functions, finances and staff connected with 29 subjects have yet to be worked out and finalized by Daman Administration.

Although no financial devolution was made to the Village Panchayats as a result of the 73rd Amendment Act and appointment of UT's Finance Commission, the wherewithal of the financial position of Village Panchayats in Daman can be seen. There are glaring disparities in the income ranges of Village Panchayats in Daman with a minimum of Rs 40,000 per annum and a maximum of Rs 17 lakh annum. The Village Panchayats, despite abundant resources/enough of income and specific schemes of development, had very limited financial powers and cannot spend more than Rs 50,001 on any scheme.

Conclusions

Following conclusions can be drawn out from the above discussion:

1. The UT of Daman had very good physical infrastructural facilities like black top roads, transport, electricity, drinking water, mark besides access to other services, viz., education, health, pub distribution system etc.
2. It is because of tax holiday in Daman, there is rapid industrialization and agriculture has been relegated to secondary position.
3. Daman is considered a tourist resort/holiday resort and excise money alone accounts for about Rs 200 crore per annum which goes to state exchequer.
4. A large number of people in Daman thrive on tourist economy industries and it is very difficult to find out a person living below the poverty line (BPL).
5. In view of the compactness of the UT, Daman is a block as well as district headquarters and easily accessible to the people living in villages.
6. The Panchayat Secretary is overburdened with work. Further, devolution of powers to panchayats only ads up to his workload. Hence, the need to strengthen Panchayat administration by creating additional posts. This apart, the Panchayat Secretary who is now under the control of the Block Development Officer (BDO) should be brought under the control of the Chief Executive Officer (CEO) for the District Panchayat to bring about organic linkages. The feeling of stagnation and lack of promotional avenues to Panchayat Secretaries should be dispelled by taking appropriate measures.

7. The overall scenario of Panchayati Raj in Daman presents that much headway has been made for the devolution of powers, functions, finances and staff to PRIs.
8. Village Panchayats in Daman had limited financial powers and they cannot expend more than Rs 50,000 on any developmental scheme without the prior approval of the district authorities despite having enough of income of their own.
9. The panchayats can improve their financial position by undertaking remunerative enterprises like shopping complexes after acquiring vacant lands from the government.
10. Instead of overemphasizing on tourist economy, economic activities can be diversified by promoting irrigation facilities and fisheries in the tanks hitherto controlled/managed by the Tourism Department.

21 Democratic Decentralization

Zila Parishad as the Apex Body in Haryana

Rajbir Singh

Abraham Lincoln has rightly stated that "democracy is the form of government, which is of the people, for the people and by the people". But, this meaning of democracy cannot be accomplished without democratic decentralization. PRIs are the main agencies of democratic decentralization in rural India, which are engaged in activities of rural development and political participation of people in decision-making process. Zila Parishad, which is the apex body of rural local government and exists at district level, has been reviewed and analyzed after 73rd Constitution Amendment Act of 1993 in the state of Haryana with special reference to Sirsa Zila Parishad. Besides the structural and functional aspects of Zila Parishad in Haryana, its financial position has been apprised. The extent of representation and participation of women and weaker sections in these bodies of local government has been assessed. What has been observed is that the Sirsa Zila Parishad consists of 17 elected members, including Chairman and Deputy Chairman, besides five MLAs, one MP and seven chairpersons of Panchayat Samitis as ex-officio members. Among the elected members, 11 are males and six females whereas their categorywise composition consists of 11 from general category, five from Scheduled Castes (SCs) and one from Backward Classes (BCs). There is full harmony in the functioning of this Zila Parishad as all the members, except one, are from the ruling party. The presence of women, SC and BC members has remained comparatively poor. The participation and attendance of elected members was low in comparison to government officials. The financial position of Sirsa Zila Parishad is very poor as it depends primarily upon government grants and its own resources are meagre. Lack of financial resources is a major constraint in the smooth and effective functioning of the Zila Parishad. There is 110 permanent staff in Zila Parishad, hence their approach towards its performance has remained casual. To check these hurdles and to make Zila Parishad as the real agency of local government, it is suggested that there should be permanent staff and adequate resources. Besides, the members should provide training and motivation for development of local leadership. Political intervention also needs to be checked.

Political participation is an essential ingredient of political development. But, the active and disciplined political participation can be ensured by giving more opportunities to people at the institutional level, which is the indicator of a healthy democracy. The idea of democratic decentralization fulfils this very goal because it provides a vital mechanism through which democracy becomes truly representative and responsive. As the institutions of local self-government are the foundation of democracy, it would be pertinent here to enumerate De Tacquville who has rightly stated: "The local assemblies of citizens are the real power of a society. Any nation can establish free government but the feeling of freedom cannot be attained without the institutions of local government". Local government is really a civic body. People are getting interested and have improved their lifestyle by undertaking responsibility by participating in the activities of local government in developed democracies like the USA, Britain, France etc. In a country like India, where majority of the population resides in rural areas, decentralization of government should not remain at local level as a mere creed, but it should be an operational imperative. After independence, the focus of the rulers shifted from regulatory to welfare administration. The crucial challenge ahead was the upliftment of the rural masses. Number of the development schemes implemented in this regard could not be pragmatic or fruitful without the active participation of the people at the implementation level. These institutions of local government in rural India are popularly known as Panchayati Raj Institutions (PRIs) and are considered as the excellent instruments to ensure people's participation at grass-roots level in the governance and a vehicle of socio-economic transformation of the rural society. Hence, democratic decentralization is the most debatable issue of the day, not only in India, but in all the Third World countries. The Government of India has taken various steps in this direction since independence and the 73rd Constitutional Amendment Act, 1993 is the latest one, which has provided constitutional apparatus to these bodies.

There is a lot of hue and cry about the autonomy of the local bodies. As these bodies are going to complete their second term after the new enactment, hence it is worthwhile to look into their functioning and procedure of work, and to get appraisal of their actual status as well. It will supplement in ameliorating the functioning of these bodies in future. Hence, a modest attempt has been made in this study to assess the actual position of these bodies with reference to the Zila Parishad in terms of its financial powers and work performance. The main focus of the study is Zila Parishad of Sirsa district in Haryana. The study is exploratory and analytical in nature in which data from 1999 to 2004 have been used.

The main objectives of the study are:

- to assess the functioning of Zila Parishad in Haryana with special reference to Sirsa district;
- to review the financial resources of Zila Parishads;
- to assess the level of participation of women and weaker sections in these institutions; and
- to provide some valuable suggestions for their betterment.

Historical Perspective

Panchayats are as old as our civilization itself and these have existed in one form or the other with more or less autonomy. But, the present idea of democratic decentralization (rural local government) is the result of Lord Mayo Resolution (1870) and Lord Rippon Resolution (1882). The Report of Royal Commission on Decentralization (1909), and the Government of India Acts of 1919 and 1935 have further contributed in this direction.[1] Mahatma Gandhi, the Father of Nation, was an ardent advocate of 'Gram Swaraj'. For him, the term comprises of the meaning of village autonomy and self-sufficiency. Thus, Gandhiji wanted to see each village to work as a small republic in which the people will not only solve their problems on their own but also formulate policies and programmes for development. On Gandhiji's insistence, a clause regarding PRIs was inserted in Indian

Constitution in Article 40 under the chapter on Directive Principles of State Policy. The Panchayati Raj system in India has evolved out of the Community Development Programme (CDP) introduced on October 2, 1952 intended to bring socio-economic development of rural masses in a democratic way. It was further supplemented by the National Extension Service (NES) in 1953. But, within a few years, it was realized that the programme has not delivered the desired results due to lack of people's participation in development programmes and it was not able to initiate the process of transformation of socio-economic life of rural masses as was expected in the First Five-Year Plan document.[2] Keeping this in consideration, the Balwant Rai Mehta Committee (1957) recommended and stressed on the need of democratic decentralization, which is popularly known as Panchayati Raj (PR). It was a three-tier system and Zila Parishad was the apex body. The committee also opined that the system could be affected by devolution of powers to these bodies and handing over the entire charge of development works within its jurisdiction.[3] The government accepted the recommendation of the committee in 1958 and the PR system was inaugurated on 2nd October, 1959 in Nagaur district to Rajasthan by the then Prime Minister, Pt. Jawaharlal Nehru. The other states also adopted this system as per their requirements and conditions. But, these institutions could not fulfil the desired goals and came to decline with passage of time due to odd or even reasons. Various committees were set up by various states to review their functioning and position. Asoka Mehta Committee (1977), appointed by the Janata Party government, was the major one, which suggested two-tier system of Panchayati Raj consisting of Zila Parishad and Village Panchayats. However, these recommendations were not accepted by the government. C.H. Hanumantha Rao Working Group (1983), G.V.K. Rao Committee (1985), L.M. Singhvi Committee 1986), Thungan Committee (1988) etc., were the other committees, which gave valuable suggestions for revamping the local bodies. The 64th and 74th Constitution Amendment Bills of 1989 and 1990 were the other abortive attempts made in this direction. Ultimately, the Congress government at the Centre, led by R.V. Narsimha Rao, succeeded to get the 73rd Constitution Amendment Bill in 1992 passed, which became an Act on 24th April, 1993, when the President gave his assent after ratification by 17 states. The salient features of this Act regarding Zila Parishad as per Article 243G are given below:[4]

1. Zila Parishad is the highest body of three-tier system of PR.
2. Direct election of the members whereas the Chairman and Deputy Chairman are elected by the members among themselves.
3. Five years tenure of each body and holding mid-term elections within six months in the event of supersession.
4. Reservation of one-third seats for women and SCs and STs as per the proportion of their population.
5. Every person, who completes the age of 21 years, is eligible to get elected as member of Zila Parishad.
6. State Election Commission to hold the elections.
7. All the chairpersons of Panchayat Samitis and the MLAs and MPs of that area are its ex-officio members.
8. Grant-in-aid from the State and Union Governments are its main sources of income.
9. The state would devolve more powers to Zila Parishads as per Eleventh Schedule of the Constitution of India to prepare plans for economic development and social justice and for the implementation of development programmes/schemes in their respective areas.

The Eleventh Schedule has been incorporated in Part IX of the Constitution consisting of 29 subjects assigned to PRIs covering the activities relating to rural areas such as agriculture, animal husbandry, minor irrigation, land improvement, small-scale industry, rural housing, drinking water, family planning, social welfare, primary and secondary education etc.[5] Thus, the 73rd Constitution Amendment Act is an attempt to revamp PR for decentralization and rural development with a view to grant power to people at grass-roots level. As per the requirements of this Act, the state governments were asked to prepare new legislation or amend the existing ones for incorporating the provisions of this Act within one year of its enactment. Keeping this into consideration the Haryana Government also passed the Haryana Panchayati Raj Act, 1994 and enforced it from April 22, 1994.[6] This Act incorporates the letter and spirit of the 73rd Constitution Amendment Act. The State Government has assigned various powers to these bodies from time to time to strengthen the process of democratic decentralization. The Government of India has constituted the Ministry of Panchayati Raj recently (2004), which will prove a feather in the cap of PRIs and work for strengthening these institutions. Simultaneously, it has been decided in the National Conference on PRIs held at Jaipur on December 18–20, 2004 that the Union Council of Ministers and the Committee of Secretaries would soon start meeting every month to monitor the progress of PRIs.

Basic Assumptions of Study

It is in the above backdrop the present study was conducted, with following basic assumptions:

— After the 73rd Amendment Act, structural and functional changes have taken place in the Zila Parishad.

— Women and weaker sections have got more representation. Zila Parishads have got more autonomy and financial soundness, which will make them viable institutions.

— Democracy has strengthened at grass-roots level.

Composition of Zila Parishad

The Zila Parishad (ZP), an apex body of Panchayati Raj, is constituted at district level and consists of (a) directly elected members from the wards in a district; (b) chairpersons of all the Panchayat Samitis within a district as ex-officio members; and (c) all the MLAs and MPs, whose constituencies are within the district or part thereof, also as ex-officio members.[7] Every Zila Parishad has ten to thirty members and one member represents at least forty thousand population. For the election of the members of Zila Parishad, the whole district is divided into wards in such a manner that the population of each ward may be the same throughout the district, as far as possible. The president and vice-president of a Zila Parishad are elected by and from amongst the directly elected members. All the ex-officio members have right to vote in the meetings, except for the election and removal of president and vice-president. In Haryana, there are 19 Presidents and 314 members in all the 19 Zila Parishads. The Sirsa Zila Parishad consists of 17 elected members whereas five MLAs, one MP and seven chairpersons of Panchayat Samitis of the district are its ex-officio members.[8] The seats for SCs, BCs and women have been reserved for the members and president of Zila Parishad, as provided in the Act. At least one-third seats have been reserved for women and for SCs and BCs in proportion to their population. Among the elected members, 11 are males and six females. Their categorywise distribution is 11 (7+4) from general category, 5(3+2) from SCs and one from BCs.[9]

Working Procedure

The president is responsible to look after the financial and executive administration and he also convenes and presides over the meetings of Zila Parishad, whereas the vice-president performs the duties of President in his absence and exercise all those powers, which are delegated to him. The president and vice-president can be removed from their offices through a no-confidence motion passed by a two-third majority of its elected members. There is total harmony in Sirsa Zila Parishad as 16 out of 17 members are from the ruling party (INLD). Hence, no problem of no-confidence motion has been observed in the last five years. Moreover, this ZP has been recommended for the best Zila Parishad Award for the year 2003–04 given by the Akhil Bhartiya Panchayat Parishad.[10] The ADC is the ex-officio CEO of Zila Parishad and DDPO acts as the ex-officio Deputy Chief Executive Officer-cum-Secretary of Zila Parishad.[11] The president exercises administrative supervision over the CEO for securing implementation of resolutions and decisions of Zila Parishad. CEO has been empowered to supervise the execution of all works and decisions of the Zila Parishad and the Panchayat Samitis in the district. Besides the CEO, the Sirsa Zila Parishad consists of the following officials: accounts officer (1), superintendent (1), accountant (1), assistants (2), clerks (2), senior scale steno (1), steno-typist (1), peons (2), sweeper (1), driver (1), and one chowkidar.[12] As there is no permanent staff in ZP and all the officials are on deputation, hence, their approach towards development remains totally casual. Thus, it can be removed by appointing permanent officials for each ZP if we really want to decentralize power and strengthen democracy at grass-roots level.

The meetings of Zila Parishad should be held once in two months and the quorum for the ordinary meetings is one-third of the total members of the Zila Parishad. But, so far as the date and agenda of these meetings are concerned, it is mainly decided by the bureaucrats and the role of elected representatives is rather poor. It can also be inferred on the basis of official record of the Zila Parishad that the presence of elected members has remained rather poor (30%) as compared to the officials (90%) in ZP meetings. The participation of women and SC members has also remained poor (about 30%) as compared to the male and general category members, which indicates that these bodies are again losing the very purpose for which these are constituted. The poor participation of members can be improved by giving them TA/DA and a fix honorarium for attending the meetings. Besides, training and motivation camps for members can do a lot, in this matter. The term for office of Zila Parishad is fixed for five years unless dissolved by a resolution passed by the state legislature, ZP can invite any district officer concerning rural affairs departments to attend its meetings with the prior permission of CEO and they can render advice relating to their departments.[13]

The Zila Parishad is required to advice, supervise and coordinate the functions of Panchayat Samitis (PSs) in the district. The various functions entrusted to Zila Parishad are: (i) to advise PSs on different matters; (ii) to consolidate and coordinate development plans prepared by PSs in the district; (iii) to ensure execution of plans, schemes, projects and other works of common interests for two or more PSs in district; (iv) to perform and exercise the powers and functions relating to developmental programmes entrusted by government; (v) to advice the government on matters relating to development activities undertaken by local authority or by government; (vi) to advice the government on allocation of works among GPs and PSs in the district; (vii) to advice the government on matters concerning the implementation of any order specially referred to Zila Parishad; and (viii) to examine and approve budget of PSs in the district. In addition to these functions, the Zila Parishad is also expected to exercise supervision and control over the performance of the administrative functions of GPs and PSs within the district whenever, it is required by the government.[14] A Zila Parishad can constitute any number of committees necessary for execution of its functions. The president of Zila Parishad is an ex-officio chairperson and CEO acts as an ex-officio secretary in each committee. A Zila Parishad can also frame rules and regulations relating to election, conduct of business and meetings of these committees.

Financial Powers

Every Zila Parishad (ZP) prepares a budget and submits it to the government for approval. The officials maintain the accounts of ZPs in prescribed manner and the authority appointed for this purpose carries out the audit. The Zila Parishad Fund, which is to be established by every ZP, comprises the proceeds of taxes, cesses, fees, rents, loans, income from property and the grants received from the government.,[15] A ZP can impose taxes with the prior permission of state government and also can levy and fix fees and cesses. However, in practice, none of the Zila Parishads in the state has imposed any tax so far and, therefore, they are totally dependent upon the grants provided by state government for all their needs and requirements. The main source of funds of ZP is the grants received from state and the central governments under Panchayati Raj schemes and Sampooran Gramin Rojgar Yojana (SGRY) programmes respectively. Under the PRIs funds, the DDPO sent only 10 per cent of it to Zila Parishad whereas for SGRY the CEO, DRDA sent only 20 per cent of its grants to Zila Parishad. Thus, ZP has a little role in this matter as most of the resources are directly allocated to Gram Panchayats and Panchayat Samitis by the concerned officials. The recent decision of the Union Ministry of Panchayati Rai to revamp the Centrally Sponsored Schemes (CSS) and making Gram Sabha at the 'centre of all CSS' will further dilute the status and functions of ZP in PRIs. The LPG syndrome, which emphasized on withdrawal of state machinery from welfare activities and opening of more avenues for market forces, has threatened the fragile fabric of PRIs, particularly that of Zila Parishad. That is why, the ZP cannot attain the desired role or position in PRIs. The Deputy Commissioner is still out of the ambit of ZP. The performance and efficiency of any organization depends upon its financial conditions. If we think that ZP will work more effectively and efficiently, its financial resources should be adequate. The ZP should generate its own financial resources and its dependency on government grants needs to be minimized. In the LPG era of 21st century, there are plenty of opportunities with ZP to raise non-tax revenues like trade tax, commercial transactions, property tax, professional tax, levies etc., which is being collected in most of the developed democracies by the institutions of local self-government. However, the state government does not seem to empower the ZP and the powers are going to be centralized more and more at government level.

Supervision and Control of Zila Parishad

The state government has the power to exercise control over the Zila Parishads. The government or any other officer, appointed for this purpose, can inspect the office or premises of works taken up by the ZP and also can examine and inspect the relevant records and documents.[16] If the government is satisfied that a ZP has defaulted in performing the assigned functions, it can fix a period for performance of these functions. In case of failure to comply with such order, the government can appoint a person to perform the functions and direct that the expenses arising out of the performance be borne by the defaulting Zila Parishad.[17] The government is also empowered to dissolve a Zila Parishad if it is found guilty of misuse of powers, is found incompetent to perform the duties or wilfully disobeys the orders and decisions of the government. When a ZP is dissolved, all powers and duties are exercised and performed by the person appointed for this purpose and all of its property has to be vested in the government.[18] Besides this, the government has power to cancel or suspend any resolution passed by ZP if it is against public interest and/or also against the provisions of the Act.[19] Moreover, a member/Vice-President/President of a ZP can also be suspended by the government, if there is any case of criminal offence or inquiry or a trial under investigation against him.[20]

So far as the structural aspect is concerned, undoubtedly, substantial changes have been noted in the Zila Parishad. After securing the constitutional status, it is no more at the mercy of the state government. The representation of women and weaker sections has increased remarkably but it is still confined to the number and their actual participation in ZP activities is not upto the mark. The rotation system of reservation restricts their tenure, virtually eliminates their chances of re-election and must water down their political ambition to acquire administrative leadership. Apprehensions regarding it have been expressed by Madhu Kishwar, the well-known feminist. Moreover, the MLAs and the MPs should not be allowed to participate in the meetings of ZP because they would not like the emergence of local leadership which can pose challenge to their very existence. In spite of this, we need not to worry and hope that with the passage of time and after getting appropriate cooperation from their family members, and training and motivation, their participation will enhance. However, the poor participation of members, dominating role of bureaucracy, rising political intervention in its activities, dependency on grants for financial outlay, lack of regular staff etc., are some of the major constraints in healthy development of Zila Parishad as a dynamic unit of local self-government. Until we overcome these restraints, the very idea of democratic decentralization cannot be fulfilled. Though certain steps have been taken, but many more are still required to accomplish the desired goals.

Notes

1. S.S. Malik, *The New Panchayati Raj,* Jaipur, Aalekh, 2002, p. 2.
2. A.Y., *Leadership in Panchayati Raj,* Jaipur, Panchsheel, 1979, pp. 7–8.
3. Hoshiar Singh, "Decentralisation Models and Responsive Administration: Need of 21st Century Administration", *Kurukshetra,* Vol. XXX–XXXI, 1996–97, pp. 2–3.
4. *The Constitution (73rd Amendment) Act, 1992,* The Gazette of India, Ministry of Law, Justice and Company Affairs, New Delhi, 1993.
5. *The Times of India,* December 24, 1993.
6. Government of Haryana, *The Haryana Panchayati Raj Act, 1994, Haryana Government Gazette,* Legislative Department, Chandigarh, 1994.
7. Ibid., Section 118.
8. Office of the Zila Parishad, Sirsa, 2004.
9. Economic and Statistical Adviser, Planning Dept., *Statistical Abstract of Haryana,* Government of Haryana, Chandigarh, 2004, pp. 42–43.
10. Director, Panchayats, Haryana, Chandigarh, Letter No. PRA-1–04/33037 38, dated 27/10/04; Secretary, AIPP, BR Mehta Panchayat Bhawan, Delhi, 8m04/2959–93 dated 20/7/04.
11. Government of Haryana, op. cit., Section 133.
12. Office of the Zila Parishad, Sirsa, 2004.
13. Government of Haryana, op. cit., Section 136.
14. Ibid., Section 137.
15. Ibid., Section 145.
16. Ibid., Section 155.
17. Ibid., Section 157.
18. Ibid., Section 158.
19. Ibid., Section 159.
20. Ibid., Section 160.

22 Panchayati Raj System

The Orissa Experiment

B.S. Bhargava and Avinash Samal

Panchayati Raj (PR) system in Orissa, during the last 48 years of its existence, has moved through many ups and downs, twists and turning points, eventually resulting in the abolition of Zila Parishads in 1968. Established as the politico-administrative institutions to provide opportunities to the people to take part in nation-building and development activities; the nature, scope and functioning of these institutions have undergone many changes depending upon the attitude of the ruling elites and the quality of their leadership. Their capacities for effective mobilization of the rural material and human resources have been very much dependent on the functioning of the governments and the way they have looked at it.

There has always been a consistent competition among the major political parties to utilize these institutions as the vote banks. As a result, the system has assumed the status of not just a state-sponsored decentralization strategy, but the institutional forum for mobilization of the people and the expansion of party bases. The way elections were held in 1992 on the one hand, and the manner in which the elected PR bodies at the lower and middle levels were dissolved by the Congress government on August 1, 1995, clearly reflect the attitude of the state governments towards Panchayati Raj Institutions (PRIs). Further, the unprecedented unity among the major political parties (including the ruling Congress) to postpone the panchayat elections scheduled to be held between 27th June and 10th July, 1996, shows the determination of the political parties to annihilate these institutions of rural local government, while adding yet another chapter to the PR history in Orissa.

It is against this background that this paper describes and analyses Orissa's experiments with rural local self-government at different points of time and under different regimes. Here, the analysis has been made in a historical perspective, tracing the evolution of PR from pre-independence period.

Evolution and Structure of Panchayati Raj in Orissa

Prior to the formation of separate Orissa province in April 1936, the region of the present state of Orissa formed parts of the Bengal presidency, Bihar Orissa province, Madras presidency, Sambalpur district and many other princely states which merged with Orissa during 1948 and 1949. Accordingly, the rural local self-government system in Orissa was regulated by the laws prevailing in all those provinces, presidencies and the districts. When the local self-government system in the districts of Cuttak, Puri and Balasore was governed by the laws of Bengal presidency and, later by Bihar Local Self-Government Act, 1885 and the Bihar and Orissa Village Administration Act, 1922; in the districts of Koraput and Ganjam and that of the district of Sambalpur, they were governed by the Madras Local Boards Act, 1920 and the Sambalpur Local Self-Government Act, 1939, respectively.

Thus, in the pre-independence period, Orissa had different Acts operating in different districts. It was a kind of three-tier structure of rural local self-government system where the District Boards stood as the apex body of rural local government at the district level, with Taluka Boards at the taluka level and Union Boards at the village level. And, the same system continued till India became independent.

Soon after independence, the Orissa government passed the Orissa Gram Panchayat Act, 1948 to establish and develop rural local self-government in the village communities of Orissa and to make better provision for their administration. As such, Orissa had the distinction of being the first state in India to introduce Gram Panchayats in the year 1948. The establishment of Gram Panchayats, as the units of self-government replacing the Union Boards constituted under the Bihar and Orissa Village Administration Act, 1992, marked the first major innovation in the field of rural local self-government in India. The provisions of the Act of 1948 extended to all except the municipal and notified areas of the state. Within a couple of years from 1948, the Gram Panchayats came to be established gradually in the areas of newly merged princely states. Thus, the Gram Panchayats at the village level combined with the already existing District Boards and Taluka Boards at district and taluka levels formed the steel frame of rural local self-government in Orissa in the initial years of independence.

With the introduction of the Community Development Programmes (CDP) and the National Extension Service (NES) in October 1952, a new administrative set-up called 'Community Development Block' was evolved to carry out the developmental programmes and projects. But, the earlier system of rural local self-government continued to work till 26th January, 1961, when Panchayat Samitis and Zila Parishads were established at the block and district level as per the provisions of the Orissa Panchayat Samiti and Zila Parishad Act, 1959. Thus, with the already existing Gram Panchayats, when the Panchayat Samitis and Zila Parishads were established on 26th January, 1961 replacing the Taluka and District Boards, a three-tier PR system was born in Orissa 11 years after India became a Republic. Subsequently, the Gram Panchayats were reorganized with suitable amendments in the existing Gram Panchayat Act of 1948 to make them an integral part of the new system. Finally, it was in the year 1964 that a new Act, i.e., Orissa Gram Panchayat Act, 1964 (Orissa Act I of 1965) was passed consolidating all the laws relating to Gram Panchayats in Orissa, which replaced the Orissa Gram Panchayats Act, 1948. Under the new Act, elections were held to the Gram Panchayats in 1967 and along with it, Panchayat Samitis and Zila Parishads were reconstituted in the same year. This system continue till 1968 when the Swatantra government abolished the Zila Parishads on 1st November, 1968, by amending the Orissa Panchayat Samiti and Zila Parishads Act, 1959.

Gram Panchayat

As per the provisions of the Orissa Gram Panchayat Act, 1964 which consolidated all the laws relating to the Gram Panchayats in Orissa, the state government was empowered to establish and constitute the 'Gram', 'Gram Sasan', 'Gram Panchayat', 'Gram Sabha' and 'Palli Sabha'. The government by notification could declare any villages or a group of contiguous villages having population between 2,000 and 10,000 to be a Gram for the constitution of a Gram Panchayat and give a name to the Gram Panchayat. It was to be a corporate body with perpetual succession and a common seal, with power to acquire, hold, and transfer property, to enter into contracts and to do all other things for carrying out the objectives of the Act, and to sue and to be sued in its corporate name. At present, there are 5,262 Gram Panchayats in the state which cover about 50,972 revenue villages.

At the base of the three-tier structure of PR system of Orissa stands the Gram Panchayat, which is the executive body of the Gram Sasan. For each Gram Panchayat, the Act provided for a Gram Sabha—a body comprising all the qualified voters of that Gram. Apart from Gram Sabha, the Act also provided for the Palli Sabhas which are the bodies consisting of all the qualified voters of their respective revenue villages/hamlets situated within the Gram. In fact, both Gram Sabha and the Palli Sabhas are the two general bodies which work within the jurisdiction of a Gram Panchayat as the institutions of direct democracy.

For the constitution of a Gram Panchayat, a Gram is divided into a number of wards ranging from 11 to 25. The voters of each ward elect from amongst themselves their ward members. The ward members along with the Sarpanch (elected directly by the voters of the Gram Sabha) and the Naib-Sarpanch (elected by the ward members from amongst themselves) constitute the Gram Panchayat. Originally, under the Act of 1964, the term of a Gram Panchayat was three years which commences from the date of the first meeting of the Gram Panchayat. However, the state government, if it deemed it expedient, could, by notification, extend from time to time the term of all or any one of the Gram Panchayats so long as the total extension did not exceed two years in the aggregate. By an amendment in 1977, the term has been raised to five years and the total period of extension reduced to one year. As per the Orissa Gram Panchayat (Amendment) Act 1991, the state government can dissolve all or any one of the Gram Panchayats. But, all such Gram Panchayats should be reconstituted by a fresh election held within a period of six months.

It is pertinent to mention here that in the Orissa pattern, the Sarpanch is not elected by the Gram Panchayat but by the Gram Sabha and comes to the Gram Panchayat directly by virtue of his already being elected as the Sarpanch of the Gram. Both Sarpanch and Naib-Sarpanch enjoy a term of five years along with other members of the Gram Panchayat. However, the District Collector can suspend them if he feels that they are abusing their powers by duty reporting the matter to the state government. The Naib-Sarpanch can also be removed from the office if two-third of the members of the Gram Panchayat pass a resolution, with 15 days notice given to the SDO by one-third of the members of the Gram Panchayat through a resolution expressing their no-confidence in him. Besides, there are several other controls exercised by the government. Even the Sub-Collector has the power to annul the resolution of the Gram Panchayat. The Panchayat Secretary is appointed by the Gram Panchayat, but with the approval of the District Panchayat Officer. Interestingly, grass roots democracy in Orissa functioned at the pleasure of the District Collector in respect of finance, tax and so on.

As regards the functions, the original Act of 1964 had provided a long list of obligatory and discretionary functions to be performed by the Gram Panchayats. Obligatory list included functions like construction, maintenance and improvement of public streets, street-lighting, sanitation, maintenance of drainage, construction and maintenance of works and means of supply of water for public and private purposes, registration of deaths, births and marriages, common grazing grounds, maintenance of records relating to cattle census, population census, and other statistics, rendering of all reasonable assistance to the Panchayat Samiti in matters of establishment and maintenance of schools for primary education, supervision and maintenance of village and field boundary marks and maintenance of village records wherever required by the state government etc. Among the discretionary functions are improvement of animal husbandry, slaughter houses, relief from famine and other natural calamities, libraries and reading rooms, ferries, fair-weather roads and cottage industries. The functions entrusted to Gram Panchayats were, thus, numerous.

So far as the functioning is concerned, the Gram Sabha is the deliberative wing of the Gram Sasan which meets twice a year—once in February and the other in June., One-tenth of its membership constitutes the quorum. At the meeting in February, the Gram Sabha considers the programmes and works to be undertaken by the Gram Panchayat during the ensuing year. It also prepares the annual budget for the Gram on the basis of the recommendations of different Palli Sabhas. Again meeting in June, it considers the Gram Panchayat's report on the progress of the programmes and works undertaken by the Gram Panchayat during the preceding year along with the annual audit report. All the meetings of the Gram Sabha are presided over by the Sarpanch. Gram Sabha, thus, stands as an institution of direct democracy where all the members (adult voters of the Gram) directly participate in the discussions and deliberations of its meetings.

The Palli Sabha meets once in a year in the month of February and gives recommendations to the Gram Panchayat in respect of the annual budget and the development works and programmes to be undertaken in the village during the ensuing year. In the case of Palli Sabha, the ward member(s) representing the Palli, preside(s) over the meetings, in order of preferences to be determined by the Gram Panchayat.

Panchayat Samiti

In the three-tier PR set-up of Orissa, the Panchayat Samiti at the block level constitutes the middle tier and is the most important body from the point of view of development works. It was in the year 1959 that following the recommendations of the Balwant Rai Mehta Committee (1957) on democratic decentralization, the Orissa government enacted the Orissa Zila Parishad Act, 1959 making provision for the establishment of Panchayat Samitis and Zila Parishads. In 1961, the name of the Act was changed to the Orissa Panchayat Samiti and Zila Parishad Act, 1959 which came into effect on 26th January, 1961. After the provisions relating to Zila Parishads were deleted in 1968 by the Orissa government the Act came to be known as the Orissa Panchayat Samiti Act, 1959.

As per the provisions of the 1959 Act, all the 314 Community Development Blocks were converted into Panchayati Raj Blocks, each having a Panchayat Samiti consisting of officials and non-officials as its members. The Panchayat Samiti, then, consisted of a chairperson, vice-chairperson, BDO, employees nominated by the government from each of the departments, Sarpanchas of all the Gram Panchayats and the chairpersons of all the municipalities and Notified Area Councils (NACs). There was a provision for representation of members from women/scheduled castes/scheduled tribes by election failing which they could be nominated.

A novel feature of the Orissa Panchayat Samiti is that the official and the ex-officio members like chairpersons of the municipalities and NACs can participate in the discussions of the meetings without the right to vote. But, after 1991 amendment, with the direct election of the members for the Panchayat Samiti who in turn elect the chairperson from amongst themselves, the Sarpanchas of Gram Panchayats have become the ex-officio members without right to vote. Again, with regard to the composition of the Panchayat Samitis, Orissa has a distinction. Unlike many other states where the BDO and his team of officers are there only to run the administration of the block (without having a place in the Panchayat Samiti itself), the Panchayat Samitis in Orissa include the BDO and his team of officers as official members to ensure the technical and administrative aspects of any decision taken by the Panchayat Samiti. While in one sense it benefits the decision-making, sometimes it might contribute to misunderstandings also.

Under the original Act of 1959, the term of the Panchayat Samiti, including all its members, was three years commencing from the date of its first meeting after the constitution of the Panchayat Samiti. But later, it was raised to five years. The Panchayat Samiti as the key tier in the PR set-up of Orissa is the centre of all developmental activities. As such, in the initial years of its existence, it was entrusted with a number of functions like planning, execution and supervision of development programmes in the block, management and control of primary education and trusts, endowments and other institutions, supervision and enforcement of laws relating to vaccination and registration of deaths and births, borrowing of money and granting of loans, supervision of Gram Panchayats and any other function assigned by the government.

The executive authority of the Panchayat Samiti is vested with the chairperson, and he/she exercises his/her powers through the BDO. The BDO, as the executive officer, is the main instrument of execution of resolutions, orders, decisions and projects. The budget of the Panchayat Samiti is prepared by the BDO with the approval of the chairperson and is placed before the body for sanction and thereafter submitted to the District Collector who has the power to modify it, if he so feels. Under the Act of 1959, the budget of the Panchayat Samiti used to be submitted to the Zila Parishad for approval. But after the Zila Parishads were abolished in 1968, the Collector had become the approving authority. Now, with the revival of the Zila Parishads (under the Orissa Zila Parishads Act, 1991), the original position has been restored.

Zila Parishad

Zila Parishads, which constitute the third-tier in the PR system of Orissa, were first constituted in January 1961 and for some time they worked well. But, unfortunately, only after seven years of functioning, they fell victims to the party politics and were abolished in 1968 on flimsy grounds. Later some alternative arrangements were made in this regard by establishing the District Advisory Councils and District

Development Committees. However, after a long spell of 23 years, the Zila Parishads were revived in 1991 by an Act called the Orissa Zila Parishad Act, 1991.

As regards the constitution of Zila Parishad, the original Act of 1959 had provided that the following will be the members of the Zila Parishad:

1. Chairpersons of all Panchayat Samitis in the district.
2. Collector of the district (as Chief Executive Officer) and other district officers of medical, education, public health, agriculture, veterinary, forest, welfare, works, cooperative and such other departments as may be prescribed.
3. Sub-Divisional Officers exercising jurisdiction within the district.
4. Chairpersons of the municipalities and NACs.
5. Presidents of Central Cooperative Banks functioning in the district.

But in the Orissa Zila Parishad Act, 1991, which has made provision for direct election of members to the Zila Parishads, following categories have been added:

6. One member elected directly on the basis of adult suffrage from each constituency of a block within the district (each block comprises of two constituencies).
7. Members of the House of the People and the State Legislative Assembly whose constituencies or major portions thereof fall within the district (an MP or MLA cannot become a member of more than one Zila Parishad at a time).
8. Members of Rajya Sabha having place of residence in the district.
9. Project Administrators of Integrated Tribal Development Agencies.
10. Project Officers of District Rural Development Agencies.
11. District Development Officers.

A Zila Parishad so constituted had a wide variety of functions. All the executive and emergency powers of the Zila Parishad were vested in the president. He was empowered to implement the resolutions and decisions. The Zila Parishad had the power to undertake schemes or adopt measures including giving of financial assistance relating to development of agriculture, industries, rural credit, cooperatives, water supply, distribution of essential commodities, rural electrification, minor irrigation, public health and sanitation including establishment of dispensaries and hospitals, communications, primary, secondary and adult education including welfare and other objects of general public utility. It also had the power to examine and approval of the budget estimates of Panchayat Samitis in the district coordinate and integrate the development plans and schemes prepared by the Panchayat Samitis in the district, and make grants to Panchayat Samitis or Gram Panchayats within the district,

After the abolition of Zila Parishads, the District Advisory Councils and District Development Committees were set up at the district level to advise and review the development and non-development works, to suggest measures for speedy and effective implementation of the development programmes. The District Advisory Council comprised of Collector as the chairperson, various district level officers, Panchayat Samiti, municipality and NAC chair-persons, Central Cooperative and Land Mortgage Bank Presidents and MLAs and MPs as members. The District Development Committee had the Collector as chairperson and various officers in the district and Block Development Officers as members. This was purely an official body. These committees were required to meet at least once in two months. But, in matters of decision-making and administration, it was not the representatives of the people who had a voice but the Collector who exercised his monopoly.

Decline of Panchayati Raj

The PR system in Orissa, like many other states, was introduced with enthusiasm and interest. It was introduced in its full structural form with a hope that it would bring democracy at the doorsteps of the rural people; that is would evoke people's participation in the decision-making and in implementation of development programmes and schemes which will determine their destiny, by and large; and that by bringing bureaucracy under local popular control it will accelerate the process of socio-economic development. Further, it was hoped that in a poor state like Orissa, where about 80 per cent the state's population live in villages with numerous problems and under conditions of poverty, unemployment, illiteracy, malnutrition and starvation, the PRIs will fulfil the long-felt need of providing rural infrastructure for development. It was hoped that through these rural local institutions the development of rural areas and specifically of the weaker sections could be brought about in a better way.

Beginning with 1961, in the initial years of its existence, i.e., upto 1967, the PRIs functioned well in most parts of the state. They created an atmosphere of enthusiasm for the people to participate in the election to the rural local bodies and take interest in the development activities. It created a sort of awareness among the people in rural areas regarding their own social and economic development. However, it was made possible because of their social solidarity and the feeling of oneness and unity among themselves, which resulted in the unanimous election of many people's representatives to these local bodies.

But this spirit of unity, oneness and fellow-feeling did not last long. Very soon it started evaporating for the interplay of a number of factors. Like many other states, the concept of party politics made its quick entry into the PR set-up of Orissa like a serpent in the Garden of Eden. The entry of political parties into the PR system polluted the environment, broke the traditional bond of unity and disturbed the rural society and their relationship. And finally, it diverted the PRIs from its main task of rural development through people's participation.

Almost all political parties in order to strengthen their party bases, started taking keen interest in the PR elections. Since the PR bodies provide a solid base for the political parties, by any means, they wanted to retain their hold over these institutions. The individual leaders, in order to make their position strong in the party, went on with a mission to create 'personal vote banks' in the rural local institutions. As a result, the main task of rural development through popular participation was relegated to the background. In providing the developmental assistance to the people, political considerations became the first priority and not the needy and poor. The benefits meant for the cross-sections of the society were cornered by the party cadres and economically well-off and socially higher-ups of the society.

In a sense, the PRIs in Orissa had become moribund when Biju Patnaik's (the then Congress leader) grip over state and politics declined after the mid-sixties. The first attack on PR came in 1968 when Zila Parishads were abolished by the Swatantra-led coalition government of Orissa. Whatever may be the argument forwarded by the government in defence of its action, the fact was that the then coalition government of Orissa wanted to weaken the hold and influence of the dominant Congress Party over these rural local bodies. Hence, on the plea that Zila Parishads without any power of execution are creating bottlenecks in speedy execution of works by delaying the distribution of the government grants to Panchayat Samitis, it abolished the Zila Parishads. However, this enabled many state level politicians, especially those of the ruling party, to keep their hold tight over the rural local bodies.

However, the Swatantra-led coalition government is not the only government to be accused of playing politics in the working of the PRIs. It is also true with the Congress government of Orissa which was in power for a fairly long period of time. In December 1983, when elections were held to the Gram Panchayats, the then J.B. Patnaik government of Orissa was accused of utilizing the official machinery and the money and muscle power for securing the seats of power in these institutions.

Even the Biju Patnaik-led Janata Dal government (1990–1995), which claimed to have taken the credit for conducting elections to various PR bodies after a gap of nine years, is not free from such criticisms. In May-June 1992, when elections were held to the newly reorganized PR bodies, it really shocked the people of Orissa and took the observers and the people of neighbouring states by surprise. Altogether, it claimed 16 lives (official report) and had left more than 100 injured. The people of Orissa would always remember the panchayat elections of 1992, it not for anything else but at least for the violent incidents that rocked most of the districts during the polls.

Janata Government and Panchayati Raj Reforms

After a gap of ten years, in 1990 State Legislative Assembly elections, the Janata Dal returned to power with absolute majority under the leadership of the veteran leader, Biju Patnaik. Having committed to provide a better administration when a determined Biju Patnaik wanted to awaken the state from its backwardness and apathy, he realized that devolution of power to the people through PRIs is a must for the development of rural Orissa without which nothing could be achieved. It may be recalled that it was the same Biju Patnaik under whose stewardship in the state in the early sixties, PRIs flourished in Orissa. Once again, after assuming power in March 1990, Biju Patnaik-led Janata Dal government in Orissa started taking steps to revitalize the PR system in the state.

In an attempt to reform the PR system, the Orissa government in 1991 passed three important Acts, namely, the Orissa Gram Panchayat (Amendment) Act, 1991, the Orissa Panchayat Samiti (Amendment) Act, 1991 and the Orissa Zila Parishad Act, 1991. The passing of these three Acts was a landmark event in the history of PR in Orissa. With many radical provisions, the new Acts of 1991 ushered in a new era for the PRIs and entrusted them with overwhelming powers to bring about rural development through people's participation and cooperation. Not only the government passed the Acts, but it also showed its sincerity by conducting elections to Gram Panchayats and Panchayat Samiti in 1992 as per the provisions of the amended Acts of 1991.

Unlike the old Acts of 1959 and 1964, the amended Acts of 1991 had made elaborate provision for the reservation of seats for the scheduled castes and scheduled tribes in the panchayats at all levels on the basis of their population.[4] Further, the reservation of one-third of the seats for women (including those belonging to SC/ST groups) in the Panchayats at all levels on rotation basis was a revolutionary step. In fact, Orissa was the first state in the country to implement 33 per cent reservation for women in municipalities and panchayats at a time when the centre was still deliberating on the issues. Thus, following the 1992 elections to municipalities and Panchayats, Orissa had about 480 women representatives in the 94 municipalities. They numbered more than 35,000 in the 5,262 Gram Panchayats and 314 Panchayat Samitis.

Compared to the Constitution (73rd Amendment) Act, 1992, the Orissa government had not only made one-third of the seats reserved for women, but also had gone a few step ahead in reserving the post of vice-chairperson for women in the panchayats at all levels, if the chairperson elected was not a woman. This step was a radical one considering the fact that neither the Constitution (73rd Amendment) Act of 1992, nor any of the states had a provision as progressive as that of Orissa. The amendment made with regard to the direct election of the members of all the PR bodies was a 'radical step' taken to make the PRIs more democratic and responsible. Devolving more and more powers and functions to the PRIs in the field of rural reconstruction and development, and the provisions for the constitution of a state level Finance Commission to look into the financial position of PRIs showed the government's interest in the PR system. Moreover, the passing of the Zila Parishad Act, 1991, to revive the abolished institution of Zila Parishad, was certainly a commendable job done by the government to make the PR system a three-tier set-up. In reforming the PR system, the Orissa government had, thus, shown its imagination and in a sense, when the Constitution (72nd Amendment) Bill, 1991 was still waiting for its fate to be decided, the implementation of the above reform measures placed Orissa's PR system at a higher pedestal.

The famous PR convention organized by the Orissa government on 5th March, 1993 at Bhubaneswar and the declaration of 5th March (birthday of Biju Patnaik,) as the *'Panchayati Raj Divas'*, further substantiates the government's commitment and interest in the development of PRIs. Looking at the attitude of the government towards PRIs at that time and the one it had shown in the past (during Biju Patnaik's reign in the early sixties), people of Orissa and that of the rest of the country were hopeful that the measures taken by Biju Patnaik government for the revitalization of PRIs will go a long way in making these institutions capable of ushering a new era in field of rural development through people's participation.

Congress Government of 1995 and the Status of Panchayati Raj

Things became different with a change in the guard at Bhubaneswar. When the Congress (I) came to power in March 1995, it was feeling uncomfortable with the Gram Panchayats and the Panchayat Samitis which were seen as the legacy of Janata rule in the state. The Congress (I) leaders in the state were looking at PRIs through suspicious eyes. Whether the elephants make love or they fight, it is the grass that suffers. And that is what exactly happened to the PRIs when the Congress (I) government, in August 1995, dissolved all the panchayat bodies depriving and denying the people of Orissa of their right to rural local self-government. The dissolution of the PRIs by the Congress (I) government, thus, marked the beginning of another crucial chapter in the history of PR by bringing the three-year old PR of Janata government in Orissa to an abrupt end.

Though Article 243E (3b) of Indian Constitution elections to constitute the panchayats were due before February 1996 but the government seemed to have turned a blind eye towards the constitutional proprieties. For one reason or the other, it has always tried to postpone the elections to PRIs.

Besides, it was mainly the Janata Dal led by late Biju Patnaik which took the lead for the cancellation of the polls. Interestingly, it was the same Janata Dal government under the leadership of Biju Patnaik which had taken the lead in reforming the PR in Orissa.

Thanks to the political parties and to the wisdom of the so-called champions of devolution of power, that ultimately elections were held in January 1997. Though the elections to the panchayats were marked by violence in as many as 19 districts in the coastal Orissa which claimed nine lives and left 200 injured; for the first time elections to all the 81,108 posts of ward members, 5,262 Sarpanchas and Panchayat Samiti members and 854 Zila Parishad members were held after a period of three decades marking the emergence of a three-tier PR system in Orissa.

Concluding Observations

As has been mentioned earlier, the nature, character and functioning of the PRIs vary depending on the attitude of the ruling elites, quality of their leadership, governmental control exercised upon these bodies from time to time and finally, the way government looks at these institutions. What emerges from the above discussion is that when the political bosses at the state capital have always been eager to capture the seats of power in these rural local government bodies, at the same time they have never shown any interest in the successful working of these institutions in achieving the goals for which they stand. On the other hand, they have become suspicious about the emerging leadership in these institutions. They see in these leaders a potential threat to their hegemonistic leadership and hence, do not take any interest in conducting regular elections. The fact that elections were held after a gap of nine years (in 1992) and the manner in which elections were postponed in May 1996, proves the point.

The unprecedented show of unity among the major political parties including the ruling Congress and the main opposition Janata Dal to postpone the panchayat elections, has not only exposed their duality in character but also demonstrated the truth that their call for decentralization of power through PRIs was nothing but an empty talk. It has shown that the political parties for their petty personal interest can go to the extent of endangering the very base on which the edifice of our larger political system stands. Just to capture the seats of power at the PRIs, the political parties can go to the extent of postponing the elections time and again, even if the timing of the elections does not suit them.

The fact that elections to the three-tier PRIs were ultimately conducted in January 1997 is not without reasons. Among other factors contributing to the holding of elections, constitutional compulsions on the one hand and the 'political expediency' on the other are considered important. Since the PR bodies were dissolved in August 1995, the Congress government could not have deferred the elections further for an indefinite period. The pressure from the NGOs and the people at large might have also forced the Congress government to conduct the elections one and half years after their dissolution.

Now that a three-tier PR system has been established in Orissa, the question that remains to be answered is: How is it going to work? What kind of environment the government is going to provide for the PRIs to function for the all-round development of the people at the grassroots? All this is difficult to say in the absence of any field based research conducted on the functioning of PRIs. It is hoped that the scholars would draw their attention to this rather neglected area and suggest the ways and means for providing a sustainable rural local self-government for the people of Orissa.

References

Beuria, S.T., (1996). "Parties Unite to Put Off Panchayat Polls", *Deccan Herald,* June 11, Bangalore.

———, (1997). "Panchayat Elections Marked by Violence", *Deccan Herald,* January 24, Bangalore.

Bhargava, B.S. and K. Samal, (1996). "Panchayati Raj System in Orissa: Problems and Prospects" in V.S. Mahajan (ed.), *Agriculture, Rural Development and Panchayati Raj: National Level Strategies and Policies,* Deep and Deep, New Delhi.

Government of India, (1993). "The Constitution (73rd Amendment) Act, 1992", *Gazette of India,* Extra, Part 11, Section 1, 20th April.

Government of Orissa, (1991). *Orissa Zila Parishad Act,* 1991.

———, (1991). *Orissa Gram Panchayat* (Amendment) Act, 1991.

———, (1991). *Orissa Panchayat Samiti* (Amendment) Act, 1991.

Jena, B.B., (1995). "Orissa" in *Status of Panchayati Raj in the States of India,* Concept, New Delhi.

Mathew, George, (1994). "Orissa Leads the Way" in *Panchayati Raj From Legislation to Movement,* Concept, New Delhi.

———, (1996). "Panchayats in a Death Trap", *The Hindu,* June 14, Madras.

23 Implementation of Panchayati Raj in Rajasthan

In the Light of 73rd Constitutional Amendment Act

G.S. Narwani

Rajasthan was the first state in India where a three-tier Panchayati Raj (PR) system was inaugurated by the late Prime Minister Pt. Jawahar Lai Nehru on 2nd October, 1959. It worked with great enthusiasm during the sixties when agriculture, animal husbandry, medical, cooperatives, primary education, social education, and women and child welfare were integral parts of the PR system. People's representatives were actively associated with rural development activities. Regular elections of PRIs were held in 1960 and 1965 only. Thereafter, in 1978, after a long spell of 13 years, elections were held only for Panchayats. In Panchayat Samitis and Zila Parishads, officials worked as administrators. Subsequent elections were held in the years 1981, 1988 and 1995.

People's representatives in Panchayati Raj Institutions (PRIs) became so popular and strong in rural areas that most of the chairpersons got elected as MLAs and became ministers. It was cause for worry among the legislators who always remained interested in weakening the PR structure.

Bureaucrats under the garb of World Bank assistance created departmental kingdoms through agricultural extension projects and green revolution, operation flood and dairy plants, ICDS, watershed development etc. PRIs were rendered weaker and weaker administratively as well as financially.

Rural development programmes for employment generation and poverty alleviation were also centralized in District Rural Development Agency under the chairmanship of District Collector. The Government of India routed all funds for DDP, DPAP, wasteland development, JRY, Indira Avas, IRDP, employment assurance, lift irrigation, TRYSEM etc., only through the agency of DRDA. It rendered Zila Parishad a weak institution at the district level.

Most of these programmes were implemented through various departments like soil conservation, forest, irrigation, ground water, PWD etc. PRIs had little share in these funds in the form of JRY, IRDP, Jeevan Dhara or Indira Avas. In fact, the PRIs were left at the mercy of DRDAs for rural development, employment and poverty alleviation programmes. The Zila Parishad remained as an administrative body only for selection of teachers and as an intermediary between the State Government and the Panchayats.

Thus, during the eighties, PRIs remained neither the institutions of self-government nor of democratic decentralization of power as envisaged in Article 40 of the Constitution of India.

It was in such a sorry state of affairs that our late Prime Minister Rajiv Gandhi tried to revive the PRIs. It was through his sincere efforts eventually that the 73rd Constitutional Amendment could see the light of day on 23rd April, 1993. All the state governments were required to amend their respective laws within one year. Accordingly, the Rajasthan Panchayati Raj Act, 1994 was passed on 23rd April, 1994 incorporating all the provisions of 73rd Constitutional Amendment Act.

The Rajiv Gandhi Foundation organized a national seminar on Panchayati Raj at New Delhi on 22–23 December, 1997 to find out whether PRIs have indeed emerged as institutions of self-government as envisaged in Article 243–G. A survey by task force on Panchayati Raj revealed that the overall picture was far from encouraging. The basic ideology was ignored by state legislatures.

Status of Panchayati Raj in Rajasthan

Powers of Gram Sabha (Article 243-A)

It was left at the discretion of state legislature to entrust such powers and perform such functions to the Gram Sabha as it deemed proper.

Section 3 of the Rajasthan Panchayati Raj Act, 1994 provides for meetings of Gram Sabha to be held twice a year in the first and last quarter of the year. The Gram Sabha has been vested with the powers to identify beneficiaries for IRDP and Indira Avas, propose annual plan, discuss budget and audit report, review progress and observations of vigilance committee. But, decisions of the Gram Sabha are not binding on the Panchayati, which is the real executive body. The Gram Sabha has more or less an advisory role, hence elected representatives hardly care for it. Moreover, the Gram Sabha is not held in every village. It is held only at Panchayat headquarters, hence surrounding villages at a distance of 7–8 km generally do not participate. The Gram Sabha does not have the power of settling local disputes of field boundaries, local pathways, minor offences etc., which old Gaon Sabha used to exercise so as to avoid resort to police and courts. The Gram Sabha should be stronger in all areas including tribal areas as provided in Panchayats (Extension to Scheduled Areas) Act, 1996.

Panchayats at Village, Intermediate and District Levels (Article 243-B)

Sections 9, 10 and 11 of the Rajasthan Panchayati Raj Act, 1994 provide for constitution of Panchayats at all the three levels. They were already existing in Rajasthan since 1959.

Composition of Panchayats through Direct Elections (Article 243-C)

Relevant provisions are contained in Sections 12, 13 and 14 of the Rajasthan Panchayati Raj Act, 1994. Sarpanch and Panchas at village level and members at Panchayat Samiti and Zila Parishad levels are elected directly by the people. The Pradhan of Panchayat Samiti and the Pramukh of Zila Parishad are elected by and from amongst these elected members. Prior to such direct elections, Sarpanchas of Village Panchayats became members of Panchayat Samiti and Pradhans of Panchayat Samitis became members of Zila Parishad. Such linkage is missing now. Directly elected members of Panchayat Samiti and Zila Parishad feel frustrated since they do not find any function to perform. To remove this anomaly, the Rule 37 of Rajasthan Panchayati Raj Rules, 1996 authorized members of Panchayat Samiti and Zila Parishad to participate in meetings of Village Panchayat in which such members ordinarily reside. Through an administrative order of 21st December, 1996, the Sarpanchas were made invitee members in Panchayat Samiti and Zila Parishad respectively. They can participate in discussions only without any power to vote on any matter.

Reservation of Seats for SCs/STs/OBCs/Women (Article 243-D)

Section 15 of the Rajasthan Panchayati Raj Act, 1994 provide and for reservation of seats for SCs/STs in proportion to population, 15 per cent for OBC and where total reservation for SCs/STs does not exceed 50 per cent, and one-third seats for women in every category.

Similarly, Section 16 provides reservation for chairpersons at all levels. Weaker sections of society have definitely come to power but they will be effective only after proper training, experience and education. Illiterate chairpersons have to depend on their secretaries whereas lady Sarpanchas and Pradhans take assistance of their husbands, sons or other dependable relatives. Even during meetings, husbands of women chairpersons generally participate unofficially. A study is needed as to how women representatives can become more effective in delivering goods in rural areas. Their participation is casual, passive and ineffective in most of the cases in Panchayats in general and insignificant even in programmes of child and woman development, nutrition, vaccination, rural sanitation, rural water supply, family planning etc.

Regular and Timely Election through State Election Commission (Articles 243-E and 243-K)

Section 17 of the Rajasthan Panchayati Raj Act, 1994 provides for regular elections of PRIs to be held every five years and reconstitution within six months in case of dissolution. The State Election Commission has also been constituted for the purpose under Section 199 of the Rajasthan Panchayati Raj Act, 1994.

Age Relaxation of 21 to Contest Election (Article 243-F)

Section 19 of Rajasthan Panchayati Raj Act, 1994 contains this clause.

Endow Panchayats with powers and authority to enable them to function as institutions of self-government (Article 243-G).

The State Government was required to endow powers to the Panchayats out of items as mentioned in Schedule XI of the Constitution of India. Devolution of powers and responsibilities with respect to:

1. the preparation of plans for economic development and social justice, and
2. implementation of schemes in relation to 29 matters listed in the Schedule XI has not so far been implemented in Rajasthan. In all, 17 items out of 29 are included in the Schedules 1, 11, 111

regarding powers to be exercised respectively by Panchayat, Panchayat Samiti and Zila Parishad as per Rajasthan Panchayati Raj Act, 1994, and relevant Sections 50, 51 and 52 provide that such powers as mentioned in the above schedule of powers shall be exercised by respective PRIs, of course subject to certain conditions as laid down by the State Government. A period of more than four years has already passed since the enactment of Rajasthan Panchayati Raj Act, 1994 but not even a single notification has so far been issued for transferring any subject like agricultural extension, fruit and vegetable cultivation, veterinary care, fisheries, health programmes, rural water supply, minor irrigation tanks, women and child development, social welfare, rural employment and poverty alleviation programmes, conventional energy, district and rural roads, upper primary schools etc. DRDA and women development agency are still functioning as separate entities outside the purview of Zila Parishads at the district level. Political will is completely lacking in this respect under the pretext that elected representatives at village level are not matured and experienced enough to discharge such functions efficiently. Thus, Rajasthan has failed to follow the spirit of Article 243-G of the Constitution of India. Promise on paper has not at all been translated in practice. Thus, the overall picture is very dismal and not encouraging. A study is required how it should be implemented in practice in Rajasthan.

Powers to Levy Taxes etc (Article 243-H)

No compulsory taxes have been prescribed by the Rajasthan Panchayati Raj Act, 1994. Village Panchayats have been invested with powers to levy house tax, octroi, toll tax, vehicle tax, tax on commercial crops etc., as per Section 68 of Rajasthan Panchayati Raj Act, 1994. Rates of taxes and fees have been specified in Rule 68 (Fees), Rule 70 (Country Liquor), Rule 73 (House Tax), Rule 78 (Octroi), Rule 94 (Commercial Crop), Rule 98 (Water Levy) and Rule 103 (Vehicle Tax). A Panchayat Samiti can collect entertainment tax (Rule 71), profession tax (Rule 72), education cess, tax on fairs as per maximum rates specified in rules as per Section 68 of the Rajasthan Panchayati Raj Act, 1994. A Zila Parishad can levy surcharge on stamp duty upto 5.5 per cent on mandi tax as per Section 69 of the Rajasthan Panchayati Raj Act, 1994. But reluctance on the part of people's representatives to levy tax and fear of losing votes in election have deterrent effect on raising tax resources in PRIs. Grant-in-aid at the rate of Rs 11 per capita per year to Village Panchayats and at the rate of Rs 1.25 per capita per year to Panchayat Samitis is given.

State Finance Commission (Article 243-I)

Section 118 of the Rajasthan Panchayati Raj Act, 1994 provides for appointment of the State Finance Commission. In Rajasthan, the Commission was appointed but it was not possible to decide the quantum of funds due to non-transfer of any function specified in Schedule XI of the Constitution of India. It had to recommend that as and when these powers and functions are transferred from various departments to PRIs, concerned staff and budget shall also be transferred to PRIs. As regards share of taxes out of state revenue, only 2.18 per cent out of net collection of taxes was transferred to PRIs which is a very meagre sum. Thus, PRIs have been left at the mercy of State Government without any right for substantial share in state tax revenues.

District Planning Committee (74th Constitution Amendment)

Though Section 121 of Rajasthan Panchayati Raj Act, 1994 provided for constitution of district planning committee under the chairmanship of the Pramukh, Zila Parishad, but Rule 352 gave it power of preparing of plan only. Execution, monitoring, review or evaluation of district plans have been kept out of their purview. Thus, it is only a powerless committee.

Deficiency Areas

Neither Finance nor Staff at Panchayat Level

The spirit of Article 40 of the Constitution of India has still been ignored that the state shall take steps to organize Village Panchayats and endow them with such powers and authority as may be necessary to enable them to function as units of self-government. The Village Panchayat is financially weak to discharge the civic functions and become a unit of self-government. The Panchayat does not have an exclusive Secretary to discharge functions. The Gramsevak-cum-Secretary looks after at least two Panchayats. Hence, with handicaps of finance and staff, the Village Panchayat cannot be an effective PRI at village level.

Powers and Authority Still Not Transferred

Article 243-G provided that preparation and implementation of schemes of economic development and social justice as listed in

Schedule XI of the Constitution of India may be entrusted to PRIs by state government. Though Schedules 1, 11, 111 of Rajasthan Panchayati Raj Act, 1994 provide for 17 functions out of 29 to be transferred to PRIs and Sections 50, 51 and 52 make it mandatory but the state government has still been sleeping over it. Not a single notification has so far been issued in compliance of Sections 50, 51, 52 of the Rajasthan Panchayati Raj Act, 1994.

Meagre Share in State Tax Revenues

The State Finance Commission failed to specify share of PRIs in state tax collection. A small share of only 2.18 per cent cannot make PRIs self-reliant.

Lack of Training for SC/ST/Women Chairpersons

Reservation for chairpersons, specially women and SC/ST, can prove beneficial only after intensive training programme and refresher courses every year. After one training of Pradhans of Panchayat Samitis and Pramukhs of Zila Parishads, they were abandoned due to fear of agitation for powers by newly elected leaders. No specialized NGOs were entrusted with training responsibilities at district or Panchayat Samiti level to train chairpersons of reserved categories or women representatives. Training is needed on a large scale for efficient management of PRIs.

Weak District Planning Committees

The District Planning Committees have been rendered ineffective since powers of execution, monitoring and review have been withheld from them.

Weak Zila Parishads

DRDA, DWDA, FFDA are still independent of Zila Parishad. The Collector is the chairman of all these district level agencies meant for rural development, women development and fisheries development.

Weak Gram Sabhas

The Gram Sabha has only an advisory role. Its decisions are not binding on Village Panchayat. The Gram Sabha is not empowered to decide local disputes of field boundaries, village pathways or minor offences etc.

24 Panchayati Raj in Tamil Nadu

Santishree D.N.B. Pandit

Panchayati Raj Institutions (PRIs) in Tamil Nadu or the erstwhile Madras State can be traced to beginnings in 1871. Though claims are made that Village Panchayats have always formed an integral part of social life from times immemorial. The Cholas had Village Panchayats functioning as self-contained economic and administrative units. They were little republics enjoying a great deal of local autonomy with powers of taxation for local purposes. They were great centres of cultures and corporate life.[1]

The Local Fund Act of 1871, though nascent, was responsible for creating the district boards. The need to undertake local works like laying roads and digging wells gave rise to the idea that funds have to be raised locally for local purposes. These included land cess, house tax and tolls. The Madras Local Boards Act was passed in 1884. This Act created district, taluka and union boards. The members were elected and nominated in part in the ratio of 1:2 respectively. This made the nominated members to dominate in local policy making.

The 'dyarchy' experiment brought into effect the Madras Village Panchayat Act, which came into effect in 1920. This Act placed Village Panchayats on a separate statutory footing, distinguishing it from district, taluka and union boards. It enfranchised all men over twenty-five years of age and provided for the election of all members of the panchayats. A post of Registrar General of Panchayats was also created to supervise the panchayats. Non-official organizers aided him. The Local Boards Act of 1930 repealed the Madras Panchayats Act of 1920 and abolished local boards.

Independence in 1947 brought changes for PRIs, which were linked with rural development administration. It was in keeping with the constitutional vision of power to the people that the Madras Panchayats Act of 1950 was passed. It came into force from April 1951. This Act sought to give effect to Article 40 of the Constitution of India which enjoined that the state shall take steps to organize panchayats and endow them with such powers and authority as may be necessary to enable them to function as units of self-government. This Act enabled every village or hamlet with a population of 500 and above to have a panchayat. Every panchayat was divided into wards, subject to a minimum of two, for the purpose of election of members. The term of office of the president and members was three years. The Village Panchayats were enjoined with certain obligatory functions like construction, repair and maintenance of public roads, lighting of streets and public places, construction of drains, cleansing of streets, removal of garbage, provision of public latrines, provision of protected water supply, sinking and repairing of wells, ponds or tanks and taking preventive and remedial public health measures.

Tamil Nadu was one of the few states which took initiative in the implementation of the Community Development Programme and the National Extension Service. Under this, the establishment of over 370 Community Developments Blocks in the state created a cohesive administrative and organizational framework. There were many debates on the issue of radical reform of local government. A committee was set up by the state government in 1951, under the chairmanship of Muttikrishna Menon to study the issue of abolition, retention or replacement of district board or, in case of their retention, to suggest improvements in their performance. The committee submitted its report in 1953.[2] The committee's recommendations came in handy to reduce the powers of the district boards in the 1958 Act, where it became an advisory body only. This was mainly done to curtail the powerful district boards and resolve once for all the conflict between the state government and district boards, in favour of the former.

Following the acceptance of the recommendations of the Balwant Rai Mehta Committee of the Government of India, the Madras government passed the Tamil Nadu Panchayats Act, 1958.[3] This was a significant step towards the achievement of democratic decentralization in Tamil Nadu. This Act that was in force till the recent Tamil Nadu Panchayats Act 1994 was passed to give effect to the 73rd and 74th Amendments to the Constitution of India.[4]

The Tamil Nadu Panchayat Act, 1958[5] created a three-tier system of Panchayati Raj in the state. The first two tiers, viz., Village Panchayat and Panchayat Union were elected bodies. The third tier, that is, the District Development Council was presided over by the District Collector who coordinates all the developmental activities in the district. The term of office for the elected members of the first two tiers was five years.[6] Members from the scheduled castes, scheduled tribes and women can be co-opted if they are not elected. Thirty per cent of the seats of the Village Panchayats were reserved for them. Every co-opted member had all the rights, powers and privileges of the elected members.[7]

The functions of Village Panchayats have been clearly drawn out in the 1958 Act under Sections 63 and 64. They are the construction, repair and maintenance of the village public roads, the lighting of public roads and public places in built-up areas, the construction of drains and the disposal of drainage water, the cleansing of streets and garbage removal, the provision of public latrines and arrangement to cleanse latrines whether public or private, the opening and maintenance of burial and burning grounds and the sinking and repairing of wells, the evacuation, repair and maintenance of water works, ponds or tanks.[8] In addition, a Village Panchayat is responsible for the planting and preservation of trees, the opening and maintenance of public slaughter houses, reading rooms, literary centres and other works of public utility.[9]

The Panchayat Unions, which function at the second tier, i.e., at the block level, have been assigned functions under Section 65 of the Act.[10] They are responsible for the establishment and maintenance of dispensaries and the payment of subsidies to rural medical practitioners, of maternity and child welfare centres including family planning programme, the construction and maintenance of houses for poor, the training and employment of vaccinators, the removal of congestion of population and the provision of house sites, the opening and maintenance and expansion or improvement of all elementary schools, preventive and remedial measures connected with any epidemic, veterinary relief, the extension of village sites and the regulation of buildings, the opening and maintenance of village sites and the regulation of buildings; the opening and maintenance of public markets, the maintenance of statistics relating to births and deaths, improvements of agriculture, agricultural stock and the holding of agricultural shows and the promotion and encouragement of cottage industries.

Section 3 of the Act enables the formation of Village Panchayats and Town Panchayats. This does not exist in the nearby states. The classification of Town Panchayats contemplates urban characteristics as one of the norms. In practice, while the Village Panchayats are upgraded as Town Panchayats only the norms of population and the minimum financial income requirements are adopted. There are 12,616 panchayats classified as Village Panchayats.[11] The presidents are executive authorities with ministerial assistance through group clerks. The Village Panchayats are under the control of the Director of Rural Development.

A Town Panchayat can be formed for all the above areas having a population of not less than 5,000 and an annual income of not less than Rs 10,000. They are classified as Grade I, Grade II, and Selection Grade depending on their income level. At present, there are 632 Town Panchayats. The number of panchayats under each grade is as follows:[12]

Grade	*Number*	*Population*	*Annual Income (Rs)*
I	263	5,000	40,000
II	80	5,000	10,000
Selection	289	5,000	1,00,000

The Town Panchayats function with regular administrative machinery headed by the Executive Officer and the complementary staff. Section 4 of the Act enables the government to declare any village or town or any specified part thereof to be township if it is an industrial or labour colony or a health resort. There are 16 townships constituted under this provision functioning with an Executive Officer and complementary staff. Both the Town Panchayats and townships are under the control of Director of Town Panchayats.

Most of the Town Panchayats still have more of rural background and they have been so classified for administrative reasons. The Town Panchayats had become ineligible for the assistance from Government of India under the poverty alleviation and other schemes as the

Central Government had assumed that these areas have been classified as urban and are eligible to be assisted only under urban development schemes. After considerable persuasion, the central government agreed to place the Town Panchayats under the category of rural and urban and rural Town Panchayats were given assistance by the Government of India. The differentiation as rural and urban had been dispensed with from 1990 and all the poverty alleviation schemes are extended to all the Town Panchayats.[13] This position is due to the nomenclature adopted, classifying them as Panchayat Towns. This was done seeing the states of Kerala and Karnataka which do not have any such classification in the panchayats, which got all the benefits of the central schemes from the very introduction of the schemes for all the panchayats, irrespective of the size, population and income.

The formation of a separate Directorate of Town Panchayats exclusively to look after the Town Panchayats brought several demands from these bodies. They wanted to be excluded from the purview of the Panchayat Union Council. They also wanted a separate organizational structure and even a separate District Development Council on the grounds that they are miniature municipalities. At the same time they wanted all the benefits that accrue to the Village Panchayats on the grounds that they have only rural characteristics.[14]

The Panchayat Union Council at the block level is the second tier that is directly elected. There are 384 Panchayat Unions, one for every Panchayat Development Block, classified into six categories with reference to per capita land revenue of the Panchayat Development Block. The number of Panchayat Unions under each category is as follows:[15]

Category	*Number*	*Per Capita Land Revenue*
I	40	Above Rs 4
II	36	Between Rs 3 and Rs 4
III	64	Between Rs 2 and Rs 3
IV	132	Between Re 1 and Rs 2
V	47	Between 75 p. and Re 1
VI	65	Below 75 p.

The Panchayat Unions are looking after the statutory responsibilities like formation and maintenance of roads linking villages, establishment and maintenance of dispensary etc. They are made the focal point and implementing agency for all the development works by way of entrustment. Now, they also look after all the social welfare programmes like family welfare, eye camps, and maintenance of noon-day meal centres among other things. They also review the various departmental programmes implemented in their area. The organizational structure of the Panchayat Union Council consists of directly elected chairman and the presidents of the Village and Town Panchayats as members. The Block Development Officer (BDO) is the executive authority called as the Panchayat Union Commissioner. He functions with complementary staff both from the government and the Panchayat Union side. The Director of Rural Development controls them.

At the district level, there is the District Development Council (DDC) which is headed by the District Collector. The members included MLAs, MLCs and MPs, and Panchayat Union Chairman. There are district officers who attend the DDC as official members. It is not an executive body. It is an advisory and a coordinating body at the district level.

The Tamil Nadu Panchayats Act, 1958 has clearly indicated the resources available to the Panchayat Union by way of local taxation and other finances.[16] It also enlists the government grants being paid to the Panchayat Unions and Panchayats on a statutory basis. The government also gives grants to Panchayat Unions to supplement their statutory functions. Apart from this, for the execution of Community Development Programmes, the government pays Panchayat Unions grants subject to the Panchayat Unions matching them with contributions for some of the programmes as fixed by the government.

The existing sources of revenues of Panchayat Unions are:[17]

1. *Local Cess*: Local cess is collected as per the provisions of Section 115 of the Act of 1958 at a uniform rate of 45 paise in the rupee of land revenue in the state. This is sharable between Panchayat Unions, Village Panchayats and Town Panchayats.
2. *Local Cess Surcharge:* Section 116 provides for the levy of local cess surcharge at such rate as may be considered suitable, subject to a maximum of Rs 2.50 in the rupee of land revenue as an addition to the local cess levied under Section 115. The rate of levy is to be fixed by the Panchayat Union Councils concerned.

3. *Entertainment Tax and Show Tax:* Under the Tamil Nadu Local Authorities Finance Act, 1962[18] as amended, a scheme of payment of a fixed tax per show in respect of permanent and semi-permanent theatres in panchayat villages and panchayat town is envisaged. The income is shared between Panchayat Union and Village/Town Panchayats on equal basis.
4. *Local Cess Surcharge Matching Grant:* Sections 129 and 116 stipulate that the government pays a matching grant to the Panchayat Union.
5. *Local Roads Grant:* This grant is given to the Panchayat Union as per provisions under Section 131 to enable it to maintain Panchayat Union roads. This is given partly based on population and partly with reference to the length of the roads.
6. *Grant for Maintenance of Maternity Centres:* The responsibility for the maintenance of maternity and child welfare centres by the Panchayat Unions ceased with effect from 30 September, 1982. The Panchayat Unions were ordered to continue the function. They are meeting out the expenditure on rent, current consumption charges and on employment of *ayahs* who are treated as Panchayat Union employees. An amount equal to the two-third of the above expenditure is met by an annual grant from government to each Panchayat Union.
7. *Maintenance Grant for Dispensaries:* Each Panchayat Union is eligible for financial assistance from government by way of grants-in-aid to cover 50 per cent of the expenditure on the maintenance of one regular dispensary subject to a ceiling of Rs 5,400.[19] In respect of new dispensaries, the government has decided to give 100 per cent grant subject to the financial position of the Panchayat Union.
8. *Development Grants:*
   (i) *Village Works Grant:* The categories of works permitted to be executed under this grant are water supply, link roads and construction of elementary, primary and secondary school buildings. The grants are released on matching contribution basis.
   (ii) *Social Education Grant:* This grant is given for the supply of periodicals and journals for Social Education and Information Centres.
   (iii) *Women and Child Welfare Grant:* This scheme is executed on the basis of the programme drawn up for the purpose by the

Director of Social Welfare and the grant is controlled and released by that department.

(iv) *Local Irrigation Grant:* This is made available to the Panchayat Unions to enable them to maintain the minor irrigation tanks transferred from the Revenue Department.[20] The grant is based on actual need with reference to five year cycle maintenance.

(v) *Animal Husbandry Grant:* To carry out this programme each Panchayat Union should come forward with a matching contribution specified for the concerned scheme.

The existing sources of income for Village Panchayats and Town Panchayats from revenues, taxes and grants are as follows:

1. *House Tax:* Under Section 119(i), the levy of house tax by panchayats is compulsory. This source of income accrues to the Village and Town Panchayats.
2. *Other Compulsory Taxes:* The profession and vehicle taxes are levied by both the Village and Town Panchayats.
3. *Stamp Duty Surcharge:* This is credited to the Village Panchayats Consolidated Fund and to the Town Panchayats Funds on intimation from the Inspector General of Registration regarding the amounts payable quarterly to the panchayats after taking into account the amount of deduction on account of the collection of transfer duty to be credited to government in respect of the instruments registered. The amount due to Village Panchayats is pooled and distributed on the basis of land revenue.[21]
4. *Village House Tax Matching Grant:*[22] This is a matching grant corresponding to the house tax collected by the Village Panchayats.[23] This is payable in two half-yearly installments. This is not available to Town Panchayats except in Kanyakumari district and Shencottai taluka in Tiruenlveli Kattabomman district.
5. *Minor Local Revenues:* These cover market fees, license fees, fishery rentals, quarry revenue, encroachment fees, avenue produces etc.

The unstable and uncertain financial position of the panchayats is mainly due to the following reasons: One, their income is unpredictable from the statutorily earmarked resources like house tax, profession tax and vehicle tax. The income from these items of taxation is not likely to increase due to various administrative and political constraints. Two, the assigned revenues due from government like local cess, quarry receipts, patta income, sale of avenue produces, fishery rentals and other minor revenues like encroachment fees are also unsteady. As they depend upon the adjustments to be made by the government to the Panchayat Unions and in turn by the Panchayat Union to the panchayats. Three, the income from entertainment tax is not available to all panchayats. Four, the collection of licence fees etc., could not be properly done for the want of proper collecting machinery.

On the other hand, the responsibilities of the local bodies to provide amenities to the public is increasing day by day. The people are now conscious of their rights and demand better amenities on par with the nearby urban areas like protected water supply, black topped roads and better street lighting.

The general financial position of the Panchayat Unions as per the receipts and expenditures for the year 1988–89 reveals a per capita receipt of Rs 12.89 and expenditure of Rs 11.81. The income from local taxation accounts for Rs 2.15 per capita. The other income is mainly by way of apportionment and grants from government. The Panchayat Unions have very little role in local taxation and they have only one source, namely, local cess surcharge which has been exploited to the maximum level by 369 Panchayat Unions. The income due to Panchayat Unions mainly depends on the land revenue, which is unpredictable. The expenditure on administration and particularly the cost of the staff takes away about 70 per cent of the total income. The analysis of the finances of the individual Panchayat Unions in the year 1988–89 reveals the following results:[24]

Range of Surplus Deficit	*Number of PUs having Surplus*	*Number of PUs having Deficit*
Less than Rs 1 lakh	30	46
Rs 1 lakh to Rs 3 lakh	59	93
Rs 3 lakh to Rs 6 lakh	49	45
Rs 6 lakh to Rs 10 lakh	28	13
Above Rs 10 lakh	17	4
Total	183	210

These Panchayat Unions took up large investment programmes under self-sufficiency schemes in 1980s with government grant and a matching contribution. The portion of contributions payable was met by short-term loan from the government in about 136 Panchayat Unions and their present financial conditions do not permit them to discharge this liability which is already overdue to the extent of Rs 42 crore.

All plan formulation is done at the state level. The planning is ad hoc. The funds are given to the Executive Officers of the Panchayat Unions the BDOs. There has been very little popular participation in the planning process.

The administrative personnel involved at the state level are the Minister for Local Administration and Rural Development, then, the Secretary, followed by the Director of Rural Development who is the real executive head. Six Additional Directors, two Joint Directors and five Assistant Directors assist him. At the district level, it is the Collector who looks after both revenue and development. The Personal Assistant to the Collector supervises most of work. At the block level, it is the Block Development Officer who is aided by an Assistant Block Development Officer, extension officers and village officers. The Community Development Programmes are carried out with the BDO as the team leader, for it is to him that funds reach from the State Government. There are also block officers deputed from other departments like cooperation and welfare. At the village level, there are Mukhya Sevika and Gram Sevika. All officials are on deputation. There have been instances of corruption and political interference. The official-non-official relations have been cordial. The State Government has both administrative and financial control over the local bodies. The local bodies and their leaders have to maintain good relations with the state leaders.

Elections to panchayats were held in 1961 in three phases. The Congress won most of the seats. It is the 1965 election that marks a watershed. The Congress was again able to comfortably win. The third elections were held in 1970. The elections were fought on party lines. A regional party—the DMK—won the elections. These local bodies lapsed in 1976. The fourth elections were not held until 1986, when the DMK-Congress alliance won more seats than the ruling party in the state—the AIADMK. There were direct elections for the posts of vice-president and president of the panchayats. The then Chief Minister, M.G.R. Ramachandran mooted the idea of recall for elected representatives of the local bodies. The idea was dropped because of fear of the panchayats being in permanent phase of elections. One reason for the delay in holding elections from 1976 to 1986 was because the Chief Minister announced reservation of seats for scheduled castes, scheduled tribes and women. This was challenged in the Madras High Court and dragged on. Some observers feel that the judiciary in the state was hand in glove with the state government in postponing panchayat elections.[25]

Leadership from the village, block and district levels have never challenged the state leadership. It is prior to the 1958 Act that District Board Presidents posed a threat to the state leadership. To remove this threat altogether the district level or the third tier is ineffective, as it is not an elected body with any executive power. Most of the leadership that emerged with regional parties like DMK and AIADMK, which have ruled the state since 1967 has come from the films. The political culture has given a very strong value to the audio-visual medium of cinema. With charismatic leaders at the helm, the state has had all other ministers or local leaders as the chosen few and loyal followers of the leader.

The issue of corruption in the functioning of the panchayat system was first raised in 1963. A question regarding the number of cases involving embezzlement of panchayat funds was raised in the State Legislature. It was found that on an average, there were ten cases in each district. The question was not replied as it had lapsed.[26]

With only four elections conducted under the 1958 Act to the PRIs in Tamil Nadu, the PRIs have been plagued with allegations of financial irregularities, casteism, official interference and dominance on behalf of the party that was in power in the state. The prevalence and increase in corrupt practices amongst the elected members and nominated officials of the panchayat system is well known. As in every case of corruption, it is very difficult to verify all that is said or alleged, let alone vouch for it.

The principal avenues where corruption was alleged was the malpractices in elections including bribing the voters. Money also played an important role in the elections of presidents and vice-presidents of the panchayats and chairmen and vice-chairmen of the Panchayat Union Councils. Then, there is corruption among the elected representatives in the management of rural works like roads, water supply projects, school buildings etc. The Panchayat Union Council Chairmen handle no executive functions and thus no money. The only possibility is what is known as gratification money while making appointments. Misbehaviour of these elected representatives with women, especially teachers, has been alleged. Complaints against the panchayat staff have been made. Very few cases have ended in suspension or dismissal after an inquiry.[27]

The 1958 Act, which enabled co-option of members from the scheduled castes, scheduled tribes and women, becomes a farce. For, only those who are from the rich families could get elected. Very few SC persons became Panchayat Union Chairmen. Their experience has been very pessimistic. One such person alleged that meetings were held at the dominant caste member's house and the minutes were only sent for his signature. Women and scheduled castes cannot disobey caste rules.[28]

In 1983, certain changes were made in the 1958 Act which adversely affected the morale and enthusiasm of PRIs. They were:

1. The Government of India introduced centrally sponsored schemes like Small Farmers Development Agency (SFDA), Marginal Farmers and Agricultural Labourers Project (MFAL) and Drought Prone Area Programme (DPAP) which were to be implemented directly by the departments of State Government without involving PRIs.
2. Continuous postponement of elections to the local bodies.
3. Dissolution of PRIs after the introduction of President's Rule in Tamil Nadu in 1976. Now, the PRIs were dissolved when their term ended in 1991. Elections have been promised but have been postponed by the latest ordinance until January 1996.[29]
4. Transferring vital subjects like agriculture, education, public health etc., from the purview of PRIs to the line departments of the State Government.
5. Curtailing the term of offices of the members of the Panchayat Union Council, chairman and vice-chairman to three years.[30]

These changes prevented them from functioning as effective instruments of development and change.

In 1989, certain amendments were made to the Act to provide for the restoration of powers to the Panchayats and Panchayat Union Councils. These changes introduced greater responsibilities and powers which brought about great involvement of PRIs in the decision-making and implementation of policies.[31] The subjects taken away from PRIs, like agriculture, elementary education and public health, in 1983, were returned to them. The term of offices of Panchayat Union Chairman, the Village Panchayat President and members in the local bodies had been extended from three to five years.

Keeping in view the poor financial position of the local bodies, the State Government had decided to create two corporations for giving financial assistance to the local bodies. The proposed Tamil Nadu Municipal Finance Corporation would give assistance to the municipalities/corporations. The proposed Tamil Nadu Panchayat Finance Corporation would give financial assistance to the PRIs. It was hoped that they would serve as effective instruments for channelizing requisite financial assistance to the local bodies in the state.

Elections had to be conducted within a period of six months in the case of dissolved or superseded PRIs and the elected members in such cases were to hold office for the remaining duration. Thirty per cent of the seats in every panchayat were reserved for women. Perhaps, the then Chief Minister MGR was the first to introduce the reservation for women as way back as 1982. Provision was made for constituting an Expert Committee to review the financial position of PRIs and make recommendations to the government with regard to the improvements of their finances. Provision was also made to entrust the responsibility of execution and implementation of schemes, programmes and activities relating to economic development to the Panchayat Unions. The review of schemes and activities of various implementing agencies by the Panchayat Unions was also made.

The Legislative Assembly election of 1991 gave a landslide victory to the AIADMK-Congress alliance led by Jayalalitha. The Tamil Nadu Panchayat Bill, 1994[32] was introduced in the State Assembly on 18 April, 1994. The Bill repealed and re-enacted the Tamil Nadu Panchayats Act of 1958. The aim, as enunciated in the preamble, was establishing a three-tier Panchayati Raj system in the state to the elected bodies at the village, intermediate and district levels in keeping with the Constitution (Seventy Third Amendment) Act, 1992, relating to panchayats for greater participation of the people so as to make them institutions of self-government and for more effective implementation of rural development programmes.[33]

The present two-tier system of PRIs in the state is sought to be replaced by a three-tier system. The 1994 Act would set up at the district level a District Panchayat, which will have under its jurisdiction the entire district excluding those areas included in municipalities or Town Panchayats. It will consist of elected members, MPs and MLAs from the district and Chairmen of Panchayat Union

Councils in it, who are to be elected in the strength of one-fifth of the total number of the elected members. The number of Panchayat Union Council elected members is to be determined on the basis of the population of the district. For the purpose of election, the government is to divide the District Panchayat area into wards. The ward is to be a Panchayat Village or a panchayat union or part to a panchayat village or panchayat union. The electoral roll is to be same as that for the assembly election. The District Panchayat is to have a chairman and a vice-chairman who are to be elected by its directly elected members.[34]

The two lower tiers are the Village Panchayat and the Panchayat Union Council. While a Village Panchayat is to constitute for each panchayat village with a minimum population of 500, a Panchayat Union Council I will roughly correspond to a development block. The minimum strength of the Village Panchayat is to be five and the maximum 15 depending on the population.[35]

The Panchayat Union is to consist of elected members, MLAs and MPs whose constituencies comprise the Panchayat Union wholly or in part, the Rajya Sabha member registered as elector within the Union and presidents of the Village Panchayats chosen for the Council. One-fifth of the strength of the elected members is reserved for the presidents of the Village Panchayats. The elected members are to be persons elected from the wards of the Union as may be notified from time to time by the State Election Commission at the rate of one member for every 5,000 population. The president of the Village Panchayat is to be elected by persons on the electoral rolls of the Village Panchayat. The vice-president is to the elected by the Village Panchayat from amongst its elected members. So also, the election of chairman and vice-chairman of the Panchayat Union Council.

The term of office of the PRIs at the three levels is five years. If they are superseded, election has to be held within six months. Reservation of seats for scheduled castes and scheduled tribes is in proportion to their population. One-third of the total number of seats is reserved for women at all the three levels. It also provides for reservation of offices of chairpersons at all the three levels for scheduled castes, scheduled tribes and women.

A new body called Gram Sabha[36] in every panchayat village, comprising all the voters of the panchayat village, is to be established. The Gram Sabha is to meet at least thrice a year, but six months shall not intervene between any two meetings. Its tasks include approving the village plan, the village budget for the year and reviewing the progress of the implementation of all the schemes entrusted to the Village Panchayat.

The Bill provides for the constitution of a State Election Commission to conduct elections, a Finance Commission to recommend grants-in-aid from the State Government in lieu of the shared state taxes in the light of a review of the financial position of the panchayats and a district planning committee for every district for consolidating the development plan of the district as a whole. The Bill was passed after a day's discussion when the leader of the opposition, S.R. Balasubramaniam (INC-1) staged walkout.

In conclusion, all political parties have made pious declaration and deep commitment to the philosophy and policy of strengthening the local bodies at all levels in order to make them efficient and effective instruments of public services. That the two Dravidian parties, the DMK and AIADMK which have held power since 1967, swear by the name of their revered leader, C.N. Annadurai, who had this to say: "Village Panchayats, and the Panchayat Unions constitute the bedrock of Indian democracy and unless we strengthen the Village Panchayats and Panchayat Unions, our democracy cannot become strong and vibrant".[37] This is in total contrast to the praxis for these very parties have been defaulters. That in their twenty-seven years in power they have held elections to local bodies only twice, that is, in 1970 and 1986. A state which had a political culture of hero worship, servility to authority and populism, it is very difficult to ensure the realization of decentralization of power.

Notes

1. Nilakanta Sastri, *The History of Colas* (Madras). It refers to the Uthiramerur inscription on the walls of the Vaikunta Perumal Temple in the Chengai-Anna district.
2. *White Paper on the Reform of Local Administration,* 1957, Government of Madras, p. 3.
3. See S. Saraswati, *The Madras Panchayat System* (1974) for a review of the implementation of the Balwant Rai Committee Report, 1956 and G. Ram Reddy (ed.), *Patterns of Panchayati Raj in India,* Macmillan: Madras, 1977.
4. *Tamil Nadu Panchayats Bill,* No. 10 of 1994, Part IV, Section 1.
5. *The Tamil Nadu Panchayats Act,* 1958, Tamil Nadu Act XXXV of 1958, Government of Tamil Nadu, 1991.
6. Ibid., Section 17 (1), p. 23.

7. Ibid., Section 16 (3–A), p. 22.
8. Ibid., Chapter III, Section 63, p. 72.
9. Ibid., Chapter III, Section 64, pp. 72–73.
10. Ibid., Chapter 111, Section 65, pp. 73–74.
11. *The Report of the Expert Committee on the Financial Position of the Panchayats and Panchayat Union Council in Tamil Nadu,* Government of Tamil Nadu, 1990.
12. Ibid., pp. 15–16.
13. n. 10, Chapter 111, Section 68, p. 75.
14. n. 12, p. 18.
15. *Grama Valarchi*, Vol. 6, 1989, p. 8.
16. n. 10, Section 74, pp. 80–81.
17. Ibid.
18. Tamil Nadu Act 152 of 1961.
19. n. 10. Section 65, pp. 73–74.
20. Ibid., Section 85(1), p. 86.
21. Ibid., Section 124, pp. 107–08.
22. Ibid., Section 132, p. 111.
23. Ibid., Section 120, pp. 101–02.
24. n. 11, p. 64.s
25. *The Hindu,* Madras, 5 January, 1982.
26. G.O. 1321, Rural Development and Local Administration, 19 November, 1962.
27. K. Palaniswamy, "People's Participation in Rural Development" (Unpublished Ph.D. thesis, Anna Centre for Pubic Affairs, University of Madras, 1993), pp. 31–39.
28. V. Kanappau, "Caste and Democratic Decentralization in Tamil Nadu", Paper presented at a seminar at University of Madras, 17–18 November, 1994.
29. *Indian Express,* Madras, 11 November, 1994.
30. *Background Papers* (State Institute for Rural Development, Maraimalai Nagar, 1992).
31. Government of Tamil Nadu, *Performance Budget 1989–90*, Community Development, 1989, p. 1.
32. n. 4, pp. 162–274.
33. Ibid., p. 171.
34. Ibid., Section 163 and 24 to 32.
35. Ibid., Section 164 and 4 to 21.
36. Ibid., Chapter 11, Clause 3.
37. n. 15, pp. 10 11.

25 People-Centred Governance

The Panchayati Raj Experience in Uttar Pradesh

S.N. Singh

Democratic governance by definition has to be participative and people-oriented. Since India opted for democratic governance after attaining independence from the British rule, it opted for a people-centred governance by choice. This could be evident if we see through the Constitution of India which very clearly provides for the grass-roots level organization of village panchayats. This provision is incorporated in the chapter on Directive Principles of State Policy in the Constitution. In pursuance of the philosophy of people-centred governance, the Government of India launched the Community Development Programme (CDP) in the year 1952. The CDP precisely based itself on the concept of people-centred governance. It can, therefore, be argued that the experiment about people-centred governance began in the initial years of the independence itself which is continuing even today in one form or the other.

Within few years of its launching, the CDP started showing problems and soon it was declared that the community development in India could not get the desired success, rather it has 'failed'. In view of the failure of the community development, the Government of India appointed a committee on democratic decentralization under the chairmanship of Balwant Rai Mehta in the year 1957. The committee went into the details of democratic decentralization through elected office bearers and recommended for a three-tier structure of Panchayati Raj in the country.

One of the factors that led to the failure of community development has allegedly been reported to be lack of proper participation in the decision-making process—the very basis of community development. The Balwant Rai Mehta Committee, therefore, tried to ensure people's participation in the governing process at the level of district and below. It provided for an organic linking of all the three tiers with a direct election to the lowest tier and the rest linked indirectly. Thus, the Panchayati Raj system proposed by the Balwant Rai Mehta Committee got introduced first in Rajasthan and then in other states. In Uttar Pradesh, a separate Act—U.P. Kshetra Samiti and Zila Parishad Adhiniyam, 1961 was passed which provided for the constitution, powers and functions of the two upper tiers of the Panchayati Raj system. The Village Panchayats were being already governed through a separate Act known as the U.P. Panchayati Raj Act, 1947.

The Panchayati Raj system proposed by Balwant Rai Mehta Committee remained in operation for about 20 years when another committee under the chairmanship of Asoka Mehta was appointed by the then Janata Party government in the year 1977 to review the Panchayati Raj system in the country and suggest measures for making the system effective. Before making observation about the Asoka Mehta Committee's report, it may be worthwhile to examine the way the Panchayati Raj system worked during the two decades since the recommendations of the Balwant Rai Mehta Committee report were made operative in various states including Uttar Pradesh.

After the passage of the U.P. Kshetra Samiti and Zila Parishad Adhiniyam in the year 1961, the first elections to these bodies were held in the year 1963. It was the first effective measure towards people-centred governance in the state. The Act provided for a direct election to the lowest tier and indirect election to the two upper tiers. Thus, the Pradhan was directly elected by the adult members of the village. The Pradhan became an ex-officio member of the Kshetra Samiti along with other members. The Kshetra Samiti then elected its Pramukh. The Pramukh became the ex-officio member of the Zila Parishad which elected its chairman. This system remained in operation till be 73rd Constitution Amendment Act became operational wherein some changes were introduced in the Panchayati Raj system of the state.

The Kshetra Samiti and Zila Parishad functioned as constituted under the said Act till 1977 when these bodies were superseded and placed under the control of the state government. These bodies were again constituted in the year 1988–89. During this long period, the Zila Parishads remained under the control of the state government. This affected the democratic functioning of these bodies as they were governed by the officials of the state government present in the district. The system of people-centred governance, thus, suffered a setback as there were no elections during this period. It was, by and large, the Collector and his staff in the district which managed the show without any popular control at that level.

The concern for decentralizing power to local bodies was indirectly shown by Rajiv Gandhi, the then Prime Minister, who talked of power to people, in the 1980s. Attempts were made towards making the administration responsive through people-centred governance. The efforts thus indicated by Rajiv Gandhi took their own time before they could be formally propounded. It was only during Narsimha Rao's period that the 73rd Constitution Amendment Act could be framed in the year 1992 as earlier efforts during the tenures of V.P. Singh and others could not succeed.

The 73rd Constitution Amendment Act, 1992 is considered historic in many respects. After several decades, a comprehensive effort was given shape so far as people-centred governance in the country is concerned. As stated earlier, the failure of community development and the Panchayati Raj in the country has generally been due to lack of people's participation, which was central to the success of these programmes. It is also central to the idea of people-centred governance. For one reason or the other, these programmes failed to register effective participation of the people. There was lack of delegation of powers, financial and otherwise, due to which these bodies could not grow in the real sense. The state government continued to intervene in their affairs. The cumulative impact of all this was an ineffective system of decentralized governance. Often, a lack of faith in these bodies has also been observed. Under such circumstances, the 73rd Constitution Amendment Act, 1992 was seen as a real departure from earlier efforts. A number of provisions were made under this Act for the first time. Some of the important provisions are as under which would ensure de facto people-centred governance:

1. The Act provided for 33 per cent reservation for women in the Panchayati Raj bodies.
2. It provided for creation of a State Election Commission to ensure regular election to the Panchayati Raj bodies.
3. It provided for a State Finance Commission to recommend distribution/sharing of resources between the state and local bodies.

These three provisions in the Central Act tried to ensure people-centred governance. In Uttar Pradesh, thus, an Act was passed in the year 1994 taking cognizance of the provisions of the Central Act of 1992. The Act of 1994 in Uttar Pradesh constituted the State Election Commission on 23rd April, 1994. The following are some of the important features of the State Act:

1. All the three tiers will be known as panchayats incorporating their level, i.e., Village Panchayat, Kshetra Panchayat and Zila Panchayat.
2. Direct election to various levels, i.e., for the members of these bodies.
3. The Pramukhs and Adhykshas to be elected from amongst the members.
4. Constitutions of a Gram Panchayat with a population of 1,000.
5. It further provided appointment of nine members upto 1,000 population, 11 members upto 2,000 population, 13 members upto 3,000 population and 15 members above 3,000 population.
6. Reservation for Scheduled Castes and Scheduled Tribes as per population, 27 per cent for OBCs, one-third for women.
7. The Act further provided for five years' term of these bodies.
8. The creation of State Election Commission and State Finance Commission is another important feature of the new Panchayati Raj system.

With the above major features, the Panchayati Raj system with a new approach became operative since 1994. It is eight years now that the system has been in operation. The second elections to these bodies were held in the month of June 2000. We have, therefore, some exposure to the new system. The further analysis is based on that exposure. The next section would deal with the problems faced and the issues identified in the working of the new Panchayati Raj system in Uttar Pradesh.

The Problem and Issue Areas

There is no denying the fact that the 73rd Constitution Amendment Act, 1992 made a genuine effort towards people-centred governance involving such sections of the population which had so far little role in the process of governance. One would like to emphasize on the point of reservation for women which accounted for 33 per cent. It is interesting to observe that during the last fifty years of the history of Panchayati Raj in the country, women had very little role in the governing process. This single provision in the said Act attempted to almost revolutionize the established social order in rural India. The purpose and objective of this provision was clear but far-reaching. We are aware that rural India provides for a social order in which woman's role in the decision-making process is negligible and she is generally confined to the household affairs and not the public affairs. The provision of this Act anticipated a future role for rural women in the governing process.

After the first election to the Panchayati Raj bodies in the year 1994, women took positions of authority in the Panchayati Raj system in the state. During this six years of working of these bodies, several opinions have come to the fore which provide mixed signals so far as the working of these bodies is concerned. The women who till yesterday were confined to the four walls of the households, suddenly found themselves in a new role—a role of managing public affairs. In this role, therefore, they had taken help from male members of the family, be it their husbands, brothers or other relatives. They generally remained passive players while the male members tried to dominate the proceedings. On the contrary, it has also been found that some of the women have really taken initiatives in the affairs of the local body. It can, therefore, be stated that even though the women may not have played any significant role so far in the governing process, but a beginning has been made which would go a long way in the people-centred governance in the states.

It was hoped that with modification suggested in the 73rd Constitution Amendment Act, 1992, the people-centred governance should improve. We have briefly discussed the changes experienced in the working of Panchayati Raj system in the state after providing 33 per cent reservation for women. As mentioned earlier, it provided for a shift in existing social structural value system. An attitudinal change and modification has been initiated which will take some more time to settle down to influence the people-centred governance in the state.

In the analysis of the people-centred governance, we can examine the issues from these distinct viewpoints or using the three variables, namely, structure, process and behaviour, and see how far we have been able to enforce the people-centred governance in the state. As has been briefly analyzed earlier, the 73rd Constitution Amendment Act, 1992 provided for certain structural changes to ensure participation of people in the governing process in the Panchayati Raj system. Following this, the Uttar Pradesh government passed an Act in the year 1994 incorporating the structural changes required under the said Act. Prominent among these changes has been the question of 33 per cent reservation for women in the Panchayati Raj system to ensure rational public-centred governance in the country. It can be observed that the state government has also taken steps to ensure the people-centred governance structurally.

The second variable on which one can analyze the question of people-centred governance in the state is that of ensuring the process. In this connection, it can be observed that in order to ensure the process of people-centred governance in the state, the government has taken steps to ensure that people's participation is there in the decision-making process of these bodies. For the purpose, therefore, the state government constituted the State Election Commission. It is the business of the Commission to get the elections to these bodies conducted regularly. It has been found that so far the elections to these local bodies have been conducted on schedule. The first election was conducted in the year 1994–95 whereas the second election in June 2000.

The third variable to be considered for analysis in this context is the of behaviour and attitude of people who are connected with the system of governance at the local level. The analysis of people-centred governance in the state would not be complete unless we try to analyze the attitude and behavioural pattern of people who man the Panchayati Raj system. We have observed that the bureaucracy is still playing a dominant role in the governing process at that level. The non-officials and the elected representatives lack the kind of orientation and training required for the purpose. For most of the things, these people generally depend on the bureaucracy. On the one hand, it could be argued that since the representatives of the people lack the knowledge and information needed for effective participation in the governing process, they have no other option but to depend on the bureaucracy for the purpose. To the extent that the elected representatives are dependent on the bureaucracy, the people-centred governance gets a setback. Traditionally also, they seem to depend more on the officials than the non-officials. Thus, the process started for the people-centred governance has yet to take roots in the state.

It is interesting to note that while, on the one hand, there is an effort on the part of the government to create a people-centred governance, on the other there are little efforts to provide enough financial resources and powers to these bodies. The District Rural Development Agencies (DRDAs) continue to be the main agency for funding rural development programmes. In Uttar Pradesh too, DRDAs operate as the main implementing agency for rural development programmes. Since DRDAs are mainly an official-oriented body headed by the District Collector, there is little scope for people-centred governance. After the 73rd Constitution Amendment, it was hoped that the Panchayati Raj bodies would become more effective vis-à-vis the DRDAs. However, the desired change is yet to take place. An effort has been made by the state government to make the chairman of the Zila Parishad the chairman of DRDA also. But, the move is opposed in certain circles and real change in this regard is yet to take place. Unless there is change in the thinking about the role of the DRDAs vis-à-vis the Panchayati Raj bodies, the stalemate regarding people-centred governance may continue.

The state government, therefore, constituted a State Finance Commission to oversee the financial resources of these bodies and also to ensure proper distribution of resources between the state and local bodies. It is hoped that this would provide some vitality to the local bodies who otherwise were generally financially starved for several decades. Finance is an important factor in the governing process and in its absence governance can suffer. The Finance Commission has now recommended the sharing of income between the state government and the local bodies which would help them in course of time.

Conclusion

It can, therefore, be concluded that during the post-independence period, efforts have been made by the Government of India as well as the state government towards people-centred governance. There has been a realization that democratic system does need a people-centred governance at the local level too as in its absence, the higher structures would not be able to sustain themselves. In this paper, therefore, we have tried to make an objective analysis of the efforts made so far towards attaining people-centred governance with particular focus on Uttar Pradesh. We have seen that of late there is serious effort on the part of the state government towards ensuring reservation for women in these bodies as well as ensuring regular elections to these bodies. However, we have found little change so far as the attitudinal change amongst the male members is concerned. At the same time, it is concluded that a beginning seems to have been made to restructure the earlier traditional social order through reservation for women in the local bodies of the state. A beginning towards the change seems to have struck and it would take some time before it could be made more effective and realistic. The women in the state have slowly started asserting themselves which should be seen as a signal of change that would be witnessed in few year time from now if the process begun is allowed to continue and flourish. So far as the statutory provisions are concerned, they have already been made. It is now the question of allowing these provisions to be implemented. A wave of change has begun its journey and it would soon be witnessed in the rural Uttar Pradesh.

Section IV

Envisioning Decentralization in Rural Governance

26 Decentralization in Rural Governance

M. Veerappa Moily

I am delighted to be here today to participate in the National Colloquium organized by the Administrative Reforms Commission along with the Institute of Social Sciences, New Delhi to discuss local governments and approaches towards reforms of Panchayati Raj system in the country.

It is widely held today that the colonial legacy of district administration, while it may have its strong points when it comes to regulatory functions such as maintenance of law order, has been unable to restructure itself into a responsive and transparent agency to implement development programmes in post-independence India. There is a view, therefore, that what is required is a wholesale replacement of the existing framework by a third tier of government in order to usher in 'grass roots democracy' so that development and civic functions at the local level can be discharged by this "third tier of government". This school of thought also seeks a separate 'local list' in

---

This is a slightly edited text of the speech delivered at the National Colloquium on Decentralization in Rural Governance organized at Institute of Social Sciences, New Delhi in collaboration with the Second Administrative Reforms Commission, Government of India on 1–2 March 2007. It is being published with the consent of Second Administrative Reforms Commission and its Chairman, Shri M. Veerappa Moily.

the Constitution for the third tier of government in order to provide for 'exclusive functional domains' backed up by adequate financial resources for the panchayats. It is stated further that these institutions should not only be autonomous in their respective domains but that their relationship with the first and second tiers of government at the central and state level respectively should be in the form of cooperative federalism with each tier respecting the autonomy of the others. This may be described as the 'maximalist approach' towards the whole issue of devolution of functions and resources to the local bodies.

The other 'minimalist approach' takes the contrary position, i.e., that in a vast country with huge regional disparities in development, endowments and cultures, the notion of Panchayati Raj Institutions (PRIs) being able to successfully discharge a wide variety of regulatory and developmental roles, is a romantic rather than a practical idea. In order to ensure greatest good for the greatest number, factors such economies of scale, as well as technical and institutional capacities that cannot be diffused at all lower tiers of government, have to be taken into account and, therefore, only certain minimal civic functions such as primary education, primary health care, sanitation, implementation of poverty alleviation programme etc., can be successfully devolved to PRIs.

The whole issue of democracy and development has been the subject of much academic debate given the varying experiences of different countries in Asia and Africa in the post-colonial era. The experience of 'guided democracy' in Singapore and the transformation it has brought to the development status of the city state, and which has been replicated in a large measure in China through a one-party state, appears to indicate that development goals can sometimes be addressed faster in an institutional set-up wherein decision-making is not subject to the daily pulls and pressures of a raucous democracy, others have argued, however, that even apart from the issue of respect for human rights, a democratic path to development has inherent advantages and points to India's success in preventing large-scale deaths due to famine in the post-independence era as compared to China, where deaths on massive scale due to famines were being reported even in the seventies.

The existing district administration does not take into account the fundamental change in the character of the state. The dichotomy between the democratic system at the centre and the state headquarters and the opaque, non-accountable and non-responsive district administration still continues to be an unsolved conundrum in the Indian polity and governance system. It is said that there is democracy at the central and state levels, whereas at all lower levels there was only bureaucracy.

In most parts of the world, the role of the local government remains confined to the delivery of civic services. The post-73rd Amendment panchayats are functioning, like before, within the framework of what may be called 'permissive functional domain'.

In any case, India has chosen the path of democracy to achieve its developmental goals and has stuck steadfastly to it. India has never seen democracy and development as mutual exclusive choices. As far as the issue of devolution of functions to local level PRIs is concerned, here too, we must follow a 'middle path' on the basis of recognized principles of subsdiarity. This has to be done in a pragmatic manner, based on the list of subjects mentioned under the Constitution (in the eleventh schedule) and by mapping the activities in relation to each of these subjects which could best be transferred to the local bodies among the different tiers of the PRIs. Such activity mapping would have to be based on objective criteria such as economies of scale, capacity available for performing an activity, externalities relating to that activity etc. Once these activities are mapped, these should be transferred to the concerned local bodies along with staff responsible for these activities and with the concomitant resources to enable them to implement such activities.

The core functions of the local level PRIs comprising civic functions, such as elementary education, primary health, local roads and rural infrastructure and implementation of poverty alleviation schemes should constitute the autonomous functional domain of the PRIs for which they should be armed with the requisite technical, financial and human resources to carry out these tasks in an effective and accountable manner. Whether this set of functions should ultimately constitute a separate 'local list' to be inserted into the constitution, is for this colloquium to consider although extensive re-writing of the constitution is a subject on which one tends to have reservations.

As per Article 243ZC, Part IX of the Constitution is not applicable to areas included in the fifth and sixth schedules. The fifth schedule provides for the administration and control of scheduled areas and scheduled tribes excluding those of the states of Assam, Meghalaya, Tripura and Mizoram. The sixth schedule stipulates provisions for the administration of tribal areas in the states of Assam, Meghalaya, Tripura and Mizoram. However, the parliament may by law extend the provisions of Part IX to these scheduled areas [Article 243ZC(3)]. Accordingly, the parliament has enacted 'The Provisions of the Panchayats (Extension to the Scheduled Areas) Act 1996' (PSA) extending the provisions of Part IX to areas under the Fifth Schedule. However, it has been mandated that the legislature of a state shall not make any law which is inconsistent with the customary law, social, religious and traditional practices of the community. But no law has been passed for extending provisions of Part IX to the areas included in the Sixth Schedule. Out of the districts, 63 districts have areas in the fifth schedule and six districts have areas in the sixth schedule. The development of model guidelines for conferring original jurisdiction on Gram Sabhas as envisaged in the PESA was examined by the expert group on "Planning at the Grassroots Level". In the report it has been highlighted that powers statutorily devolved upon Gram Sabhas and Panchayats are not matched by the concomitant transfer of funds and functionaries resulting in the making the panchayats ineffective. To tackle the problems of this unique area and to preserve the democratic traditions and cultural diversity of its people, the framers of the Constitution conceived of the instrument of tribal self-rule. This stands embodied in the sixth schedule to the Constitution.

Careful steps should be taken to devolve political powers through the intermediate and local level traditional political organizations, provided their traditional practices carried out in a modern world do not deny legitimate democratic rights to any section in their contemporary society. The details of state-wise steps to devolve such powers will have to be carefully considered in a proper representative meeting of traditional leaders of each community, opinion builders of the respective communities and leaders of state and national stature from these very groups. A hasty decision could have serious repercussions, unforeseen and unfortunate, which could further complicate and worsen the situation. To begin with, the subjects given under the sixth schedule and those mentioned in the eleventh schedule could be entrusted to the Autonomous District Councils (ADCs) The system of in-built safeguards in the sixth schedule should be maintained and strengthened for the minority and micro-minority groups while empowering them with greater responsibilities and opportunities, for example, through the process of central funding for plan expenditure instead of routing all funds through the state governments. The northeastern council can play a central role here by developing a process of public education on the proposed changes, which would assure communities about protection of their traditions and also bring in gender representation and give voice to other ethnic groups.

Traditional forms of governance must be associated with self-governance because of the present dissatisfaction. However, positive democratic elements like gender justice and adult franchise should be built into these institutions to make them broader based and capable of dealing with a changing world.

The implementation of centrally funded projects from various departments of the Union Government should be entrusted to the ADCs and to revive village councils with strict audit by the Comptroller and Auditor General (CAG) of India.

All the states have chosen to assign functions to the PRIs not through the statute but by delegated legislation in the form of rules' executive orders. The task of assigning functions to the panchayats was given to the state legislatures, but the same seems to have been usurped by the state governments. The Constitution did not guarantee assignment of a set of exclusive functions for the panchayats. (The Eleventh Schedule is only an indicative list.) Hence, the kind of role they would be expected to play in the system of governance depends on the policies of the regime that controls the government of a state. In other words, as before, the issue of empowerment of panchayats still remains at the mercy of the state governments. There should be an exclusive functional jurisdiction or an independent sphere of action for each level of panchayats. There may be a sphere of activities where the state government and the panchayats would work as equal partners. There may also be a sphere where PRIS would act as agencies for implementing state or central government schemes or programmes. Among these three spheres, the first two should predominate. The agency functions should not be allowed to overshadow the other two spheres of action, for it is in the latter sphere that the local government institutions will have autonomy. Panchayat at each level is an institution local government. Hence, there cannot be a hierarchical relationship between a higher level panchayat and a lower level panchayat. There cannot be principle a hierarchical relationship between the PRIs and the state government also.

Whether certain types of regulatory functions could also be devolved to the panchayats should also be considered by this colloquium. Ideally, certain types of regulatory functions, such as birth and death registration, building by-laws, community policing and even local level courts could be considered for then under the domain of PRIs.

The whole approach to devolution has to be built around the twin criteria of speed and simplicity instead of an overtly ideological approach. The fact is that over the years, a certain level of institutional and technical capacity, as well as departmental fiefs, have been built up at state levels and for these to be dismantled and decentralized from the state to local levels is not a painless process, has also to be recognized. Focused implementation of core functions would ensure building up of the capacity as well as the trust in these institutions to carry out the functions entrusted to them. At the same time, it would be essential to bring in accountability for the functions that are devolved to the local level institutions because it is almost inevitable that decentralization of functions will in the initial phase be accompanied by "decentralization of corruption". For ensuring accountability, ensuring rigorous annual audits, empowering the Gram Panchayats, providing a framework for social audit and substitution of oversight of panchayats by government officials or the state governments by means of a statutory ombudsman with full authority for taking action against defaulters and institutions would need to be considered.

There are five important issues which I would like this national colloquium to address in some detail.

First, we have to bear in mind that democratic decentralization can greatly enhance the capacity of the state to accelerate local development and reduce poverty, but only if it is effectively designed. PRIs need considerable autonomy, including fiscal autonomy, as well as considerable support and safeguards from the government. Moreover, they need mechanisms to ensure high levels of participation in the design and monitoring of the programmes and policies by all sections of the population to be served. Are the existing PRIs designed to do these?

Second, the PRIs need fiscal autonomy to plan their activities. But locally raised revenues are often a small part of the budget of the PRIs, weakening ownership of locally designed policies, threatening their sustainability. For example, at present, the PRIs own revenues as a share of their revenue expenditure is just 9.26 per cent on average and they are entirely dependent on the state/central grants for their functioning. In order to strengthen these institutions from the financial point of view, setting up of a State Finance Commission every five years in order to provide an institutional basis for the fiscal relationship between the state and local bodies would have to be ensured. It is also equally important that while the PRIs need an adequate budget base, enforcement of hard budget constraints is also essential in order to make them accountable. The local bodies themselves would need to get away from their dependency-prone mindsets towards responsible fiscal behaviour by not only making adequate use of the existing process of revenue but also mobilizing additional sources of both tax and non-tax revenues including user's charges.

The third important issue relates to the need for strengthening administrative and managerial capabilities in the PRIs. Studies of successful democratic decentralization indicate the importance of creating administrative capacity. Almost all PRIs lack the administrative capacity for large-scale decentralization and need training in accounting, public administration, financial management, communications and community relations. Let me also hasten to add that if PRIs have strong administrative capacity and accountability mechanisms, then it can reduce the scope for corruption. If they do not, it can increase corruption as has been the experience in Central Asia, the South Caucasus and the Baltics.

The fourth issue is about elite capture of the PRIs. Safeguards need to be put in place to monitor financial probity and discourage the capture of PRIs by powerful elites. Given the unequal power structure, which is the characteristic feature of most Indian villages, we have to ensure that the process of democratic decentralization is to not made to subserve the vested interests of the rich and powerful in rural India to the detriment of the poor and the marginalized.

Last but not the least, the PRIs should play a very critical role in resolving social fragmentation and conflict at the local level and in the local context. This, to my mind, is the most critical determinant of the success of the PRIs. Unless the PRIs offer forums for mediating inter-group rivalries and forging cross-cutting ties among diverse competing groups, these cleavages can lead to conflicts, tearing a society and economy apart, leaving everyone vulnerable to poverty. Breakdowns in governance and in institutions of conflict resolution create conditions for social unrest and further conflict. In order to create a functioning society, we need the PRIs to be institutions of conflict mediation, which, I am afraid, our PRIs have not been. So, the important question is: What can be done to make the PRIs the institutions of conflict resolution at the local level as well as in the local context.

Putting in place a well-delineated activity mapping, allocating specific activities between the state as well as different tiers of the panchayats should be the starting point of the proposed reforms. Funds and functionaries need to be devolved upon each tier with clear responsibility and accountability.

Grants to the PRIs must be untied so that they can decide their own priorities.

Decentralized planning starting from the Gram/Ward Sabha has to be strictly enforced and the Planning Commission while giving approval to the state plans must verify whether the state plans have incorporated the panchayat plans at appropriate places.

While making financial provisions for implementing schemes in respect of the subjects entrusted to the panchayats, it must be ensured that the allocated funds go directly to the panchayat concerned from the state exchequer without being routed through the concerned state departments, whose role should be limited to monitoring and evaluation of the implementation.

The central and state governments may function as funding agencies for projects to be approved by them, but their role should be like that of any other funding agency. They may periodically evaluate and monitor the projects to ensure that the objectives set forth in the approved projects are fully achieved.

The central ministries and state departments dealing with the activities that are entrusted to the PRIs should be deliberately downsized over the next five years. In any case, sanctioning additional staff in these ministries should be prohibited forthwith. There shall be no further recruitment of the field staff at the cutting-edge level by the state governments. This should be left to the local governments themselves.

Capacity building of panchayat functionaries—the elected representatives and the officials—should be given high priority to enable them to discharge their roles effectively.

The panchayats can also arrange interaction of the service providers with the beneficiaries to create an enabling atmosphere for better performance. A disturbing feature noticed in several states in the fact that the service providers responsible for physical delivery of benefits are not fully accountable to the PRIs. The only relationship between these officers and the panchayats is that they are ex-officio members of the concerned sub-committees of the panchayats and are therefore obliged to attend the meetings of the sub-committees.

Several structures and bodies have been in existence for delivering sectoral benefits in rural areas prior to the 73rd Constitution Amendment. In the presumed interest of unity of command, professional integrity, operational efficiency and achievement of sectoral targets, departments, boards, authorities and corporations in each sector grew into large numbers creating their own vertical hierarchy down to the local level. These parastatals continue to exist even after the constitutional amendment, without being integrated into the new system. A conscious decision has to be taken to annul these parallel structures or to bring them under the respective tier of PRIs, by amending the relevant sectoral legislations.

Neither the National Planning Commission nor the State Planning Boards are constitutional bodies. In that context, making DPC a constitutional entity is somewhat incongruous. Secondly, in a developmental state, planning is an essential function of government at any level. If a committee is needed for undertaking the exercise of planning, the concerned government itself can constitute the same creating a separate authority independent of the structures of governance for undertaking the exercise of development planning has no logic. Thirdly, DPC is the only body in the decentralization scheme of the Constitution where at least one-fifth of the total members can be nominated. A nominated member can also be the chairperson of DPC. Nomination is a convenient tool available to the Riling party of a state to induct members on narrow political considerations. Some states have taken the liberty to nominate a minister as head of the committee, thus converting the DPC as a power centre that is stronger than the elected local bodies. Fourthly, DPC is a stand-alone committee within the panchayat-municipal system and there is no organic linkage between the two. Last but not the least, the very legitimacy of the DPC is doubtful, because it has no accountability. Being constituted partly through indirect election and partly by nomination, it is neither accountable to people directly, nor to the PRI-municipal system system. With all these odds against it, DPC in its present form is hardly making any contribution to the project of democratic decentralization. This needs to be debated.

District Panchayat as District Government

In the strict sense of the term, only the Gram Panchayat and the municipality qualify for being regarded as local government. It is also significant that taxing power, which is an indicator of governmental authority, is enjoyed by these two bodies among all the local bodies. On the other hand, traditionally, district has been an indispensable unit of our country's administration. Hence, if democratization of local administration is the goal, then, there has to be a representative body at the district level.

- The district tier of local government may represent both rural and urban population.
- Article 243(d) needs to be amended facilitating election of a single representative body at the district level for both rural and urban population.
- Article 243 ZD may be deleted, since with district tier representing both rural and urban areas, DPC in its present form will be redundant.

The factors that would have to be taken into consideration for determining the minimum size of a Gram Panchayat (GP) may be: (a) potentialities of local resource generation, (b) sustainability of maintaining essential staff for service delivery, (c) suitability as a unit of planning for the core functions, (d) geographical cohesiveness, and (e) terrain conditions and the communication facility within the GP area. It is necessary that each state, which has small-sized GPs (population below, say, 6,000 in the non-hilly regions), should undertake detailed exercises to reconstitute them after considering the factors mentioned above. The oversized GPs also have problems, for normally, the population of a GP should not exceed 15,000, unless habitation patterns demand otherwise. Large GPs pose problems for popular participation. Here, instead of Gram Sabha, emphasis should be given on Ward Sabha for encouraging participation. Appropriate solution will have to be evolved.

In the paradigm shift as obtained after the 73rd Amendment to the Constitution of India, it needs to be debated whether there is any scope left for the continuation of the office of District Collector/Deputy Commissioner which will negate the democratic ethos contemplated under the amendment. It should also be debated whether the role of District Magistrate/Collector could be assigned to the CEOs of Zila Parishads (ZPs) as a delegated power from the state government in addition to the duties to be discharged as CEO of ZP.

Controlling Power of the State Government

Some of the traditional methods of supervision and control are as follows:

- Powers of sanction of budget.
- Powers of suspension and cancellation of resolution and orders.
- Powers of suspension and removal of chairpersons, vice-chairpersons and members.
- Powers of suspension and supersession of PRIs.

A highly coercive instrument at the hands of the state government is the power to suspend and remove the chairperson or vice-chairperson and also members of the panchayats.

The very idea of removing an elected person by the executive on the basis of its own judgment is a relic of the colonial practice that is still not abandoned.

There should be uniform provisions in the State Panchayat Acts that an elected person can be removed only on two grounds: (a) 'no-confidence' motion passed by the elected members against the office bearers, and (b) being subject to any of the disqualification clauses.

The strongest coercive power at the hands of the state government to control the PRIs is the power to supersede the elected local body. Immediately thereafter it should refer the matter to an independent tribunal or ombudsman.

Accountability and Transparency of Panchayats

These are: (a) accountability for what, (b) accountability to whom, and (c) means of ensuring accountability of the institution.

Thus, in designing the components of accountability of the PRIs, it is necessary to focus on the following:

- Integrity in the use of resources and preventing rent-seeking tendencies of public officials/representatives.
- Exercise of administrative powers of officials and political executives in a fair manner.
- Responsiveness of the PRIs to the urgent needs of people.
- Performance of the PRIs in terms of efficiency and effectiveness.

There may be various ways by which the accountability of panchayats can be ensured—both upward and downward.

One of the weak links in the system of rural governance has been in the field of human resource. Maharashtra has the distinction of creating 'district service' (technical and general) of all panchayats. This needs to be studied carefully to evolve a system of human resource in rural governance.

The resource mobilization is yet another aspect which has not been properly addressed. The fiscal powers of the PRIs may be strengthened by empowering them to (a) levy and collect some taxes, (b) by assigning to them certain taxes levied and collected by the state government, and (c) by expanding the sources of non-tax revenue. The non-tax revenue may be collected from various sources: (i) tolls and various kinds of fees, (ii) various user charges, and (iii) return from remunerative assets.

In reality, most state governments have so far failed to adopt rational and consistent policies in this regard. Major reform issues involved in the matter of inter-governmental transfer of resources appears to be as follows:

— Most of the panchayats of the country are operating with tied funds either schematic funds or specific purpose grants. Activities related to the schematic funds are agency functions. Very meagre funds are available with the PRIs to discharge the activities assigned to them. The quantum of untied funding has therefore to be increased in order to enable the PRIs to discharge their core functions and improve the delivery of basic services in terms of both coverage and quality.
— There is no predictability and consistency in allocating funds to the local bodies. The state governments should frame legislations defining the principles and formulae to allocate specific purpose and untied grants to the different tiers of PRIs. The principles of funding should have a direct relationship with the devolution of activities.
— There should be a local body component in the budgets of every state government indicating the allocations to each local body.
— The state governments do not demonstrate seriousness in considering the reports of the SFCs or in implementing their recommendations. There should be legislations defining specifically the responsibility of the state government with regard to the

consideration and implementation of the recommendations of the SFC within a definite time frame.

— In most cases, the periods covered by the SFCs and the Central Finance Commission do not coincide. This creates difficulties for the Central Finance Commission in assessing the requirements of resources of different states for transfer to the local bodies. It is necessary to synchronize the two periods. In order to realize this objective, it is necessary to empower the state governments to set up the SFCs not only "at the expiry of every fifth year" as envisaged in Article 243–1, but also at earlier time. Accordingly, this Article may be amended by inserting the words "or at such earlier time as the governor considers necessary" after the words "at the expiry of every fifth year". Such amendment will bring Article 243–1 in conformity with Article 280.

The quality of all SFC reports is not good. Nor do they cover same grounds, making inter-state comparison possible. It is necessary that each Central Finance Commission gives a guideline to be followed by the future SFCs.

Honestly, I expect great things from the deliberations of this national colloquium. I hope that through the instrumentality of this colloquium, the Administrative Reforms Commission will be enabled to not only engender an illuminating debate on the issues of local government in India but would also be in a position to glean from its proceedings some practical, simple and meaningful suggestions that can help enrich development in India's rural landscape.

List of Contributors

Abdul Aziz, Former Project Director, Institute for Social and Economic Change, Bangalore.

Pawan Kumar Banta, Research Scholar, Department of Public Administration, H.P. University, Shimla.

A.P. Barnabas, Former Professor, Indian Institute of Public Administration, New Delhi and UNDP Expert, 27, Konark Apartment, Pocket A-4, (DDA Flats), Kalkaji Extension, New Delhi.

B.S. Bhargava, Former Professor and Head, Development Administration Unit, Institute for Social and Economic Change, Bangalore and now Senior Fellow, Institute of Social Sciences, Bangalore.

Rakesh Hooja, Additional Chief Secretary (Training) Government of Rajasthan and Director, HCM Rajasthan State Institute of Public Administration, Jaipur.

Rakshat Hooja, Associate Director, Minnesota Studies in International Development—India Programme, Jaipur.

Sunita Kale, Department of Political Science and Public Administration, University of Poona, Pune.

Mats Kihlberg, Chief, Research Division, Swedish International Development Authority, Stockholm, Sweden.

R.S. Kumat, Former Chairman, Board of Revenue, Government of Rajasthan, Ajmer.

M. Veerappa Moily, Chairman, Second Administrative Reforms Commission, Government of India, New Delhi.

G.S. Narwani, Former Director of Rural Development and Panchayati Raj and retired IAS officer, 23, Krishna Colony, Amba Bari, Jaipur.

Pranab Kumar Pandey, Lecturer, Department of Public Administration, University of Rajshahi, Rajshahi, Bangladesh.

Santishree D.N.B. Pandit, Reader, Department of Public Administration, University of Poona, Puns.

Sujit Kumar Paul, Lecturer, Department of Social Studies and Rural Development, Visva Bharti Sriniketan, Birbhum.

D. Ravinder, Associate Professor, Department of Political Science, Osmania University, Hyderabad.

Avinash Samal, Research Assistant, Development Administration Unit, Institute for Social and Economic Change, Bangalore.

Satish C. Sharma, Post-Doctoral Research Associate, Texas Tech. University, USA.

Y. Sharma, Former Deputy Secretary, Finance, Government of Rajasthan, Jaipur.

Ramesh C. Shrivastava, Faculty Member, HCM Rajasthan State Institute of Public Administration, Jaipur.

Rajbir Singh, Reader, Department of Public Administration, Choudhary Devi Lal University, Sirsa (Haryana).

S.N. Singh, Professor of Public Administration, Lucknow University, Lucknow.

K.V. Sundaram, Former Joint Advisor in Multilevel Planning, Planning Commission of India, New Delhi and Chairman, Working Group on Decentralized Planning and Panchayati Raj, State Planning Commission, Government of Tamil Nadu.

Shashi Ranjan Tewari, Reader in Public Administration, Lucknow University, Lucknow.

C.P. Vithal, Faculty Member, National Institute of Rural Development, Hyderabad.

John J. Williams, Associate Professor and Chair of Research, Faculty of Economic and Management Science School of Government, University of Western Cape, South Africa.

Editors

Ramesh K. Arora, Visiting Professor, Centre for Good Governance, HCM Rajasthan State Institute of Public Administration, Jaipur.

Meenakshi Hooja, IAS, Principal Secretary to His Excellency the Governor of Rajasthan, Jaipur.